Creativity in Indian Dance: Uday Shankar's Autumn Years, 1960–1977

Heralded as the father of Indian Creative Dance, and India's cultural ambassador, Uday Shankar (1900–1977) was a dancer and choreographer who created a vibrant new Indian dance form without any ethno-regional centricity. Over time, Shankar's art evolved from being a representation of the exotic East, to a narrative of modern India. This book provides a detailed study of Shankar's works in his autumn years (1960–1977), which remain largely un-documented. It discusses the form and content of Shankar's style, and its basic tenets – something hitherto unexplored. It also analyses Rabindranath Tagore and Uday Shankar as path-breakers of the duality in Indian performing arts traditions. The productions explored in detail are *Samanya Kshati* (1961), Shankar's tour of the USA, Canada and Europe in 1962, and India's cultural diplomacy, as well as *Prakriti Ananda* (1966), Shankar's last tour of the USA (1968), his last masterpiece, *Shankarscope* (1970, 1971 and 1972), together with Shankar's legacy.

This book is an essential read for scholars and researchers of dance history, art history, critical theory, artists' biographies, creative arts studies, theatre and Asian performing arts studies, as well as students of International Relations theory – primarily those interested in cultural diplomacy and soft power.

Sulakshana Sen is a senior faculty member at Symbiosis School for Liberal Arts, India. She has a doctorate in History, a master's in International Relations and Strategic Studies, and an undergraduate degree in Political Science. She teaches courses across specializations of International Relations, Political Science, Literature and Performing Arts (Dance). She has traversed the trajectory of being a student, performer, teacher and researcher of Uday Shankar's style of creative dance over the last four decades; and is also an exponent of the Indian classical dance form, *Odissi*. Her other research interests include community-based academic learning, sustainability, higher education and diplomacy.

Creativity in Indian Dance
Uday Shankar's Autumn Years,
1960–1977

Sulakshana Sen

LONDON AND NEW YORK

First published 2024
by Routledge
4 Park Square, Milton Park, Abingdon, Oxon OX14 4RN

and by Routledge
605 Third Avenue, New York, NY 10158

Routledge is an imprint of the Taylor & Francis Group, an informa business

© 2024 Sulakshana Sen

The right of Sulakshana Sen to be identified as author of this work has been asserted in accordance with sections 77 and 78 of the Copyright, Designs and Patents Act 1988.

All rights reserved. No part of this book may be reprinted or reproduced or utilised in any form or by any electronic, mechanical, or other means, now known or hereafter invented, including photocopying and recording, or in any information storage or retrieval system, without permission in writing from the publishers.

Trademark notice: Product or corporate names may be trademarks or registered trademarks, and are used only for identification and explanation without intent to infringe.

British Library Cataloguing-in-Publication Data
A catalogue record for this book is available from the British Library

ISBN: 978-1-032-20655-4 (hbk)
ISBN: 978-1-032-56078-6 (pbk)
ISBN: 978-1-003-43377-4 (ebk)

DOI: 10.4324/9781003433774

Typeset in Sabon
by Apex CoVantage, LLC

Contents

Preface   *vi*
Acknowledgements   *xxx*

    Introduction: Uday Shankar – Till the Autumn of His Life   1

1 Uday Shankar's Style of Creative Dance – The Form and Content   12

2 Paying Tribute to Tagore through *Samanya Kshati*   30

3 The Watershed Year – 1962   58

4 Revisiting Tagore   73

5 Revisiting the USA and Looking Forward   88

6 The Last Masterpiece   98

7 Uday Shankar's Style of Creative Dance – Its Impact and the Legacy   114

Bibliography   *127*
Index   *140*

Preface

The Five W's

As this book is an extension of my doctoral dissertation, I wanted to share the five W's – the Who, What, When, Where and Why in the Preface, so that the readers can gain an understanding of what compelled me to undertake this research, and how I went about it. This section is also written with the hope that it may be of some help to young dance scholars who are working their way forward in dance scholarship.

Hailed as India's cultural ambassador in a public reception by the Mayor of Calcutta in 1933,[1] Uday Shankar's emergence as a dancer and choreographer in the field of Indian dance was akin to a revolution. He was the father of Indian Creative Dance. Through his style, Uday Shankar not only represented Indian culture to the world at large, but his art was also representative of the idea of a new resurgent India. With the newly emerging idea of nationhood in the early twentieth century, Uday Shankar's dance was a natural corollary of modern India. The vibrant, new form that he created had never before existed in Indian dance traditions. Be it in terms of themes, music, movements or stagecraft, his style was not only unique, and made a tremendous contribution to Indian performing arts traditions, but was also an inimitable medium of narrative for stories never told before, through the form of Indian dance. He gifted to India, the third genre of dance – that of the creative form.

What is now referred to as classical dance forms is often indicative and reflective of the understanding of the Indian equivalent of Western classical dance forms.[2] The term classical in the context of Indian dance is a postcolonial construct; for during the British Raj, all dance forms had been clubbed together as *nautch*. During this period, the women dancers, who were essentially court dancers, were referred to as the *nautch* girls. The term *nautch* being a distortion of the colloquial Hindi and Bengali word *naach*, meaning dance. The term, however, according to Dr. Pallabi Chakravorty, represented a cultural and political transformation under British colonialism as all dance forms were lumped together under the one word.[3] Not only was regional diversity and the purity of the art forms lost, but the audiences expected to see only the beauty of the dancers and not their dancing.[4]

Indian classical forms have been referred to as neo-classical by the late Kapila Vatsayan, one of India's primary dance scholars, in view of the ongoing reconstructions of the various forms,[5] as they had lost their essence during the colonial period. These traditional dance forms of India were known as *Shastriya Nritya*, since they had their roots in the *shastras* or sacred scriptures of ancient India.[6]

With around 5,600 verses,[7] Bharat Muni's *Natyashastra*[8] forms the basic treatise of the structured Indian dance forms, traditionally performed in temples, which we now term as the classical dance forms of India. Apart from items based on pure dance movements or *nruta*, set to select *ragas*,[9] Indian classical dance forms interpret and translate mythology and the works of immortal poets. They are also instrumental in the translation of the *shlokas*[10] and the *stotras*[11] and played an important role in conveying them to the common man in a medium other than the written word – as the ancient texts were written in *Sanskrit* – a language, essentially within the purview of the *Brahmins*[12] solely, in ancient times. Indian classical dance also played the inherent role of carrying forward traditional knowledge from generation to generation through the aural–oral and visual medium.[13] This depiction of the lyrics of the *shlokas* and *stotras* was and is still carried out through *nritya*[14] and/or *abhinaya*.[15] Defined and structured within the framework of the *navarasas*,[16] the *mudras*,[17] *pada bhedas*,[18] neck movements, eye movements and basics of stagecraft, classical dance forms of India were rigid and set in their ways. However, even with this rigidity in structure, holding on to the purity of the form posed to be a challenge against the decadence and depths of depravity that dance had sunk to, becoming relegated to *kothas*[19] – due to lack of patronage under the British Raj.

Unlike the traditional temple dance forms, the folk form on the other hand was an expression of joy to mark religious festivals and other social occasions. Whether it was performed to celebrate a good harvest, or to augment the rituals of a wedding or to herald the New Year, the form always entailed happy, joyful and vigorous dance movements. According to Kapila Vatsayan, who explores the regional diversity of the folk dance forms of India, folk forms can be broadly divided into seven categories. The first category, according to her, is hunting and animal imitation dances of the nomads and food gatherers. The second form would be the dances related to fertility rites, rituals, magic propitiation and trance of shift cultivators and others. The third would be the functional and occupational dances of the peasants. Next would include dances related to seasonal cycles and thereby dedicated to particular festivals. The fifth would be dances which were an enactment of myths and epics like the Ramayana and the Mahabharata. She also includes in her classification, as the sixth and seventh forms of folk dance, devotional dances set to semiclassical music, as well as traditional dance-drama forms existent in rural and urban settings.[20]

Both the traditional dance forms – that is to say the folk dance forms as well as the classical dance forms – played an integral role in bringing the community together. The folk form brought the community together in the form of a celebration, while the classical dance forms, like *Kathakali*, for example, brought the local community together, whenever performances were presented.

Uday Shankar took on the mantle of storytelling without excessive use of *mudras* and the other rigid structures and grammar, as put forth in the *Natyashastra*, thereby bridging the gap and revolutionizing Indian dance with the introduction of the third genre – the creative form. Shankar's form had a universal appeal as it could be grasped by a global as well as an Indian audience, all of whom were not well versed with the text of the *Natyashastra*. It was nonetheless, quintessentially Indian. A storyteller par excellence, his form of narrative evolved by creating movements that would tell stories – be it that of villagers, farmers or labourers, or any incident from the daily lives of any strata of society – as well as that of Gods and Goddesses. Inspired by movements from daily life and at times by music, Shankar created artistic impressions that could be used to narrate the stories he wanted to tell, all the time keeping in mind the basic tenets of his style – the three fundamentals of beauty, power and simplicity.[21]

According to Edward W. Said, the traditional connotation of the term Orientalism refers to the "high-handed executive attitude of nineteenth-century and early-twentieth-century European colonialism," whereby, as far as the Europeans were concerned, the Orient was a "place of romance, exotic beings, haunting memories and landscapes, remarkable experiences."[22] A study of the trajectory of Uday Shankar's performances and choreography from the early years in the 1920s and 1930s till the 1970s reveals that during the initial years, the content of the maestro's art form in terms of the themes of the items produced was more of a representation of an exotic India to the West. However, the difference between the oriental dances as presented by Westerners in the early twentieth century and those that Uday Shankar presented, in that period, primarily lay in the fact that Shankar's childhood was spent in India and he had been exposed to various dance traditions, especially the folk dancers in present-day Uttar Pradesh and Rajasthan, as well as the dancers in the court of Jhalawar,[23] which was renowned for its patronage of the arts. With time, the movements that he used and the stories that Shankar told, evolved to become a narrative of the socio-economic–political–cultural and technological evolution of the times that he was witnessing.

Another extremely important element that Uday Shankar contributed to Indian dance is the pan-Indian nature of his form. Both folk dance forms and classical dance forms of India have a regional dimension. Whether it be *Bharatnatyam*,[24] *Odissi*,[25] *Manipuri*,[26] *Kathak*[27] or *Kathakali*,[28] or any other classical dance form, they are intrinsically linked to a particular region of India. Therefore, unconsciously or subconsciously, they are identified with certain regions and, in independent India, states, where the dance forms originated. The same ethno-regional centricity is applicable with regard to the folk dance forms – be they *Bhangra*,[29] *Bihu*,[30] *Madia*[31] or *Santhal*.[32] They immediately bring to mind a certain region, community, language and culture. Uday Shankar's style of creative dance went beyond this provincialism. There is no denying that most of the items performed in his repertoires are quintessentially Indian in nature, but they cannot be identified with any particular region of India. This approach, however, was not well received by some traditionalists. In an article in the New York Times, John Martin writes how Uday Shankar was criticized by traditionalists like Mr. Sheshagiri, who felt that this was an example of the type of decadence in society due to deterioration in taste, as Uday Shankar's dance form had nothing Indian about it as per the *Natyashastra* except the costumes. In the same article, Shankar's response is carried, where he says that the only way to progress in any field was to adopt the best from the past and mould it to the requirements of the present.[33] The timeframe that this article was written in, and responded to by Shankar, is the 1930s, and Shankar's dance is reflective of the idea of a united modern India that is fighting to shed the shackles of Western imperialism. This idea of a united India is reflected in the concept of the idea of India during the early twentieth century, when "Nationalism could only be Indian. And Indian meant that which was above all the smaller loyalties to religion, caste, ethnicity and region."[34]

As far as the source of his form is concerned, Shankar himself spoke about the Indian-ness of his art form many times. In his own words,

> I made categories of movements, such as decorative, devotional, martial and so forth. I must tell you for my folk dances I created the movements. I do not think you will find these movements anywhere, but still you will see they are folk. Somewhere, I must have seen some folk movement and then imagined and allowed something to be born of me. Often, seeing one movement gave me the idea of a completely new and different movement. When you see my folk-dances you will always think they are folk dances. But if you wish to find out from what part of India my movements are taken, you will find no answer. You will agree they are folk, they feel folk, but they cannot be identified.[35]

Given the advice Uday Shankar received from both Anna Pavlova and William Rothenstein,[36] two major influencers in his life, during his early years – who urged him to focus on his own Indian heritage – Uday Shankar always consciously presented all that was Indian. He says,

> I was very aware and conscious not to get anything from European and American movement – I mean even movement in life – nor from Western way of thinking. Except the method of composition, the placing of dancers on the stage patterns etc., everything I did was my own.[37]

Apart from his own innovative and unique creative form, Uday Shankar also took upon himself to showcase India's rich cultural heritage. Be it the classical or the folk form, be it through dance, music or costume, whether they were folk dance forms from Punjab in North Western India, or the dance of the Nagas from North Eastern India, or *Madia* from Madhya Pradesh in central Asia, or be it classical dance forms like *Manipuri*, they found their way in his repertoires at different points in time. His film, *Kalpana*, also portrays this, thereby making him truly the cultural ambassador of India.

Seminal studies on Uday Shankar till date have been undertaken primarily by Dr. Joan L. Erdman, Professor Emerita of Anthropology and Cultural Studies, Columbia College, and Associate, Committee on Southern Asian Studies, University of Chicago. Through her paper titled "Performance as a Translation: Uday Shankar in the West,"[38] Professor Erdman looks at the early life of Uday Shankar and the influences in his upbringing that enabled him to translate his experiences and culture into his dance form. In her review of Mohan Khokar's book titled "His dance, His Life: A Portrait of Uday Shankar,"[39] Prof. Erdman touches on the idea that few of the present generation are aware of the importance of Uday Shankar in the renaissance of performing arts in India and the maestro's innate ability to communicate to his audiences in both the East and the West.[40] In her article, "A Comment on Dance Scholarship,"[41] Dr. Erdman contends that writing dance history is a complex project as it involves an intense study of not only the artist but also the context, contact, colleagues, locales, events and other factors. The questions raised by her specifically on his work during the 1960s and 1970s went a long way as a deciding factor for me, to work on this period of Shankar's productions.

One of the most detailed biographies on Uday Shankar, "His dance, His Life: A Portrait of Uday Shankar," by Mohan Khokar, while focusing Shankar's life and work in great detail in the 1960s, skims over the period 1960–1977, which witnessed three new productions, namely, *Samanya Kshati* (1961), *Prakriti Anando* (1966) and *Shankarscope* (1970). These productions also witnessed Shankar's slow transition to donning the mantle of a choreographer rather than a performer. This too compelled me to take up this project, to enable a detailed look at this period.

Most of the other literature again, be it Ashoke Kumar Mukhopadhyay's book titled *Uday Shankar – Twentieth Century's Nataraja*[42] or noted dance scholars, Dr. Sunil Kothari and Mohan Khokar's jointly edited book, *Uday Shankar – A Photo Biography*,[43] do not detail either the productions of the period 1960–1967 or the international tours undertaken by Shankar and his troupe in 1962 and 1968. It is the same even with Satyen Chatterjee's book, *Padma Parer Manush Ebong Uday Shankar*[44] which is more of a memoir and personal reminiscences of Chatterjee's association with Shankar, as the manager of his troupe. Similar lacunae are present in Sudhiranjan Mukhopadhya's *Uday Shankar*[45] and Shankarlal Bhattacharya's *Udayer Pathey*,[46] where the focus has essentially been on Shankar's life and work till the 1960s.

Even *Shankarnama: Smritichitrey Amala Shankar*, a memoir of Amala Shankar, penned by Bishakha Ghosh,[47] which is a compilation of the series

Preface xi

brought out under the same name by Ananda Publishers in their bi-monthly magazine *Sananda*, sometime in the early 1990s, does not detail the productions for the period 1960–1977, as Amala Shankar was not associated with Shankar's productions after 1962. Some inaccuracies also exist regarding observations of Shankar's productions and tours during this period. For example, on page 235 of the book,[48] it is written that the members of Uday Shankar Ballet Troupe, travelling to the USA with him, during the tour of 1968, were not trained in Indian classical dance forms. However, the fact remains that Shanti Bose, along with Pranati Sengupta nee Guha, Polly Guha, Sadhan Guha, Dhurjati Sen, who had all accompanied Uday Shankar in the tour of 1968, and some of whom were also a part of the performances from *Samanya Kshati* in 1961, had studied at the Academy of Dance, Drama and Music, which later became known as, and a part of Rabindra Bharati University.[49] The Academy, which had been set up in 1956, under the aegis of the then Chief Minister of West Bengal, Dr. Bidhan Chandra Roy, was housed in Tagore's ancestral home at Jorasanko, Kolkata.[50] Uday Shankar himself was the Dean of Dance at the Academy for the first couple of years when it was established. However, he resigned as the creative and performing artist in him found the rules and regulations of a government organisation too binding to offer him the freedom to work as he deemed necessary.[51] When Rabindra Bharati University was established under the Rabindra Bharati Act of 1961, to commemorate the birth-centenary year of Rabindranath Tagore, again under the aegis of Dr. B. C. Roy, this was housed in the same premises as the Academy and it was merged with Rabindra Bharati University. At present, the Academy of Dance, Drama and Music falls under the Department of Fine Arts at the University.[52] For the three-year course offered by the Academy, in Dance (before it was merged with Rabindra Bharati University), during the first year and second year, students had to pursue the three classical styles of *Kathakali, Manipuri* and *Bharatnatyam*. This was compulsory. Practical classes on these three subjects were conducted alongside classes on theory. Apart from this, the students had to also study and appear for a paper on the History of Indian Dance. They had to choose any one of the three compulsory subjects, as their specialization for the third year, and opt for any one of the remaining styles as their pass subject.

Prof. T. S. G. Namboodri – son of Guru Shankaran Namboodri, whom Uday Shankar considered his Guru, used to teach *Abhinaya* and *Mudras* as applicable in *Kathakali*. Prof. N.K. Shivashankaran, an erstwhile member of Uday Shankar's troupe, who re-joined Shankar's troupe for the productions of *Prakriti Ananda* and *Shankarscope*, used to conduct classes for *Kathakali*. Guru Maruthappa Pillai taught *Bharatnatyam*, while Guru Nadia Sigh trained the students in *Manipuri*. Sri. Bal Krishna Menon used to teach the paper, "History of Indian Dance."

The lament of the reviewer for the book, *Shankarnama*, Swapan Shome, as published in *Ananda Bazar Patrika* itself is that a complete account of the maestro's work is yet to be published in Bengali, and this is something that is not only sad but also something to be ashamed of.[53] The fact, however,

xii *Preface*

Figure 0.1 This official photograph from the Faculty of Dance, Academy of Dance, Drama and Music, showcases the faculty members, staff and students from all the three batches as of 1958. Dhurjati Sen and Shanti Bose can be seen standing in the last row, third and fourth from the left, respectively. Pranati Sengupta nee Guha is standing third from the left in the third row. Prof. T.S.G. Namboodri is seated third from the right in the second row. Seated second from the right in this row is Guru Nadia Singh. Seated second from the left in this same row is Prof. N. K. Shivashankaran. Next to him, third from the left in this row, is Prof. T. K. Maruthappa Pillai. Seated next to Prof Pillai, fourth from the left, is Sri. Bal Krishna Menon.

Source: Courtesy, private collection of Shanti Bose

remains that a complete detailed account of all the maestro's works is not available in English either.

In her article, "Who Remembers Uday Shankar,"[54] Prof. Erdman opines that the two major considerations while writing on Uday Shankar should include "the impact of this Indian choreographer and dancer on his times, and the significance of his life and works for our times." In this article, Dr. Erdman puts forth that Uday Shankar's style was neither recognized nor given due importance despite the role it played in being the initiator of modern dance traditions in India. According to Dr. Erdman, Uday Shankar reinvented Indian dance almost single-handedly by placing it "on stage in technically up-to-date settings."

This book seeks to add to the existing literature on Uday Shankar a documentation in detail of Shankar's work in the period 1960–1977 while contextualizing Shankar's art form as a mirror of modern India through the stories that he narrates using his art form. The need to look in depth at the

Preface   xiii

productions during these two decades stems from the fact that even though a major chunk of India's social movements and history is presented by Shankar through his art form, they are not documented. This book therefore explores Shankar's works during the period 1960–1970, reflecting the:

- socio-economic and political conditions of modern India, which were mirrored through Shankar's creativity and reflected in his compositions during this period
- technological advancements and innovations introduced in the global cultural arena in post-1950s, which were introduced and harnessed for creativity in performing arts for the first time in India by Shankar
- introduction of new movements in dance and the basic tenets of Uday Shankar's technique and style of dance/movement
- impact of Uday Shankar's art form on performing arts traditions of modern India

As is evident through his film *Kalpana* which released in 1948, not only did Uday Shankar's art reflect the dynamics of a resurgent India as it came into being as a new nation-state but also the problems faced by independent India. The shift in his compositions from representing the mythology of India and its exoticism to telling tales of the struggle of the newly independent nation represents a shift in his dynamism as a creator, as well as the perception of India by the Occident. Shankar's tremendous ability to observe daily life and represent it through his dance makes him a visual chronicler of the life and times of the common man, and therefore the history of the period.

In a paper presented at the annual conference of the Society of Dance History Scholars, Barnard College, New York, on June 21, 1997, Dr. Joan L. Erdman, as mentioned before, who was an anthropologist and taught at Columbia College, Chicago, and conducted research as an associate of the Committee on Southern Asian Studies at the University of Chicago, opined that there is a "smug dismissal of Uday Shankar which characterized his (Uday Shankar's) latter years."[55] This depressive evaluation is evident in the usage of the terms "grey years," "helpless," "pathetically dependent"[56] and so on, despite the fact that this period witnessed three original projects undertaken by the maestro, namely

- *Samanya Kshati* (1961)
- *Prakriti Anando* (1966)
- *Shankarscope* (1970)

To be noted is that the years mentioned in brackets against the productions only signify the years that the production was first launched in and not the subsequent performances.

These productions were path-breaking in nature and played an immensely important role in changing the perception of performing arts in India. They created a new path which is still used widely, yet remains unacknowledged.

xiv *Preface*

According to Dr. Erdman, all the twists in the "Uday Shankar pathway . . . are integral to any analysis of his works, as well as to his continuing presence in the world of Indian dance and modern ideas of choreography in India."[57] It is this knowledge gap that the book will address.

I am sharing at this point how I went ahead with my research in the hope that it will be of help to future dance scholars. Drawn from the French word, *rechercher*, which literally means to search again, this re-look or re-search, it could involve putting together, something that has not existed before – a new area of knowledge, thereby bridging a knowledge gap; or it could imply taking a re-look at knowledge that already exists. Therefore, research may imply, either finding out new evidence or data or adding new interpretations to existing data. The starting point of any research nonetheless remains the ability to raise questions.

As the objective of this research was to take a re-look at the existing data, on Uday Shankar's works between 1960 and 1977, which has not been delved into in detail, my work was focused on re-interpreting the period by delving into unexplored material, which, when studied in detail, revealed a new perspective to the one that was already in existence. The other aspect that I explored was the impact of Shankar's form on performing arts traditions in India. I also contextualized Shankar's work within the framework of times and conditions of modern India.

As far as the Analytical and Synthetic operations of Methodology are concerned, I aligned my position on methodology with that of Intellectual History. This stance stemmed from the fact that Intellectual History is

> an especial interest in the history of thought and expression . . . characteristic of transitional ages in the lives of cultures; it arises when received traditions in thought and mythic endowments appear to have lost their relevance to current social problems or their presumed coherency . . . During such times, thinkers may try, by means of what is usually called "historical perspective," to gain some purchase on their cultural legacy.[58]

For me, the understanding of the field Intellectual History reverberated with the course introduction to Intellectual History on the website of the University of Pennsylvania. The understanding that

> Intellectual History investigates the history of human thought, culture, and expression – in short, the things that have allowed human beings, alone among the species, to mediate their relationship to the natural world with their minds and their media of communication. It includes a central concern with the texts that have helped to shape human history, with intellectual communities, with the great debates within and across cultures, and with the history of all forms of human expression, including the visual arts and music. It is a field that offers contact with other minds in other times, places, and contexts.[59]

This, to my understanding, extends to all creative forms, including performing arts and thereby to the field of dance as well. For my doctoral thesis titled *Creativity in Independent India: Uday Shankar, 1960–1977*, as I explored the maestro's productions in context of the times that he created them in, the contention that his work was therefore influenced by and became a reflection of the socio-political economic trajectories of the period, was well aligned to the field, scope and framework of Intellectual History.

I also viewed Shankar's works through the lens of Cultural History, as Shankar's productions during this period are very much a part of India's cultural history. They bring "to life a past time and place. In this search, cultural historians study beliefs and ideas, much as intellectual historians do."[60] This bringing to life of the past time and place can not only be identified through the items based on myth and mythology which he continued to perform – although to a lesser extent during this period – but also in his interpretations of Tagore's works during the period under study. Any artist is a product of the times he or she lives in, and their creativity in turn is a reflection of the same. So too was the case with Uday Shankar, as his productions during this period were a reflection of the times he lived and worked in, as is evident through the items performed in *Shankarscope*. According to Raymond Williams, "culture has two aspects: the known meanings and directions, which its members are trained to; the new observations and meanings, which are offered and tested."[61] Thus, the experimentation offered by Uday Shankar in terms of form and content of his productions through his inimitable style during this period was his observations of society, offered through his creativity.

For the purpose of this study, the ambit of the material researched included both performative and illustrative texts. For purposes of data collection, the method of data collection for the performative texts involved recording oral history primarily from Shanti Bose, who was hailed as "Shankar's heir apparent" by the Houston Post, in a review of the troupe's performance in November 1968.[62]

The recording of oral history as a form of data collection is in keeping with the traditions of Salvage Ethnography, which has been a well-established research method in the Social Sciences from the early twentieth century. It entails the recording of oral history as a way of documenting cultural history that is slowly becoming extinct. The Dictionary of the Social Sciences published by Oxford University Press in 2022, edited by Craig Calhoun, President of the Social Science Research Council in New York and a professor of Sociology and History at New York University, states that it was Franz Boas (1858–1952), one of the founding fathers of modern Anthropology, who in reconstructing American Indian traditions and cultures paved the way for Salvage Ethnography as a research method. This method is primarily based on reminiscences and long-term participant observation.[63] Shanti Bose is the only surviving direct associate of Uday Shankar, who has worked with the maestro for 17 long years, through all the productions from 1960 to 1977, initially as a dancer in the troupe and subsequently as the lead male dancer

xvi *Preface*

and Ballet Master of Shankar's troupe. Bose is also the only surviving artist who shared stage space and performed with Uday Shankar in all his productions in the 1960s and the 1970s. Moreover, Bose's position as the Ballet Master of Shankar's troupe from 1965 makes oral history recordings of his insights on Shankar's form and productions of the period under consideration, all the more valuable, as like any Ballet Master, his job required him to teach, prepare and rehearse dancers for productions and performances,[64] and sometimes extended to choreographing as well. As the souvenirs, pamphlets, flyers, paper clippings, photographs of the period and images from the various souvenirs reflect, Bose also played an important role in the troupe as a male dancer and was the Assistant Director of Shankar's last production of *Samanya Kshati* in 1972. Therefore, the recording of oral history of Shanti Bose is well in keeping with the traditions of the research method of Salvage Ethnography as the art form and the movements devised by Shankar are slowly dying and Shanti Bose fulfils the required criterion of reminiscences resulting from long-term participant observation.

As mentioned earlier, this book is an extension of my doctoral thesis, and I would also like to point out that Salvage Ethnography as a research method was recognized, accepted and praised not only by the Supervisor for this research but also by the external panel of senior historians in their reviews, as all the oral history recordings provided were and are supported by archival material. This also included establishing Bose's role as a long-term participant observer.

Shanti Bose initially joined Uday Shankar's group as a male dancer and troupe member in 1960 for the production of *Samanya Kshati*. He travelled with Shankar's troupe both across India for the production of *Samanya Kshati* and for Shankar's international tour of the USA and Europe in 1962, in the same capacity. Bose went on to become the Ballet Master of Uday Shankar's troupe in 1965, for the production of *Prakriti Ananda* and Shankar's subsequent productions and tours at the national level as well as international tour of the USA in 1968. Bose continued in the position of the Ballet Master for the productions of *Shankarscope* in 1970 and 1972 (whereby he was also the Assistant Director for the segment of *Samanya Kshati* staged in *Shankarscope*). This is evident in advertisements of *Shankarscope* (1972) in November, 1972, in popular newspapers of the time in Kolkata, including Ananda Bazar Patrika,[65] Yugantar[66] and Amrita Bazar Patrika.[67] Therefore, Bose was associated with Shankar during the period 1960–1977, thereby fulfilling the requirement of long-term participant observation, as required in the use of the method of Salvage Ethnography.

As far as the illustrative aspect of the productions was concerned, the texts that were explored were the photographs and souvenirs of the productions of the period, from the private collection of Shanti Bose. As far as the souvenirs are concerned, I considered the text of the souvenirs – in terms of both the write-ups and the images, as content that Uday Shankar wanted to convey to his audience when they came to watch the performances. Apart from the

Preface xvii

Figure 0.2 A page from the souvenir of *Samanya Kshati* for the production in 1961, showcasing the male dancers of Shankar's troupe. Shanti Bose, then known by his given name Amarendra Bose, is reflected in this cast of dancers. The caption also states that Bose joined the troupe in 1960.

Source: Courtesy, private collection of Shanti Bose

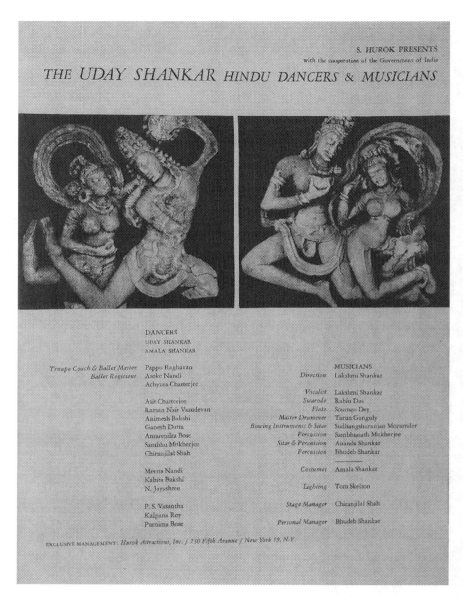

Figure 0.3 A page from the souvenir of Shankar's tour of the USA in 1962, reflecting Shanti Bose in the cast of dancers, as per his given name Amarendra Bose.

Source: Courtesy, private collection of Shanti Bose

main souvenirs for the productions, brochures, pamphlets, flyers as well as other promotional materials with respect to different performances on different dates and locales were also considered in the same light.

Apart from souvenirs and photographs, newspaper clippings of content written and published about the productions during the period 1960–1977

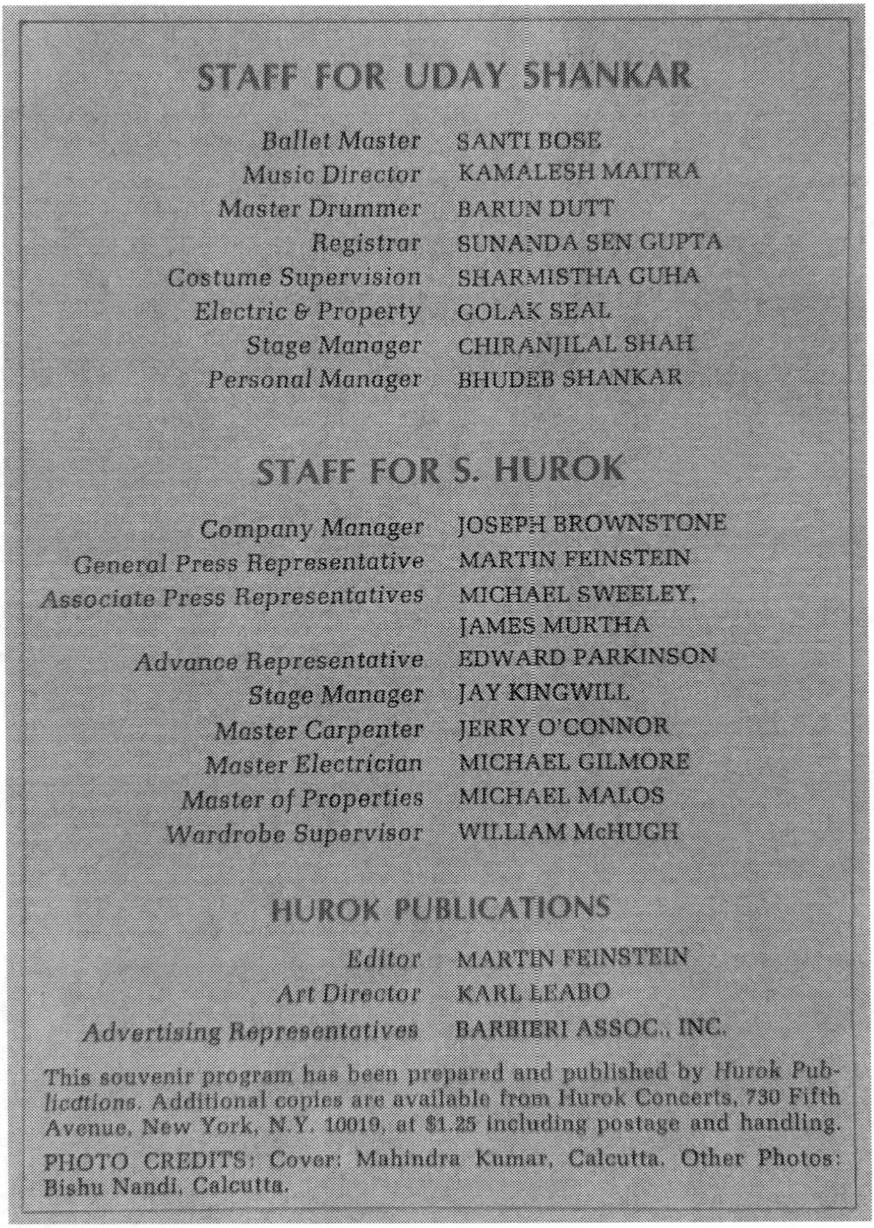

STAFF FOR UDAY SHANKAR

Ballet Master	SANTI BOSE
Music Director	KAMALESH MAITRA
Master Drummer	BARUN DUTT
Registrar	SUNANDA SEN GUPTA
Costume Supervision	SHARMISTHA GUHA
Electric & Property	GOLAK SEAL
Stage Manager	CHIRANJILAL SHAH
Personal Manager	BHUDEB SHANKAR

STAFF FOR S. HUROK

Company Manager	JOSEPH BROWNSTONE
General Press Representative	MARTIN FEINSTEIN
Associate Press Representatives	MICHAEL SWEELEY, JAMES MURTHA
Advance Representative	EDWARD PARKINSON
Stage Manager	JAY KINGWILL
Master Carpenter	JERRY O'CONNOR
Master Electrician	MICHAEL GILMORE
Master of Properties	MICHAEL MALOS
Wardrobe Supervisor	WILLIAM McHUGH

HUROK PUBLICATIONS

Editor	MARTIN FEINSTEIN
Art Director	KARL LEABO
Advertising Representatives	BARBIERI ASSOC., INC.

This souvenir program has been prepared and published by Hurok Publications. Additional copies are available from Hurok Concerts, 730 Fifth Avenue, New York, N.Y. 10019, at $1.25 including postage and handling.

PHOTO CREDITS: Cover: Mahindra Kumar, Calcutta. Other Photos: Bishu Nandi, Calcutta.

Figure 0.4 From the souvenir of Shankar's 1968 tour of the USA, reflecting Shanti Bose's name, spelt as Santi Bose, as the Ballet Master of the troupe. Santi is an alternative spelling of the Sanskrit word *Shanti*, as per the International Alphabet of Sanskrit Transliteration.[68]

Source: Courtesy, private collection of Shanti Bose

xx *Preface*

Figure 0.5 A page from the souvenir of Shankar's production of *Shankarscope* in 1970, with Shanti Bose's name as the Ballet Master of Shankar's troupe.

Source: Courtesy, private collection of Shanti Bose

from the private collection of Shanti Bose were also studied. A televised interview of Uday Shankar from the early 1970s, conducted by thespian Shambhu Mitra[69] telecast on DD Bharti, a documentary on Shanti Bose titled *Uday Pather Shanti*, produced by the Government of West Bengal and Rabindra

Bharati University, as well as televised interviews of Ravi Shankar and Shanti Bose both on *Doordarshan* (the autonomous public service broadcaster of Government of India) and on other private networks were also viewed and reflected on. Books and articles on Uday Shankar in peer-reviewed journals were also studied.

With Uday Shankar himself being no more, all his thoughts and ideas that went into these productions cannot be directly understood, and I often found myself wishing that I had the opportunity of interviewing him in person, for in trying to contextualize Shankar's productions of the period with reference to the socio-economic–political time frame, I was required to step into the realms of speculative history. Despite this limitation, I moved ahead with my study keeping in mind that all history is relative to the historian who writes it and the historian in turn is relative to his historical and cultural background.[70] According to E. H. Carr, it is important to study the historian before studying history, in order to understand the historian's historical and social environment, as history "is a continuous process of interaction between the historian and his facts, an unending dialogue between the present and the past."[71]

According to Charles A. Beard as well, "the historian cannot know or explain history as actuality"[72]. Every historian's work is based on a selection and organization of a frame of reference of what is deemed necessary and desirable"[73]

It is on the basis of these ideas that I viewed Uday Shankar as a chronicler of the times through his art form and contextualized his works within the framework of modern India to prove this contention.

The book has been divided into seven chapters apart from the, Preface, Acknowledgements and Introduction. The *Preface: The Five W's* essentially looks at the need for the study, the research methodologies opted for and the analytical lens used. It introduces Uday Shankar and his art form which was akin to a revolution in Indian performing arts traditions, be it in terms of themes, music, movements or stagecraft. His unique style which bridged a gap in both form and content was an inimitable medium of narrative of stories never told before. The segment discusses the important literary works of Uday Shankar till date, leading to the identification of the knowledge gap which is essential with regard to his work during the autumn years of his life, namely 1960–1977. It states the objective of the book, which is to showcase that Shankar's productions between 1960 and 1977, document major socio-economic, political conditions and technological advancements and innovations of modern India; and has had an immense impact on performing arts traditions of contemporary India. It brings into discussion the broad analytical frameworks used to understand and explore Shankar's work, and the oral recordings of primarily Shanti Bose, in keeping with the traditions of Salvage Ethnography, as he was associated with all of Shankar's productions of the period 1960–1977.

The segment titled *Introduction: Uday Shankar – Till the autumn of his life* traces Uday Shankar's life from his birth in the city of Udaipur in 1900,

xxii *Preface*

till the late 1950s, and the various socio-cultural and economic influences on him. This section is more in the form of a biography and traces the trajectory of his life from his childhood days divided between Udaipur and Nasrathpur (which was his maternal grandfather's home), to being a student at the J.J. College of Arts in Mumbai, then a student at the Royal College of Arts in London. Shankar's interaction with Sir William Rothenstein and Anna Pavlova, and his subsequent transition from a painter to a dancer and choreographer are also included in this segment. It highlights his performances and choreography during this period, as well as the various people he came into contact with, who influenced him and his work immensely. It also looks at Shankar's return to India in the early 1940s, after having spent almost two decades in the West, the setting up of the Uday Shankar India Culture Centre at Almora; the socio-political as well as economic conditions both in India and the global order at the time, the move to Madras and the creation of *Kalpana*, and then finally the move to Kolkata. This segment also explores the transition in his compositions from being based on mythology and reflecting exotic India in the initial years to mirroring and questioning the socio-economic, religious and political order of modern India, which is reflected in his film released in 1948, *Kalpana*. Given the fact that the period and content of this chapter is beyond the focus of the main study, this segment is more of a dawn-to-dusk narrative based essentially on secondary literature review, which sets the background for a detailed analysis of Shankar's work in the autumn of his life. It has been written primarily on the basis of review of the existing literature on Uday Shankar; and Shankar's write-ups in the various souvenirs of the period 1960–1977, as well as a televised interview of Shankar by the theatre personality Shambhu Mitra – where Shankar talks of his life and what influenced him.

The first chapter, titled *Uday Shankar's Style of Creative Dance – The Form and Content*, outlines what Uday Shankar's style of creative dance entails and its basic tenets. It examines the maestro's own contention of what his style comprises. This is gathered and collated through his writings in the souvenirs of his productions, as well as his interviews both in print and on television. It moves on to consolidate this narration with the learnings from his Ballet Master, Shanti Bose's recording of oral history, as he was responsible for perfecting movements of the troupe members during the period 1965–1977. The uniqueness of form and content and the evolution of the style; the introduction of the ballet form to Indian dance traditions; the focus on body language compared to excessive usage of *mudras* or hand gestures and facial expressions for the purpose of emoting; as well as the foundation of the form, which provides the anchor to the creative expression, concepts of symmetry, basic considerations for choreography, the discipline he exacted from his troupe as well as the power of the form are discussed in this chapter as well. Shankar's creative vision of the performance as it should appear on stage, together with his innate understanding and use of stagecraft – whether it be the usage of lights or costumes or sets, to the best advantage – also finds

Preface   xxiii

space for discussion in this section. As does the revolutionary change that he brought in terms of the content, to the stage.

Paying Tribute to Tagore through Samanya Kshati, the second chapter of the book, explores Uday Shankar and Rabindranath Tagore as the two path breakers of their time as far as performing arts of modern India is concerned. They are also both harbingers of social change, concerned with India's education system, humanists and universalists in their thought and action – and this is apparent through their work. They have also paved the way for social upliftment of performing arts and artists, from the manner in which they had come to be viewed during the British era, when every form of dance had been clubbed under the word *nautch*, a distortion of the word *naach*, meaning dance. The production of *Samanya Kshati* and *Udara Charitanam*, the ballets which Shankar creates based on Tagore's poems by the same name, sees Shankar's creativity take off from Tagore as these were created to pay tribute to the Nobel Laureate poet on his birth centenary. The chapter also speculates as to why Uday Shankar chose for his production these particular pieces as performative texts. It examines the performative and illustrative texts of the production itself, delving into the storytelling, the additions to Tagore's narrative made by Shankar, the experiments with costume, lights and other stagecraft as well as the technology used – which was far ahead of its time. It also glimpses into the professionalism brought to the art form by Uday Shankar and identifies the locales, occasions and periods that the performances were carried out in and for. It highlights the fact that Shankar managed to bring together on a common platform, a team which comprised a veritable who's who from the world of Indian classical music, to create and perform the music of *Samanya Kshati*, which was composed by none other than his brother, the late sitar maestro, Pandit Ravi Shankar.

The third chapter, *The Watershed Year – 1962*, delves into Shankar's tour of the USA, Canada and Europe in the year 1962. This was a watershed year not only in world politics but for India as well. On the one hand, October of the year witnessed the world coming to the brink of a nuclear war, with the Cuban Missile Crisis, on the other hand, in October itself, India faced its first military invasion from China. The chapter follows the trail of Shankar's tour of the USA, Canada and Europe with his troupe, which set off sail for the West, before either the Cuban Missile Crisis or the Sino-Indian War began. They performed at the Seattle World's Fair 1962, where they represented India. President John F. Kennedy opened the Fair with a speech delivered on telephone but was unable to do so during the closing ceremony on October 21, due to the fact that the world was then on the brink of a nuclear war. The performance at Seattle World's Fair as well as the performances across Europe, were all sponsored by the Government of India. This reflects the soft power initiatives of the Indian government under its first Prime Minister, Jawaharlal Nehru, and the status of performing arts and artists, as well as the establishment of the ICCR as a means of institutionalizing cultural diplomacy. The performances across the USA were hosted by the then notable impresario, Sol Hurok, which was another experience in itself and has not been documented in detail in any literature on Uday Shankar. The chapter also looks at the preparation that the troupe underwent for this tour, the items performed along with the ballet *Samanya Kshati,* as well as the novel experiences of the troupe during their travels, spanning a period of almost five months. An important point to be noted is that Amala Shankar ceased to be a part of Uday Shankar's performances after the tour of 1962, and this is reflected in her autobiography as well.

Uday Shankar disbanded the troupe once they returned to India in February 1963. Many of the erstwhile members of Shankar's troupe now came together to form the Indian Ballet Troupe (IBT), which though primarily involved with taking forward Shankar's legacy also performed other styles as well. In 1965, together with Amala Shankar, Uday Shankar opened the "Uday Shankar India Culture Centre" in Kolkata. The institute was a reminiscence of the centre at Almora, though on a much smaller scale. It became a centre for learning not only Uday Shankar's style of creative dance but various classical styles of India as well. Shankar however was not happy. The creative artist in him soon became restless for new productions. Soon after, by the end of 1965 itself, he reached out to his erstwhile troupe members to band together, this time for the production of *Prakriti – Ananda,* based on Tagore's dance drama *Chandalika* and poem by the name *Prakriti – Ananda.* The members of the IBT were taken on as dancers for this production as many were his erstwhile troupe members, while the others were already trained in his style, given the repertoires of IBT. Shankar was also well acquainted with IBT's work. This segment, which constitutes the fourth chapter of the book, titled *Revisiting Tagore,* explores Uday Shankar's *Prakriti Ananda,* as a window to the issue of untouchability, ailing independent India, together with a consideration of the context that may have influenced the maestro to choose this particular work of Tagore as a performance piece to interpret. It also explores the performative text itself, the choreography, as well as the actual performance and tours across India.

A dynamic shift in India's foreign policy occurred with the advent of Indira Gandhi, who took over the reins of the government in January 1966. India had by then been through three wars. The Indo-Pak war of 1947, the Sino-Indian war in 1962 and the Indo-Pak war of 1965. As P. Terhal writes in the article "Guns or Grain: Macro-Economic Costs of Indian Defence," what during the pre-Sino-Indian war had been a question of guns or grains, during the war, and post that, almost seemed to become guns at the cost of grains. In such a scenario, performing arts naturally took a back seat in India's policy considerations. Therefore, unlike the previous tour of 1962, where performances in Seattle and Europe in 1962, had been sponsored by the Government of India, this time around in 1968, it was only Sol Hurok who sponsored Uday Shankar's trip to the USA with his troupe. Ill health suffered by Shankar in December 1966 could not keep the showman in Shankar subdued for long. After a year's rest, towards the beginning of 1968, he sent for all his troupe members again. He had already started preparations for what would turn out to be his last tour of the USA in 1968. Chapter 5, *Revisiting the USA and Looking Forward*, traces not only Shankar's last tour of the USA with his troupe but why and how he took this on. It delves into the passing on the baton to Shanti Bose by virtue of bestowing on him the honour of performing *Kartikeya*, a favourite of Shankar's, a study of the items performed during the tour, the composition of the troupe members, and the sequence of performances in terms of the cities they toured, till the maestro suffered a cerebral attack in San Diego and the last two performances of the tour had to be cancelled.

Shankarscope was Shankar's last masterpiece. Once Shankar returned to India after the tour of 1968, he spent a few months in recuperation. However, towards the beginning of 1970, he sent word to a few of his close associates that he wanted to embark on a new production. In the souvenir of *Shankarscope* in 1970, Shankar writes that he had been thinking of this multi-media production for almost 20 years but had been unable to take it on due to financial constraints. With Ranjit Mull Kankaria as the producer, this final production of Shankar's which used both the stage and the screen concurrently was technologically way ahead of its time, and the first time that such an experiment was undertaken in India. It introduced to India technical innovations which had not been previously used and mirrored some of the socio-economic–political challenges India faced in the 1960s and 1970s. It posed pertinent questions and even critiqued various aspects of Indian society. The themes varied from that of unemployment, to the then current trend of Bollywood movies, to questioning what comprises true beauty. The 1971 production of *Shankarscope* also witnessed the inclusion of the item *Chinna Bichinna*, based on the havoc created by West Pakistan in East Pakistan and the genocide that followed, prior to its war of liberation. The sixth chapter of the book, *The Last Masterpiece*, details the items performed, the stories they told, how they were performed, the technology used, the music recordings and the re-staging of it in 1971 and 1972. In the 1972 restaging, a one-hour reworked version of *Samanya Kshati* was also staged with Shanti Bose as the Assistant Director, and in the lead role of the King, which Shankar himself used to previously enact himself. Bose was still the Ballet Master for Shankar's troupe. Details of this production have not been recorded in any of the existing literature on Shankar.

The seventh and concluding chapter of the book, *Uday Shankar's Style of Creative Dance – Its Impact and the Legacy*, looks at the impact that Uday Shankar and his art form had on India in terms of being a new vibrant form that was a corollary of modern India. It explores how Shankar introduced new movements in dance and formulated the basic tenets of his technique and dance style, thereby creating a revolution of sorts as it broke away from not only the duality in the bifurcation of Indian dance primarily as folk and classical but also many of the existing traditions of both the classical and folk forms, nonetheless retaining the essence of both. Shankar used his dance to present an alternate portal to view the challenges of modern India and the socio-political and economic turmoil that it faced in the post-independent years as well. His form was therefore not only a window to India's problems but also a platform for creativity and innovation. It discusses how for the purposes of creativity, he harnessed technological advancements and innovations from across the world and more often than not introduced them in the arena of performing arts in India, thereby giving form to his ideas in a manner never before conceived or seen in India. It highlights the legacy of Shankar and his impact on society and performing arts in terms of his role as the harbinger of social upliftment – thereby removing the social stigma attached to dance and dancers, and elevating the status of performing arts to the respect that it demands. His thought-provoking productions on the plight of marginalized communities in society, his social awareness and his sense of social responsibility ensure that he does not use his style purely for the purpose of entertainment but to provoke his audience to reflect on the world they inhabit. These elements of change and continuity are apparent in his productions of the period 1960–1977, both through the form and content. The impact of Shankar's art form on performing arts traditions of modern India places him in the position of one of the architects of modern India, whose contribution is no less valuable and important than many other oft-mentioned names. Unfortunately, non-textual works and their contribution often remain unacknowledged in their role of nation-building. The chapter concludes with the contention that these last two decades of Shankar's life, which are often viewed as a grey phase and one of degeneration, where he worked himself into despair, was in fact one of his creative crests. Just as autumn dazzles the earth with its maturity and presents itself in glorious golden shades and warm hues, so too did the maestro's choreographies, form, content and style, mature and unfold itself, taking it to glorious heights in the autumn of his life.

Notes

1 Mohan Khokar, *His Dance His Life – A Portrait of Uday Shankar* (New Delhi: Himalayan Books, 1983), 74.
2 Uttara Asha Coorlawala, "The Classical Traditions of Odissi and Manipuri," *Dance Chronicle* 16, no. 2 (1993): 269–76, accessed June 1, 2018, url: www.jstor.org/stable/1567933
3 Pallabi Chakravorty, "Dancing into Modernity: Multiple Narratives of India's Kathak Dance," *Dance Research Journal* 38, no. 1/2 (2006): 115–36, accessed February 20, 2019, url: www.jstor.org/stable/20444667
4 Kimiko Ohtani, "Bharata Nāṭyam, Rebirth of Dance in India," *Studia Musicologica Academiae Scientiarum Hungaricae* 33, no. 1/4 (1991): 301–08, accessed February 20, 2019, www.jstor.org/stable/902452
5 Uttara Asha Coorlawala, "The Classical Traditions of Odissi and Manipuri," *Dance Chronicle* 16, no. 2 (1993): 269–76, accessed June 1, 2018, url: www.jstor.org/stable/1567933

6 Ibid.
7 Board of Scholars, eds, *The Natya Shastra* (New Delhi: Sai Satguru Publications, year of publication not mentioned), ix.
8 *Natyashastra* – Said to have been penned by Sage Bharata, by compiling all that is best in the four texts of ancient India – the Rig Veda, Sama Veda, Yajur Veda and the Atharva Veda. It is a treatise on Performing Arts as per the traditions of ancient India.
9 *Ragas* – The melodic variations based on different permutations and combinations of the seven basic notes in Indian music. Said to be reflective and associated with various seasons, emotions and *prahar* or time of the day.
10 *Shloka* – A couplet in Sanskrit where each line contains 16 syllables.
11 *Stotra* – A Sanskrit word which roughly translate to mean an ode or eulogy to a deity. It can also be a prayer.
12 Brahmins – People belonging to the upper echelon in the four main tiers of the Indian caste system.
13 Joan L. Erdman, "Performance as Translation: Uday Shankar in the West, *The Drama Review: TDR* 31, no. 1 (1987): 64–88, accessed July 9, 2017, url: www.jstor.org/stable/1145766
14 *Nritya* – Being a combination of dance movements through various postures and *mudras* or hand gestures along with facial expressions.
15 *Abhinaya* – Enactment through facial expressions and gestures.
16 *Navarasas* – The nine basic emotions and their *prayog* or application as defined in the *Natya Shastra*.
17 *Mudras* – Hand gestures both *Asamyukta Hastas* or single hand gestures and *Samyukta Hastas* or gestures made by using both hands.
18 *Pada Bhedas* – Different kinds of positioning of the feet by the dancer.
19 *Kothas* – Houses of ill repute in the red-light area of an urban space primarily in eastern and northern India.
20 Kapila Vatsyayan, *Traditions of Indian Folk Dance* (New Delhi: Clarion Books associated with Hind Pocket Books, 1987).
21 Uday Shankar, "My Love for Dance," *Souvenir of Shankarscope* (1970).
22 Edward W. Said, *Orientalism* (London: Routledge and Kegan Paul, 1978), 1–2.
23 Joan L. Erdman, "Performance as Translation: Uday Shankar in the West," *The Drama Review: TDR* 31, no. 1 (1987): 64–88, accessed July 9, 2017, url: www.jstor.org/stable/1145766
24 *Bharatnatyam* – Classical dance form associated with the state of Tamil Nadu in Southern India.
25 *Odissi* – Identified as the classical dance form of the state of Odisha, in eastern India.
26 *Manipuri* – The classical dance form of Manipur, in Northeast India.
27 *Kathak* – The classical dance form of northern India, the two main gharanas and styles being from Lucknow and Jaipur, in the states of Uttar Pradesh and Rajasthan, in northern and north-western India, respectively.
28 *Kathakali* – The classical dance form of Kerala in southern India.
29 *Bhangra* – The folk-dance form of Punjab in north-western India.
30 *Bihu* – The folk-dance form of Assam in north-eastern India.
31 *Madia* – The folk-dance form of Madhya Pradesh in central India.
32 *Santhal* – The folk-dance form of parts of West Bengal and Bihar.
33 Mohan Khokar, *His Dance His Life – A Portrait of Uday Shankar* (New Delhi: Himalayan Books, 1983), 78.
34 Romila Thapar et al., *On Nationalism* (New Delhi: Aleph Book Company, 2016), 3.
35 Mohan Khokar, *His Dance His Life – A Portrait of Uday Shankar* (New Delhi: Himalayan Books, 1983), 169.

xxviii *Preface*

36 Uday Shankar, "My Love for Dance," *Souvenir of Shankarscope* (1970).
37 Mohan Khokar, *His Dance His Life – A Portrait of Uday Shankar* (New Delhi: Himalayan Books, 1983), 170.
38 Joan L. Erdman, "Performance as Translation: Uday Shankar in the West," *The Drama Review: TDR* 31, no. 1 (1987): 64–88, accessed July 9, 2017, url: www.jstor.org/stable/1145766
39 Mohan Khokar, *His Dance His Life – A Portrait of Uday Shankar* (New Delhi: Himalayan Books, 1983), 74.
40 Joan L. Erdman, "His Dance, His Life: A Portrait of Uday Shankar by Mohan Khokar," *Asian Theatre Journal* 3, no. 2 (1986): 275–76, accessed July 10, 2017, url: www.jstor.org/stable/1124405
41 Joan L. Erdman, "A Comment on Dance Scholarship," *Dance Chronicle* 31, no. 2 (2008): 306–9, accessed July 10, 2017, url: www.jstor.org/stable/25598167
42 Ashoke Kumar Mukhopadhya, *Uday Shankar – Twentieth Century's Nataraja* (New Delhi: Rupa Charitavali Series, 2004).
43 Kothari, Sunil and Mohan Khokar, eds, *Uday Shankar – A Photo Biography* (New Delhi: Ravi Shankar on behalf of RIMPA and Uday Shankar Festival '83 Committee, 1983).
44 Satyen Chatterjee, *Padma Parer Manush Ebong Uday Shankar* (Kolkata: Satyen Chatterjee, 1993).
45 Sudhiranjan Mukhopadhya, *Uday Shankar* (Kolkata: Pratya Prakashani, 1991).
46 Shankarlal Bhattacharya, *Udayer Pathe* (Kolkata: Sahityam, 2007).
47 Bisakha Ghose, *Shankarnama: Smritichitre Amalashankar* (Calcutta: Ananda Publishers Private Limited, 2019).
48 Ibid.
49 Tapati Chowdhurie, "Mould It Like Manipuri," *www.thehindu.com*, October 18, 2016, accessed September 12, 2019, url: www.thehindu.com/features/friday-review/Mould-it-like-Manipuri/article14412584.ece
50 Nitish Sengupta, *Builders of Modern India: Dr. Bidhan Chandra Roy* (New Delhi: Publications Division, Ministry of Information and Broadcasting, Government of India, 2002), accessed January 7, 2023, url: https://archive.org/details/bidhanchandraroy00seng/page/n5/mode/2up
51 Mohan Khokar, *His Dance His Life – A Portrait of Uday Shankar* (New Delhi: Himalayan Books, 1983), 131.
52 Rabindra Bharati University Prospectus 2012, accessed September 12, 2019, url: www.academia.edu/8192030/RABINDRA_BHARATI_UNIVERSITY
53 Swapan Shome, "Jiban Je Rokom, Shey Bhabei Meley Dhorechhen," *Ananda Bazar Patrika*, August 3, 2019 (page: *Pustak Parichay*).
54 Joan L. Erdman, "Who Remembers Uday Shankar?" accessed July 10, 2017, url: https://mm-gold.azureedge.net/new_site/mukto-mona/Articles/jaffor/uday_shanka2.html
55 Joan L. Erdman, "Who Remembers Uday Shankar?" accessed July 10, 2017, url: https://mm-gold.azureedge.net/new_site/mukto-mona/Articles/jaffor/uday_shanka2.html
56 Mohan Khokar, *His Dance His Life – A Portrait of Uday Shankar* (New Delhi: Himalayan Books, 1983), 142.
57 Joan L. Erdman, "Who Remembers Uday Shankar?" accessed July 10, 2017, url: https://mm-gold.azureedge.net/new_site/mukto-mona/Articles/jaffor/uday_shanka2.html
58 Hayden V. White, "The Tasks of Intellectual History," *The Monist* 53, no. 4 (1969): 606–30, accessed March 11, 2019, url: www.jstor.org/stable/27902149
59 Intellectual History, Penn Arts and Sciences, Department of History, accessed March 11, 2019, url: www.history.upenn.edu/undergraduate/undergraduate-courses/concentrations/intellectual-history

60 Cultural History, Department of History, Yale University, accessed May 5, 2019, url: https://history.yale.edu/academics/undergraduate-program/regions-and-pathways/cultural-history
61 Geoffrey Eley, "What Is Cultural History?" *New German Critique*, no. 65 (1995): 19–36, accessed May 5, 2019, url: www.jstor.org/stable/488530
62 Charlotte Phelan, "Dance – A Review: Rattle, Roll and Shankar," *The Houston Post,* November 15, 1968, 7.
63 Craig Calhoun, *Dictionary of the Social Sciences* (New York: Oxford University Press, 2004).
64 Alonzo King Lines Ballet, accessed December 4, 2022, url: https://linesballet.org/wp-content/uploads/2021/03/Ballet-Master-Job-Description.pdf
65 Shankarscope, advertisement, Ananda Bazar Patrika, November 14, 1972.
66 Shankarscope, advertisement, Yugantar, November 12, 1972.
67 Shankarscope, advertisement, Amrita Bazar Patrika, November 10, 1972.
68 Shanti, Santi, Śāntī, Śānti, Samti, Shamti: 39 definitions, Wisdom Library, accessed December 4, 2022, url: www.wisdomlib.org/definition/shanti
69 An interview of Uday Shankar by Shambhu Mitra on DD Bharati, accessed April 28, 2019, url: www.youtube.com/watch?v=JHq-uBio5vE&t=14s
70 A. M. Frazier, "The Criterion of Historical Knowledge," *Journal of Thought* 11, no. 1 (1976): 60–7, accessed March 15, 2019, url: www.jstor.org/stable/42588543.
71 E. H. Carr, *What is History?* (London: Penguin Books, 1987), 30.
72 Charles A. Beard, "History Written as an Act of Faith," *American Historical Association*, accessed May 20, 2023. url: https://www.historians.org/about-aha-and-membership/aha-history-and-archives/presidential-addresses/charles-a-beard.
73 Ibid.

Acknowledgements

This book is a culmination of a journey of more than 40 years which saw me travel the trajectory of being a student, performer, teacher and researcher of the Uday Shankar's style of creative dance. I extend my heartfelt thanks to Antara Ray Chaudhury, Brinda Sen and the rest of the team at Routledge, Taylor and Francis, for making it possible to share not only the knowledge accumulated over the last so many decades but that too about a pioneer figure who had captured the imagination of the world with his art.

This book is an extension of my doctoral thesis, *Creativity in Independent India: Uday Shankar, 1960–1977*, and would not have been possible without the guidance of my Ph.D. supervisor, Dr. Radhika Seshan, to whom I extend my heartfelt thanks. Now my guide for life, without her patient guidance, gentle nudges, and at times tough to meet deadlines, I would not have been able to complete either my thesis or this book. It is only after I had acquired my degree that she informed me (to my surprised delight), that she found my research to be path-breaking and that I ought to get it published at the earliest, as recommended by the external examiners of my Ph.D. defense. It is she who connected me with Antara Ray Chaudhury and from then on, there was no looking back. Radhikadi, as I now call her (the adding of the "di" in Bengali reflecting respect usually reserved for an elder sister), has been by my side from the first day I met her in 2013. Our conversations whether at the university cafeteria, her office or at her home – which she and her family so welcomingly opened up for me – have enriched me tremendously, and continue to do so.

My heartfelt thanks also to Dr. Anita Patankar, Founder Director, and now Advisor at Symbiosis School for Liberal Arts (SSLA). A role model for me as someone who leads from the front, her tips on time management and smart working, together with her kind consideration and support, have enabled both my thesis and this book to see the light of the day. Over the last 11 years, Anita has become my friend, philosopher and guide, and propelled me to achieve much more than I thought myself to be capable of, after my transition from being a performing artist to academia. The transition was nudged by several injuries that prevented me from returning to stage. Her confidence in me and my work has always boosted me to push my boundaries. I am

Acknowledgements xxxi

also happy to share that with Anita's support, I was not only responsible for initiating and leading a department of Performing Arts at SSLA but that SSLA is the only liberal arts college and institute of higher education in the world, to offer a 60-hour, 4-credit course on Uday Shankar's style of creative dance. It was while teaching the style, that the lacunae of literature on Uday Shankar and his works between 1960 and 1977, propelled me to undertake the study of Shankar's work and style as an academic pursuit, as this was a period when Shankar was at his creative best as a mature artist. The online knowledge portals that I could access at the click of a mouse, by virtue of being a faculty member of SSLA, were also of immense help.

The late Dr. Joan L. Erdman, Professor Emerita of Anthropology and Cultural Studies, Columbia College, and Associate, Committee on Southern Asian Studies, University of Chicago, whom we lost in October 2021, is another person to whom I owe immense gratitude, in terms of her encouragement towards my research and writing on Uday Shankar. While writing my research proposal in 2014, her seminal writings on Uday Shankar and the questions she raised helped me identify and consolidate the knowledge gap that existed and paved the way for me to bridge it. A serendipitous meeting in 2016 (I had already commenced with my PhD by then), and again in 2018, when she encouraged me to put on paper, this period of Uday Shankar's work, i.e. between 1960 and 1977, as well as her detailed pointers on what I should keep in mind to ensure that the study is as unbiased as possible, since the art form is so close to my heart, were exceedingly crucial to this work as well.

My sincere thanks also to Dr. Ilora Basu. A family friend, she shared with me some rare and precious photographs from her private collection when she heard that I was working on Uday Shankar. These images had been clicked by her father, the late Amiyah Lal Choudhury in the early 1940s, during Uday Shankar's visit to Mymensingh, with his troupe. Her generosity in allowing me to use them both for my thesis and this book has helped add immense value to the book, as these are images of Uday Shankar, Simkie, Amala Shankar and Baba Allauddin Khan which have never before been published.

My heartfelt thanks also to my friends and family, without whose support I would not have been able to achieve any of it. My friends were always there whether I needed to talk or required any help with tech-related challenges. Dr. Shweta Sinha Deshpande and Shweta Chawla – a big thank you!

There are no words adequate enough to thank my husband, Susmit Sen, and my daughter, Sharanya Sen. Not only did they encourage me, but their patient understanding whenever I got lost in the world of Shankar be it during rehearsals, performances, research or writing, enabled me and empowered me – to be myself – and pursue my passions and dreams.

My maternal aunts, Dr. Sutapa Sengupta and Dr. Sudipta Sengupta, who are awe-inspiring academicians and achievers in their own right, inspired in me the desire to pursue academics and goals which I had once thought insurmountable. Having travelled and worked across the globe, climbed the highest peaks both literally and metaphorically, challenging all odds and living life on their own terms, they are the ones who opened my eyes to all the best that the world has to offer – be it in literature, music, films, adventures and everything else under the sun! Growing up in a joint family, the evening *addas* and conversations opened my mind to the fact that everything was connected – be it literature, art, music, dance or politics! Their constant help during the course of the writing, whenever I reached out to them, for whatever need, has helped immensely in seeing this study and book through.

My brother, Dr. Shamik Bose, and his family, albeit on the other side of the globe, their quiet assurance that they are there, no matter what, and that all will be well, also added tremendously to my peace of mind during the writing of both the thesis and the manuscript of this book.

My mother, Sunanda Bose, who is a superwoman in her own right, whom I can only hope to emulate in the multiple roles she played and continues to play – as a dancer, choreographer, teacher, mother, daughter, grand-mother, sister, home-maker (and the list is endless) – with equal dexterity, has been the force who has always pushed me to excel in whatever I pursued, and reach out for that piece sky which I always felt was beyond my grasp. My first formal dance teacher, by virtue of being the dance teacher of the primary section at Loreto House, one of Kolkata's finest schools, which is my alma mater, she helped me evolve as an artist, and feel and realize what I was learning, rehearsing and performing – all the more so when I began playing the lead roles in Tagore's dance dramas. My father, Shanti Bose, the most graceful dancer conceivable, under whom I trained as I advanced in age and received instruction in Uday Shankar's style of creative dance, is a perfectionist to the core. He refused to settle for anything less from his students and troupe members, and set the toughest bars for me. It is to him I owe my perfection and fascination for Uday Shankar's style of dance and its depths. A genius of a choreographer, and the most principled person I have ever come across, he always challenged me to put in better than my best in everything that I do, and I hope this book reflects that as well. This book, in fact, would not have taken off, but for his collection of photographs, souvenirs, newspaper clippings, memorabilia – all annotated, and the sharp memory that he still carries with him in terms of the work that he engaged in with Uday Shankar between the years 1960 and 1977. His cupboard was my archive. To thank them seems to be a grossly inadequate way of expressing my gratitude to them. I am sure they know exactly how important they were in seeing this book to its completion, and therefore to them, I dedicate this book.

Introduction
Uday Shankar – Till the Autumn of His Life

Born on December 8, 1900, in the city of Udaipur, after which he was named, Uday Shankar revolutionized Indian dance traditions, with the creation of the third genre – the creative form. His father, Shyam Shankar, was a distinguished scholar, and a connoisseur of arts. Shyam Shankar had initially come to the city of Udaipur, in present-day Rajasthan, as a tutor to the Prince, Maharaj Kumar Bhopal Singh. He was later appointed as Private Secretary to His Highness, Maharaj Rana Bhawani Singh after the latter became the ruler of the then princely state of Jhalawar. Shyam Shankar was often appointed to travel as the Home Minister to assist the Maharaj. He later became the Prime Minister of Jhalawar. Uday Shankar's mother, Hemangini Devi, often took Uday Shankar to her maternal home in Nasrathpur, a village near Varanasi, also known as Benaras or Kaashi. The stays would get prolonged if Shyam Shankar happened to be travelling for work with His Highness. Hemangini Devi's father was the *Zamindar* or landlord of Nasrathpur. A conservative and authoritarian man, he never appreciated nor understood Shankar's refusal to conform. Having spent his childhood between Jhalawar and Nasrathpur, Uday Shankar's formal education was naturally hampered. He changed schools thrice. A nature lover and a rebel, Shankar often skipped school and went around wandering in many locales considered to be unsuitable for the upper caste *Bramhins* – for that was his caste by birth. Apart from occasional forays to a Muslim friend's house for chicken, which was forbidden among the *Brahmins*, he also visited the neighbourhoods on the fringes of Nasrathpur, where resided the low-caste *chamars* or the untouchables – as society had deemed them to be.

    The music of the *chamars* and their dance, especially the movements of an old man, Matadin, captivated him. It is said that it was Matadin who inspired in Uday Shankar, the desire to dance. Years later, when Shankar returned to India after staying abroad at a stretch for more than a decade, during which he choreographed and performed pieces in many European cities, and having enchanted the world with his dance, he revisited Nasrathpur, and he threw himself at Matadin's feet.[1] In his interview with Shambhu Mitra, however, Uday Shankar says that it was his mother, who given that she did not have any daughters, used to dress him up as a girl and asked him to dance – which he did in his own fashion, much to her delight. He therefore attributes to her, his first desire to dance.[2]

He had also wanted to meet Ambika Charan Mukherjee, another strong childhood influence, but could not trace him. Ambika Charan Mukherjee used to teach art at the school Uday Shankar attended in Nasrathpur. He had been the first one to notice the artistic traits in this otherwise rebellious boy. Under Ambika Charan Mukherjee, or *Mastermoshai* as he was called, a young Uday Shankar developed his skills as an artist. Passionate about photography, *Mastermoshai* had his own camera and darkroom equipment. Shankar soon became adept at clicking photographs and developing them himself. Once back in Jhalawar, impressed by his son's keenness and talent in painting, Shyam Shankar arranged for him to have extra classes in painting. The Jhalawar court too was a centre of art, for Maharaj Rana Bhawani Singh was a great patron of art. This cultural ambience of the court, together with the festivals and colours of Rajasthan – their folk dances, their rich Rajputana heritage, skilled swordsmanship, the style of painting – all had an indelible effect on Uday Shankar's formative mind.

In 1917, Uday Shankar joined the J.J. School of Art in Bombay. While Shankar was undertaking his formal training in Bombay, Shyam Shankar became the Prime Minister of Jhalawar. Fate, however, had other plans. The Maharaja and Shyam Shankar fell apart in time, and Shyam Shankar remained in London. In the meantime, Uday Shankar completed his three-year course at the J.J. School of Art, in Bombay and set sail for England to join the Royal College of Arts for painting.

Uday Shankar's transition from an artist to a dancer can perhaps be best grasped from his write-up titled "My Love for Dance," from the souvenir of *Shankarscope*. In it, Uday Shankar states that he left India in 1919 and was a scholarship holder. He finished his five years' course in two years and got the A.R.C.A. Diploma with honours. During his tenure at the Royal College of Arts, he was the only Indian student in the history of the college till then, to receive the Spencer prize for imaginative painting and the George Clausen prize for self-portraiture. It was also as a student there, that he was profoundly influenced by the Principal, Sir William Rothenstein. One day, Rothenstein came to visit the class and after examining Shankar's work, asked him to come to his office, once Shankar had finished his work. Shankar met him accordingly. Writes Shankar, Sir Rothenstein told him,

> I was in India for a long time, and I have seen wonders in your arts and crafts. I can see in your work that you are very much interested in our European way of modern painting. Why take this disease to India? Why not keep to your Indian style and improve on it?

He handed Uday Shankar a letter saying, "Give this to the Curator of the British Museum, he will help you, and you don't need to come for a month to join your classes."[3]

Uday Shankar met the Curator. He took him to a room and showed him a large table with hundreds of voluminous books on Indian Arts and Crafts and said, "Here you are Mr. Shankar. You can go through all of them and if you want anything else, ask for me."[4] For one month, Uday Shankar went through all the books. According to him, a month was not enough. He could have spent a lifetime looking at them. For the first time, Uday Shankar realized the richness of India's heritage, in terms of art and culture; and for that he was most grateful to his Principal, Sir William Rothenstein.

During his college days in London, Uday Shankar had already started experimenting with dance, and after his performance at the Wembley Exhibition Theatre on India Day, where he performed the dance of *Shiva*, he received high praise. In his televised interview with Shambhu Mitra, Uday Shankar refers to Mrs. Sen, who put him in touch with the organizers and thereby enabled this performance.[5] Again, on June 30, 1922, Uday Shankar got a chance to dance in a garden party for His Majesty King George V. He performed a *Sword Dance* and a few other items. King George V appreciated them very much and after the performance showered him with compliments. Uday Shankar was naturally very happy. His knowledge of painting played an important role in his choreography and creation of movements. As told in a conversation with Shanti Bose, Uday Shankar had said that once looking at a photograph of *Nataraj* – the divine form of Lord Shiva as a cosmic dancer – he felt that the image of Shiva was moving towards him in a particular motion. He used the movement that he had visualized and imagined in his composition of *Indra*. In the televised interview, Shankar says that the picture of Lord Shiva in the *Nataraj* pose appealed to him so much that he tried it in front of the mirror, and in the process realized that it was not just one static posture but, rather, constituted a whole host of movements which led to that posture.[6]

In the same write-up, *My Love for Dance*, Shankar goes on to say that the renowned Russian dancer, Anna Pavlova, had left Russia and was living in London at that time. She used to live in "Ivy House" in Hampstead Heath. She was looking for someone who could help her compose two short dances based on Indian themes. She had heard of Uday Shankar from some of her Indian friends. They met for the first time in 1922, when he agreed to create two ballets for her – *The Hindu Marriage* and *Radha Krishna*. Shankar worked with Pavlova's team for three months and partnered as Krishna to Pavlova's Radha. The ballets which were presented at the Royal Opera House, Covent Garden, garnered high praise from the London press after the premiere performance.

So happy was Pavlova with the productions that she asked Uday Shankar to accompany her troupe to the USA. During his travels, Uday Shankar watched her troupe and saw how hard they worked. To them, work was their God, and this is something he not only writes in the article, *My Love for Dance*, but also says in the televised interview. He learned from them and imbibed this facet in his subsequent life and works.[7] Working with Pavlova was a tremendous learning for Shankar, for he was exposed to how a professional dance troupe functioned and witnessed first-hand the principles of organization, discipline and above all, showmanship. In her book, *Stages: The Art and Adventures of Zohra Sehgal*, authored by Dr. Joan Erdman with Zohra Sehgal, Sehgal, who was associated with Uday Shankar from 1935 to 1943, as a lead dancer at the Uday Shankar Ballet Company and Main Teacher at the Uday Shankar India Culture Centre at Almora, reminisces how it was with Shankar that she "learned the discipline of the stage, punctuality and the religious atmosphere during a performance."[8] Another extremely important aspect of Shankar's tour with Pavlova was that it was during this tour in 1922, that he met Sol Hurok, the impresario who would enable Shankar to tour the length and breadth of the USA eight times, with his own troupe, subsequently.

While touring with Pavlova for ten months in the USA, Uday Shankar one day asked Pavlova to let him learn classical ballet so that he could be more useful to the troupe. According to Shankar, hearing this, Pavlova told him,

> You should never learn our dancing. I have been in your country and seen beautiful dances there, which I will never forget. You should bring a troupe with wonderful Indian music and dances which we know so little about in the West – and that should be your job in the future.[9]

This is also something he reasserts in the televised interview.

With both Rothenstein and Pavlova urging him to turn to his roots, the next period saw Uday Shankar, in the peak of his youth, spending his days in Paris' libraries and museums to understand Indian culture, heritage and its various art forms. During this period, he struggled hard to survive in Paris. This struggle was not just for survival but a creative one as well. He worked for 13–14 hours a day, creating hundreds of movements and different kinds of steps, to suit different moods and environments. He built a complete programme with music built on European orchestra.[10] It was also in Paris, often called the city of love, that Uday Shankar met Simone Barbier. Simone was only 16 years old, but she was quite a proficient pianist. Uday Shankar engaged her to accompany him on the piano. Soon she started emulating the poses struck by Uday Shankar and ultimately became his dance partner for nearly 20 years. Uday Shankar christened her Simkie – and as Mohan Khokar writes, together they created dance history.[11] In 1928, Shankar gave his first recital in Paris to tremendous acclaim. Soon he was performing in almost every European capital. But he was not satisfied, as he felt that the music he used, when played on Western instruments, did not convey the authentic sounds and rhythms of India. He stopped his tour and returned home to India, after 11 years of stay in Europe at a stretch.[12]

The propagation of any art form requires a patron. Uday Shankar received patronage for his art form from the Swiss painter and sculptress, Alice Boner. In fact, according to Zohra Sehgal, it was Miss Boner who encouraged Shankar to return to India and form his own troupe with Indian dancers and musicians.

Alice Boner was Shankar's guide and mentor in financial and artistic matters and ran Shankar's company in partnership with him.[13] Together with Alice Boner, Uday Shankar travelled all over India for one year. In his own words,

> (I) saw the wonders of my country. I saw the dances, temples, mosques, architectures, caves, paintings etc., and studied as much as I could. I was overwhelmed with joy, seeing all these and fully realized what Sir William Rothenstein and Anna Pavlova had said about India.[14]

It was during this trip to India that Uday Shankar revisited Nasrathpur and Matadin. At the Guruvayoor temple in Kerala, Uday Shankar was taken aback by the similarity of the movements he had created with the ones used in *Kathakali* – all the more so as he had never been exposed to this ancient art form of Kerala before. After touring India and collecting various musical instruments from different parts of the country, Uday Shankar was ready to return to Europe with his own troupe of dancers and musicians. The lack of response with regard to funding for the realization of this dream led Alice Boner to shoulder the responsibility of the troupe.

The team that he brought back to Europe in 1930 comprised mostly his family members. Uday Shankar's three brothers – Rajendra, Devendra and Rabindra (Ravi Shankar) – were taken on as dancers. His uncles Kedar Shankar and Brojo Bihari Banerjee, as well as his cousin Kanaklata also joined the troupe. Shankar's music director at this point in time was none other than Timir Baran, who is referred to as the father of the Indian symphony orchestra.[15] A disciple of Baba Allauddin Khan, Timir Baran was a sarod artist who ran India's first orchestra, comprising primarily his relatives – the Bhattacharya's – another Brahmin family, who were well known for their musical traditions.

Vishnudas Shirali, a sitarist and a master drummer, joined the troupe directly in Paris. In an interview with Sangeet Natak Akademi on March 12, 1974, Shirali reminisces how during 1930–1939, when he was touring the USA, Canada and Europe with Uday Shankar, the pioneering work they created was what paved the way for Indian musicians and dancers in the post-independent era to go abroad and play independently and be accepted by the Western audiences.[16] His struggles during his stay in London, before he joined Shankar, were witness to this. Uday Shankar's mother also accompanied them. In the televised interview, Uday Shankar says that it was his mother who cooked and took care of all of them. Simkie joined the troupe soon after their arrival in Paris. The company was registered under the name *La Compagnie d'Uday Shankar Hindoue Danses et la Musique*.

Uday Shankar and his troupe performed in the USA for the first time in 1932. The 1930s saw the creation of some 45 individual items including *Kartikeya, Indra, Snanam, Yuddha Yatra, Hara Parvati* and the *Harvest Festival*. *Kartikeya* was composed by Guru Shankaran Namboodri in Kolkata in 1934. Although the dance had inputs from Uday Shankar, Uday Shankar accepted Shankaran Namboodri as his Guru. Shankaran Namboodri went back to Kerala after his stint in Kolkata, but later joined Uday Shankar at his

Culture Centre in Almora. The music for Kartikeya was created by Vishnudas Shirali. He would later join Shankar at his centre at Almora and go on to become the music director for Shankar's film, *Kalpana*.

It was during this period that Shankar first met Amala Shankar at the *Exposition Coloniale* in Paris. She was then a young girl, 11 years of age, who had accompanied her father to Paris to attend the same exhibition. Amala Shankar toured with Uday Shankar for a year and performed the role of *Kalia* in his composition of *Kalia Daman*, after which she returned to India. She later joined Uday Shankar at the centre in Almora. They got married in 1942.

After touring and performing in Europe and the USA for over two years, Uday Shankar toured India for almost three months in 1933, staging 42 performances with his Indian impresario Haren Ghosh.[17] He again returned to the West with his troupe and continued conquering his audience in different cities of Europe and the USA with his dance and his art. After accompanying Uday Shankar for five years, Alice Boner who had by now felt that she had neglected her own work for too long left Uday Shankar's troupe where she had been the co-director along with Uday Shankar.

In 1938, Uday Shankar decided to return to India and set up an All India Centre for Dance and Music. Shankar had been very impressed by the academic ambience at Dartington Hall in Devonshire. Developed by Leonard and Dorothy Elmhirst, studies on a host of subjects, ranging from agriculture and forestry to education and arts, were pursued at Dartington Hall. Uday Shankar wanted to develop a centre in India, which would not only teach dance and music but would also look at costume designing and encourage the development of India's cultural heritage.

Uday Shankar's main inspiration for opening this centre was a result of the impression made on him by Mikhail Chekov, the renowned Russian actor, who was also the nephew of the renowned litterateur, Anton Chekov. Uday Shankar had performed with his troupe on October 5, 1936 – the day the Chekov Theatre Studio had opened at Dartington Hall. After the performance, Uday Shankar attended a discussion conducted by Michael Chekov, who, along with his students, analysed Shankar's performance, which they had all seen the previous evening. The in-depth analysis of the performance, together with the free exchange of views and counter-views between the teacher and the students, impressed Uday Shankar to a great extent. He decided to imbibe this idea of free exchange of views at his centre. The Elmhirsts pitched in and helped Shankar with a starting fund of 20,000 pounds. Others who helped with the funding for the centre at Almora included Alice Boner, Mikhail Chekov, Jawaharlal Nehru, Romain Rolland, Sir William Rothenstein, Mr. Whitney and Lady Daphne Straight and Rabindranath Tagore – to name a few. Erstwhile members of Uday Shankar's troupe like Simkie, Zohra and Uzra Sehgal, Amala Nandi and Vishnudas Shirali, got together a year before the centre opened, to formulate a plan of action for the Centre. The government of Uttar Pradesh donated 93 acres of land for the centre.[18]

Named "The Uday Shankar India Culture Centre," the institute at Almora began functioning in March 1940. The centre attracted stalwarts in various fields as teachers, like Guru Shankaran Namboodri for *Kathakali*, Guru Kandappa Pillai for *Bharatnatyam*, Guru Ambobi Singh for *Manipuri* and Ustad Allauddin Khan of Maihar for music. The classes used to begin with a General Class conducted by Shankar himself. This class was attended by both students and troupe members. This was followed by a class in "Technique" taught only to the students. Rajendra Shankar conducted the theory classes, while Uday Shankar occasionally taught painting. Apart from these, there would also be classes in different Indian Classical Dance forms like *Bharatnatyam*, *Kathakali* and *Manipuri*. In the evening, another class was conducted by Uday Shankar on "Improvisation." During these classes, the students or dancers would give form to their imagination and bring forth their creativity. Monthly assessments were held where the students had to perform their own compositions, and these were then discussed and evaluated.

The exercises conducted in the general class and classes on improvisation were something that Shankar continued with his troupe members and disciples well into the mid-1960s, during rehearsals at Shankar's house for the production of *Prakriti Ananda*, in which he also integrated the improvisations in the opening scene of the dance drama.

This period in the early 1940s witnessed the creation of a few of Uday Shankar's items like *Rhythm of Life* and *Labour and Machinery*. It also saw the creation of a ballet performed in shadow – *Ram Leela*, *Kirat Arjun* and many other individual items, which were also composed during this period. The Centre, however, though conceptually magnificent, closed down according to Uday Shankar in an interview, due to the advent of the Second World War, which created a whole set of war-induced problems[19] as well as other problems which varied from a student strike and the desire to focus on the making of a film.[20]

Before moving on to the next segment of Shankar's life and his venture into film-making with *Kalpana*, I would like to share a couple of extremely rare photographs from the early 1940s, of Uday Shankar and his troupe, including Simkie, Amala Shankar and Baba Allauddin Khan. The photographs were shared with me by a close family friend, Dr. Ilora Basu, from her private collection. These images were clicked by her father, the late Amiyah Lal Choudhury in Mymensingh, which is in present-day Bangladesh, when Shankar and his troupe were touring and performing in an undivided Bengal. Although in construction business by profession, photography was Amiyah Lal Choudhury's passion. Says his daughter, Dr. Ilora Basu,

> These pictures of Uday Shankar and group were taken by my father . . . in the early 1940's. He had his own photography studio. So, these pictures were developed and printed by him too. He made three small albums, one for Uday Shankar, one for Simkie, and one for our family. After my father passed away, I found these three albums. Apparently, he never gave it to them. One day, I went to Uday Shankar's house with my uncle and gave him the album. The family copy was badly damaged and Simkie's copy is still in the family.

8 Introduction

Figure I.1 Uday Shankar with his group in the early 1940s, clicked by the late Amiyah Lal Choudhury. Uday Shankar can be seen here flanked by Zohra Sehgal on the left and Simkie on the right; with Baba Allauddin Khan, on the other side of Simkie.

Source: Courtesy, private collection of Dr. Ilora Basu

To return to the narrative, after the centre at Almora, Uday Shankar's next venture was his film, *Kalpana*. Although *Kalpana* was completed in 1947 and released in 1948, the idea for the film was conceived during the early 1940s. With inputs from the famous actor and director, Guru Dutt, who was then a student at the centre, the film was shot at Gemini Studios in Madras. Most of the actors were trained dancers from Kerala and other parts of southern India. With a storyline that was autobiographical in nature, it saw Uday Shankar himself enact the role of Udayan, the lead character of the film. The movie was produced and directed by Uday Shankar and although it did not garner much return in terms of monetary benefits, it received awards and collected accolades all over the globe. It was restored by the World Cinema Foundation and screened at the Cannes Film Festival in 2012.

Introduction 9

Figure I.2 Uday Shankar, Simkie and Amala Shankar, again in the early 1940s in Mymensingh.

Source: Clicked by the late Amiyah Lal Choudhury. Courtesy, private collection of Dr. Ilora Basu

Having stayed and performed in the West – spanning the UK, the USA and France – for most of his adult life, till the age of 38, Shankar when he forayed into dance was initially rather unaffected by the Indian socio-economic–political scenario from the 1920s till the late 1930s. It was only once he returned to India and set up his dance centre at Almora that the events of contemporary India affected him and this was reflected in his dance items. Termed a manifesto for modern India,[21] *Kalpana* opens with the scroll which reads:

> I request you all to be very alert while you watch this picture – Fantasy. Some of the events depicted here will reel off at great speed and if you miss any piece, you will really be missing a vital aspect of our country's life in its religion, politics, education, society, art and culture, agriculture and industry.

10   Introduction

> *I do not deliberately aim my criticism at any particular group of people or institutions, but if it appears to be so, it just happens to be so, that is all.*
>
> *It is my duty as an artist to be fully alive to all conditions of life and thought relating to our country and I present it truthfully with all the faults and merits through the medium of my art.*
>
> *I hope that you will be with me in our final purpose to rectify our own shortcomings and become worthy of our cultural heritage and make our motherland once again the greatest in the world.*
>
> Uday Shankar[22]

After *Kalpana*, Shankar started anew with a troupe consisting mostly of new members. He again toured the USA in 1949. Among the new items presented in this tour alongside the old ones were *Bidai, Rajput Bride, Nirikshan, Tilottoma* and *Village Festival*. Uday Shankar himself performed in the solo dance of *Naga Chief*. The tour was a huge success and not only was Uday Shankar interviewed by ABC network but his performances were also telecast by the CBS network.

Uday Shankar's most well-known production of the 1950s was *The Great Renunciation*. Based on the story of the life of Lord Gautam Buddha, this ballet premiered in New Delhi during a symposium on Buddhism on occasion of the 2,500th anniversary celebrations of Buddha's *Mahaparinirvana*. The Government of India and UNESCO jointly sponsored it. Between 1957 and 1959, Uday Shankar, together with his dance troupe, toured China and Africa.

1959 saw the headlines in the Kolkata press scream "Shankar Finished," after a fire ravaged the venue where Shankar and his troupe had performed in Kasba, in Kolkata. It was feared that his costumes, musical instruments, lights and other equipment had been damaged. Luckily, despite some minor damage, the boxes where these were stored were all waterproof and fireproof, and therefore the damage was not as much as it had initially been feared.

This segment of the book was one of the most challenging to write as it attempts to provide an overview of Uday Shankar's life from 1900 to 1960. Many details spanning across these 60 years have not been included as the focus of this book is Shankar's work from the period 1960–1977. Nonetheless, it was necessary to introduce the readers to Uday Shankar and to understand the mature artist that he became in the autumn of his life. The influences on Shankar's life in terms of the places, times and contexts all reflect and help trace the trajectory of the distinct shift in the subject matter and content of his compositions. Primarily based on existing literature on Uday Shankar, together with the write-up published in the name of Uday Shankar in the Souvenir of *Shankarscope* in 1970, titled *My Love for Dance*,[23] this segment also takes into consideration a televised interview of Uday Shankar with the thespian Shambhu Mitra on DD Bharati[24] and oral history recordings of Shanti Bose.

Notes

1. Mohan Khokar, *His Dance His Life – A Portrait of Uday Shankar* (New Delhi: Himalayan Books, 1983).
2. An interview of Uday Shankar by Shambhu Mitra on DD Bharati, accessed April 28, 2019, url: www.youtube.com/watch?v=JHq-uBio5vE&t=14s
3. Uday Shankar, "My Love for Dance," *Souvenir of Shankarscope* (1970).
4. Ibid.
5. An interview of Uday Shankar by Shambhu Mitra on DD Bharati, accessed April 28, 2019, url: www.youtube.com/watch?v=JHq-uBio5vE&t=14s
6. Ibid.
7. Ibid.
8. Joan L. Erdman with Zohra Sehgal, *Stages: The Art and Adventures of Zohra Sehgal* (New Delhi: Pauls Press, 1997), 77.
9. Uday Shankar, "My Love for Dance," *Souvenir of Shankarscope* (1970).
10. Ibid.
11. Mohan Khokar, *His Dance His Life – A Portrait of Uday Shankar* (New Delhi: Himalayan Books, 1983), 42.
12. Uday Shankar, "My Love for Dance," *Souvenir of Shankarscope* (1970).
13. Joan L. Erdman with Zohra Sehgal, *Stages: The Art and Adventures of Zohra Sehgal* (New Delhi: Pauls Press, 1997), 77.
14. Uday Shankar, "My Love for Dance," *Souvenir of Shankarscope* (1970).
15. Sharad Dutt, "Father of Indian Symphony Orchestra – Timir Baran, Millennium Post," November 30, 2019, accessed December 19, 2021, url: www.millenniumpost.in/sundaypost/beacon/father-of-indian-symphony-orchestra–timir-baran-388449
16. B. C. Deva, "Towards and Indian Orchestra: Interview with Vishnudas Shirali," *Sangeet Natak Akademi, New Delhi*, 1993, accessed December 19, 2021, url: www.indianculture.gov.in/towards-indian-orchestra-interview-vishnudas-shirali
17. Mohan Khokar, *His Dance His Life – A Portrait of Uday Shankar* (New Delhi: Himalayan Books, 1983), 74.
18. Mohan Khokar, *His Dance His Life – A Portrait of Uday Shankar* (New Delhi: Himalayan Books, 1983), 95–6.
19. An interview of Uday Shankar by Shambhu Mitra on DD Bharati, accessed April 28, 2019, url: www.youtube.com/watch?v=JHq-uBio5vE&t=14s
20. Joan L. Erdman with Zohra Sehgal, *Stages: The Art and Adventures of Zohra Sehgal* (New Delhi: Pauls Press, 1997), 111–2.
21. Nandini Ramnath, "In Dancer Uday Shankar's Rare Film From 1948, a Manifesto for a New India," *Scroll.In*, November 26, 2014, accessed December 10, 2021, url: https://scroll.in/article/691671/in-dancer-uday-shankars-rare-film-from-1948-a-manifesto-for-a-new-india
22. Kalpana, accessed July 19, 2017, url: https://indiancine.ma/BKLU/player
23. Uday Shankar, "My Love for Dance," *Souvenir of Shankarscope* (1970).
24. An interview of Uday Shankar by Shambhu Mitra on DD Bharati, accessed April 28, 2019, url: www.youtube.com/watch?v=JHq-uBio5vE&t=14s

1 Uday Shankar's Style of Creative Dance – The Form and Content

After traversing the journey of being a student, performer, teacher and researcher of Uday Shankar's style of creative dance for 40 years, the realization struck that, while the practice of it is being taken forward in its true form by Shankar's direct associates and their students, the fact remains that till date, there is no documentation on what Uday Shankar's style of dance comprises, in terms of the basics of the form and content. This chapter is an attempt to delineate in black and white, what Uday Shankar's style of creative dance entails and its basic tenets. It examines the maestro's own contention of what his style comprises through his writings in the souvenirs of his productions, as well as his interviews both in print and on television. It moves on to collate and consolidate this narration with learnings of what his associate Shanti Bose has to say. Given Bose's long association of almost 17 years with the maestro, initially as a male dancer in the troupe from 1960, with the production of *Samanya Kshati*, and then the tour of the USA, Canada and Europe in 1962; and subsequently as the Ballet Master and lead male dancer of the troupe from 1965 onwards, he was witness to the evolution of many of Shankar's movements, style and thought process. As the Ballet Master of the troupe, he was responsible for teaching and perfecting movements of Shankar's troupe members for productions during the period 1965–1977. Bose was also responsible for many of the choreographies and compositions which were performed during the aforementioned period by Shankar's troupe, after they received Shankar's inputs and approval, of course. Having been a student of the style, not only under Shanti Bose but also Sunanda Bose nee Sengupta, who was a troupe member in Shankar's productions for *Prakriti Ananda*, as well as his tour of the USA in 1968, this chapter inevitably has inputs from both my teachers, regarding the understanding of Shankar's style. The limitation of putting in print, movements of any performative art will always prevail, but nonetheless given the lack of any text on the form and content of Shankar's style, this chapter will hopefully remain for posterity, an understanding of the foundation of Shankar's form on the basis of which his style was built, and evolved over time.

DOI: 10.4324/9781003433774-2

Uday Shankar's Style of Creative Dance – The Form and Content

According to Shankar,

> From the very beginning of my artistic career, I never wanted to go on with mere repetitions, but always tried to produce something new and exclusive . . . I found that the older conception of our Indian dances have lost essential truths and their interpretation has become mechanical . . . my innovation . . . lay in that I created an altogether new technique.[1]

According to Uday Shankar, creativity implied creating and undertaking something that had "not been done yet." "My dance," he said, "I created. I got inspired by music sometimes, by movement in actual life sometimes."[2]

Though hailed as a classical dancer and choreographer, or an architect of modern dance on most of the online sources that carry information on Uday Shankar and his art, according to Shankar himself, he never cared to be classified as either.

> I had seen so much classical ballet in Europe it was shocking for me when I first saw Modern Dance. I felt it was something being done just for the sake of doing something new. Sorry, Modern Dance does not touch me. In the composition, in the way the theme, if any, is built up, I did not find anything modern. I found it more human, more natural. But I did not learn or derive anything from it. Now it is a fashion to use the word choreography in India. But I learnt this more from the Pavlova company than from anywhere else. Another thing I could learn from the West is how to compose and give ever-changing patterns of the body covering space. This, I watched carefully in their ballet and then tried to see how I could use all that in my dances and ballets.[3]

It is only with Uday Shankar that the creative form of dance emerged in India. A form that was not restricted by the rigidity of the *Natyashastra*, yet evolved to become a sophisticated style. In fact, the concept of the ballet form in India also probably came to be popularized with Uday Shankar's productions in India, for apart from Kathakali and Tagore's dance dramas, the concept of group performances with different characters performing on stage, essaying various roles to take forward the storytelling was not in practice before that. *Kathakali* with its depiction of episodes from the Mahabharata and the Ramayana,[4] with multiple performers and the interplay of characters, undoubtedly set the stage for dance dramas in India. However, the use of mudras and other fundamentals associated with the form including the language of the lyrics that the dances were performed to, made it difficult for the layman to understand what was being depicted on stage, without prior knowledge of *Natyashastra* or the language. Tagore's dance dramas incorporated what was referred to in earlier times as *bhav nritya*, given that they comprised expressions of *bhav* or the emotion expressed. Referred to as "mood dance" by Utpal K. Banerjee,[5] this *bhav nritya*, together with elements from classical dance forms like Kathakali, Manipuri and traditional forms of other countries like Sri Lanka and Indonesia, gave form to what we now know as *Rabindra Nritya* that took forward the narrative of the storyline through interplay between multiple dancers and characters. It was, however, again limited in its outreach because of the language of the lyrics – Bengali.

It is with Shankar that we see the *ballet* form brought to stage in Indian dance traditions on a professional platform, with the usage of stage space, where a number of dancers in various formations, and interplay of different characters, took the story forward. There exist a lot of debates on whether Shankar's form can be termed ballet.[6] The pamphlets, brochures and souvenirs of Shankar's productions showcase that he termed some of his slightly longer items as ballets.

The term ballet is lexically defined to include theatrical dance productions characterized by graceful, balanced movements with fully extended limbs, initiated from a restricted set of body positions. It is a theatrical work incorporating ballet dancing, music and scenery to tell a story or convey a thematic atmosphere. It is also often referred to as a company of dancers.[7] Shankar's form, apart from the technique of the ballet, which he replaced with his own creative style, encompasses all the other associated attributes of ballet. Therefore, there should ideally not be any challenge in identifying ballet to be one of Shankar's contributions to Indian dance, as many of his items and productions match the template of what may be termed ballet.

Another contribution of Shankar in Indian dance traditions was the focus on *body expressions* rather than on *mudras*, which are hand gestures enshrined in the *Natyashastra*, used to depict specific objects and emotions. At times, single-handed gestures called *Asamyukta Hastas* are used, while at other times both hands are used to form a gesture to convey a meaning, termed *Samyukta Hastas*. This shift from the mudras to body expression in Shankar's style was based on a certain rationale. In Shankar's own words,

> I have not adopted *mudras* in my dance or dance dramas unless it is very necessary. Let me tell you: when a dance or dance drama is going on, perhaps vigorously with much feeling, and the dancer suddenly stops and starts "talking" with mudras, it breaks. I tell you, it breaks for me the continuity . . . I like to show what I want to show with the body, with the body in emotion. For instance, when saying "I feel angry" the dancer flutters his hands and takes leaps. Why not just show the anger? When the body is capable of showing anger, why not let it do that? I try to avoid *mudras* as much as possible. *Mudras* are beautiful and nice, but in my kind of dancing, I go for movement of the whole body to express what I want, and with no exaggeration.[8]

According to Shankar's Ballet Master, Shanti Bose, there was another reason for this. *Dada*[9] – as he was addressed by those near to him, as well as his colleagues – used to say that *mudras* and facial expressions would be visible only to those who were seated in the first few rows of the audience. But in order to ensure that members of the audience who were seated even in the last row could make out very clearly what was being enacted on stage, body expression was a must. According to Bose, Uday Shankar used to repeatedly tell his dancers that those sitting in the last few rows were as important an audience to him, as those in the front few rows, for those seated in the last rows had spent whatever little they could afford from their meagre income to come and watch him and his troupe perform. This was also one of the reasons whereby he urged his dancers to perform expansive movements.

Only in *Kartikeya*, one of Shankar's favourite items is the usage of *mudras* pronounced as it was composed by Guru Shankaran Nambudri in Kathakali style of dance for Uday Shankar. Shanti Bose opines that his own training in *Kathakali* at the State Academy of Dance, Drama and Music is probably what helped him achieve perfection in terms of the *mudras* and gestures used in *Kartikeya* when taught by Shankar, which led to the maestro bestowing on Bose the honour of performing it for the first time under Uday Shankar's aegis during the troupe's tour of the USA in 1968 and thereafter.

Apart from *Kartikeya*, the usage of mudras to convey specific meanings is very limited in Shankar's style. The question that emerges at this point then is, if Uday Shankar moved away from the hand gestures and other aspects of the *Natyashastra*, what then, is the basis of his dance form? Did this shift imply that it was a form of do-it-yourself or a go-as-you-like style, without any foundation or basic grammar that guided its composition and led to its construction and creation? While it may be argued that by definition the term "creative" defies any form of limitation, nonetheless, it must be kept in mind that while the nomenclature may defy limitations in terms of creativity and innovation, it does not necessarily defy a foundation. Creative writing while harnessing creativity is based on the basic structure and syntax of the language in which it is being written. Creativity and innovation in business do not necessarily imply that it is not based on any management theory, practice or guidelines, but rather that it builds up practices and innovates on the foundation of the knowledge. Cinematic creativity stems only from a deep understanding of cinematic techniques and apparatus and other aspects of the craft. Similarly, Shankar's form too, although creative by design, has its basics, on which the style was not only founded but evolved.

Shankar's dance was pan-Indian in nature. The ethno-regional centricity that is reflected in both classical and folk dance forms of India is not evident in his form. This is probably a reflection of the time that he was creating his form in – when being "Indian meant that which was above all the smaller loyalties to religion, caste, ethnicity and region."[10] It was also probably a result of the fact that when Shankar was creating and showcasing his form, he was doing so in England and Europe, where he wanted to portray his idea of India.

In his interview with Shambhu Mitra on DD Bharati, a national channel dedicated to art and culture on Doordarshan (an autonomous public service broadcaster of Government of India), Shankar repeatedly said that in the initial years, he did not know what he was doing. But in the same interview he talks of the various categories of movements that he later created and how he created them. His style therefore evolved and developed over time as he matured; and by the time Uday Shankar Culture Centre started functioning in Almora on March 3, 1940,[11] these techniques were well in place and taught in the General Class by Uday Shankar himself.

After Shankar moved away from the Uday Shankar Culture Centre that had been set up in Kolkata, he wrote to the management in 1972 requesting his name be removed from the institute as it was not continuing to teach the style that had been developed by him. Addressed to Sukomal Kanti Ghosh, who was then the General Secretary at the centre, and sent to other committee members as well, this letter written by Uday Shankar is printed in Amala Shankar's memoirs.[12] Therefore, there is a definite basis for Shankar's form, which has undoubtedly evolved over the years. This evolution of Shankar's style was brought forth in discussions and debates at the Uday Shankar Shatabdi Samaroh held between 2001 and 2002, organized across India in the cities of New Delhi, Mumbai, Chennai and Kolkata, by Sangeet Natak Akademi, New Delhi. I was fortunate enough to participate in the celebrations held in New Delhi in 2001, with Shanti Bose, both as a performer and a presenter from Nrityangan.

The first and most important aspect of Uday Shankar's form is that of *posture*. As Shanti Bose, Shankar's Ballet Master recollects, according to Dada, the first thing that a dancer must know and inculcate is how to stand. The basic tenets of *chin up, chest out* and *stomach in* were almost like a *mantra* imbibed in the dancers when training in the style.

The next step involved *preparing the body for dance*. For Shankar, dance not only meant movements of the body but a connection between the body and the mind. A dancer can only achieve perfection in movements if the body is effectively controlled by the mind. In order to achieve this control, Shankar devised a series of exercises for each body joint – be it the wrists, elbows, shoulders, hips – which would ensure fluidity and suppleness, thereby making each movement appear seamless, fluid, apparently easy and simple to perform. This contributed and took forward the other basic tenet of Shankar's concept of *beauty, simplicity and power*.

As mentioned earlier, the exercises developed by Shankar were taught by the maestro himself at the Uday Shankar Culture Centre in Almora, during the General Class, which was deemed so important that it had to be attended by everyone – be it the students or the teachers. Every student, irrespective of the specialization that they were pursuing, was mandated to attend the General Class. Shankar also conducted the General Class at the State Academy of

Uday Shankar's Style of Creative Dance – The Form and Content 17

Figure 1.1 A page from the souvenir of the *Uday Shankar Shatabdi Samaroh*, where Shanti Bose presented Kartikeya and recreated Shankar's ballet *Samanya Kshati* as performed in 1972 with *Shankarscope*. The ballet was presented by *Nrityangan*, an institution founded by Shanti Bose and Sunanda Bose nee Sengupta with Uday Shankar's blessings in 1969. The image reflects Shanti Bose in a pose from *Kartikeya*.

Source: Courtesy, private collection of Shanti Bose

18 Uday Shankar's Style of Creative Dance – The Form and Content

Figure 1.2 Shanti Bose demonstrating the basic posture of Shankar's style – chin up, chest out and stomach in – at Shankar's birth centenary celebrations in Kolkata in 2002, organized by Sangeet Natak Akademi.

Source: Courtesy, private collection of Shanti Bose

Uday Shankar's Style of Creative Dance – The Form and Content

Dance, Drama and Music, which later became Rabindra Bharati University, during his tenure as the Dean of Dance at the institute.

The importance that Shankar placed on these exercises devised by him is evident from the following excerpt from his application for Nehru Fellowship on February 23, 1976, where he wrote,

> I found out with my experiences of the past, that the root of all dances of the world is the body and the mind and the past cultural heritage of the nations.... I worked out a method of my own. This is to prepare the mind and the body and to make the body an effective instrument before taking up any kind of dance of the world.... It starts with walking – just walking, and through this method of mine, some problems are created, and then one starts feeling that he has never known his body before. As he goes on, after few months, he realizes how wonderful his body is, and (that) this can create thousands of patterns, and for the first time he starts to know that he has limbs which are beautiful when they work with the mind.[13]

The benefits according to Shankar of these exercises were manifold. First of all, they helped develop self-awareness of the body and its movements, thereby leading to a conscious use and control of it. These exercises which were performed in varying tempos, also helped develop a sense of rhythm, along with fitness, alertness, discipline, concentration, a sense of how to use space, imagination, bonding and group feeling, together with a host of other benefits. According to Shankar, these were not only of immense importance to a dancer or any performing artist but also beneficial for other professions such as lawyers, teachers, politicians, public speakers and so on – whenever an interaction with an audience was necessary. According to Bose, these exercise classes were also conducted by Shankar and practiced by the troupe in 1966, before the troupe embarked on their tour of Assam as well.

Apart from exercises, *improvisation* was another important aspect that was taught by Shankar. The idea was to provoke thought and creative action on ideas and emotions, and explore the various reactions of different people that can result from a single emotion or event or action, as every individual is unique with independent thought processes. All the students and troupe members were encouraged to explore and express themselves independently – whether it be at Almora or later. This is encapsulated in the film *Kalpana* as well. Being autobiographical in nature, the film *Kalpana* shows *Kalakendra*, an institute nestled in the heart of the Himalayas, a dream of Udayan, the protagonist of the film, played by Shankar himself, where improvisation classes are held. As Bose recollects, improvisation classes were also held at Shankar's house on 38 Golf Club Road in Kolkata in 1962, before the troupe went to Madras to prepare for the 1962 tour of the USA, Canada and Europe. The importance that Shankar continued to place on improvisation throughout his life as an artist is evident in the first scene of *Prakriti Ananda*, staged in 1966.

The first dance, *nabo basantero danero dali*, saw a collation of improvised movements by individual dancers to the song, details of which will be covered in Chapter 4, *Revisiting Tagore*. Recalls Sunanda Bose, the women dancers were asked to create their own sequence of movements based on their perception of the song mentioned earlier, which describes the beauty of spring. The idea was that these improvisations would encapsulate each dancer's own and unique reaction to Tagore's lyrics and melody. Dada would then call each dancer individually to see what movements they had created. He would provide his inputs to these movements which then acquired a vastly improved and new dimension. He asked the individual dancers to remember what they had created and performed. Once he had seen all the movements and added to each dancer's composition, he called in everyone and asked them to perform together, what they had created individually. It turned into a mesmerizing scene, for it encompassed each and every individual dancer's reaction to the beauty of spring as expressed in this song by Tagore, and the different emotions that had been evoked by this song, in each dancer.

The next principle of the Uday Shankar's style that needs to be kept in mind is that Shankar always was very insistent that his dancers be aware of *where a particular movement started and where it ended*. It was only this conscious knowledge, followed by practised and controlled action, that would allow a movement to be replicated in the exact fashion every time the performer performed that particular movement. This would ensure that not only had the dancer achieved perfection in the movement but when it was passed on to another, the movement would not be corrupted. As Sunanda Bose reminisces, Dada himself used to say that while everyone talks of Uday Shankar as a choreographer and performer, only my troupe members know me for the teacher that I am. The perfectionist in him made him a brilliant teacher with an uncanny knack for pointing out where and why the movement was being performed incorrectly.

Both Shanti Bose and Sunanda Bose recollect Shankar repeatedly telling them, *dao dao . . . aro dao . . . amake na, nijeke ke dao . . . joto debey, toto tomar laabh hobey* – urging his troupe members to push themselves to perform and give their best, for they would only be serving themselves by doing so, as it would only result in their achieving perfection! Recollects Shanti Bose, in 1962, during the training sessions in Madras, with almost seven hours of rehearsals from 1 pm to 8 pm, Shankar would sometimes relentlessly, often for two to three hours at a stretch, be at them, correcting and perfecting just one single movement. Witnessing their exhaustion, Dada would say, *tomader diye je ei porishram korachhi, eta kintu laabh hochhey tomader – ei perfection ta amar noy – eta tomader – eta tomader kaach thekey keu kerey nitey paarbey na, amar laabh hochhey amar production ta bhalo hobey*, implying that though he was working his team members hard and pushing them to their limits in terms of perfecting movements, the perfection once achieved would remain with them forever and that no one could take that knowledge and perfection away from them. Shankar's only benefit would be that his production would be a perfect one! Shankar's group therefore presented picture-perfect synchronized movements, and this is also evident in every dance sequence captured in *Kalpana*.

In his interview conducted by Shambhu Mitra, Shankar talks about how he got inspired during his days with Pavlova when he realized that for her and her troupe, work was God![14] This *work ethic* inspired Shankar even till his last masterpiece – *Shankarscope*. According to Shanti Bose, who joined Shankar's troupe when the maestro was in his 60th year, the hard work that Shankar would put in each day, for the production of *Samanya Kshati* – which was staged by the way of paying tribute to the Nobel Laureate poet Rabindranath Tagore on his birth centenary – could put any younger person to shame. It was this work ethic which made him appreciate and give opportunity to anyone who was hard-working, sincere and dedicated. Bose recollects how their rehearsal sessions, be it in Madras or Kolkata, often resulted in them needing to wring out their perspiration-soaked clothes.

The golden principle that guided Shankar's choreography and composition was that *dance movements should reflect the music*, and vice versa. They should reflect the movement of the music in terms of whether it is reaching a crescendo or a high pitch, or a decrescendo or a lower pitch. The first should see the movement reflect the music through bigger expansive movements preferably stretching to the maximum possible limits, including rising on toes, while the latter should reflect and result in smaller movements, not as expansive and closer to the body.

What was also important to keep in mind, apart from the movement of music and its reflection in the movement of the body, was where it was being placed in the *sequence of movements*. Expansive movements ought to be placed towards the end of the composition so that the dance can build up and blossom slowly and then rise to a climax. Or else, the bigger and bolder movements if used at the beginning would engage the audience at the beginning of the dance, but then fail to hold on to their attention, if they became smaller in scope – unless of course, the emotion, moment or music demanded it. A recollection from Bose's treasury of memories is from the time when rehearsals for *Samanya Kshati* were being conducted in Madras in 1962, before the tour of the USA and Europe. In one of the sequences in *Samnaya Kshati*, Queen Karuna played by Amala Shankar is depicted as frolicking in the waters of River Baruna with her companions. The movements of the sequence, towards the end of the dance, are naturally very expansive and joyous; however, the next movement required the Queen and her companions to pull themselves close to their bodies as possible, as they were emerging from the river in their wet garments – so the shyness, embarrassment, chill, everything had to be reflected in that walk which was away from the audience. Shankar was not happy with anyone's movements and then demonstrated his understanding of a woman's embarrassment about emerging from waters in wet transparent clothing, in a gait, that very few were able to emulate.

Therefore, apart from the movements themselves, the emotion and reaction to situations expressed through the movement and thereby through body expression, together with *smooth transitioning* from one movement to the other whereby it seamlessly flowed into one another, was another hallmark of Shankar's style. Unless intentionally created as a sudden movement to catch the attention of the audience – or hit the audience with the idea that this was something momentous, like in the scene in *Samanya Kshati* where the King orders the Queen's companions to stay back as she has been banished from the palace, alone. The transition of movements had to be smooth no matter if it was from one movement to the other or it was a change when mirroring the left side of the movement with that on the right, as symmetry was a very important aspect in Shankar's style.

The principle of *symmetry* was in fact, of paramount importance in Shankar's form, as reflected in Shankar's movements. Symmetry enhances the perception of beauty of the movement as it provides maximum scope for the movement to be explored and expressed on both the right and the left sides. The completion of the movement on one side and its mirroring on the other side completes the entire movement. Exceptions were of course there, for example, in a few dances and movements when props were used like in *Astra Puja*, where the dancers held a sword in the right hand and a shield in the left hand, a couple of movements did not reflect the principle of symmetry in absolute terms or, for example, when it was a single sudden and extremely bold gesture to create a dramatic impact. This element of symmetry was also evident in his choreography, where his dancers created various formations and patterns on stage that were symmetrical in nature. This was evident in not only the way he used stage space in his various compositions and the resultant imageries they created but also many of the dance sequences in *Kalpana*.

Shankar created movements at times inspired by music and at times inspired by movements of daily life. An example of the former instance would be the songs for Shankar's 1966 production of *Prakriti Ananda*, which was a combination of Tagore's poem by the same name and Tagore's dance drama, *Chandalika*. Shankar retained some of the songs from *Chandalika* but took the story forward through instrumental music so that it had a universal appeal, overriding the limitations and obstacles of language barriers. In such an instance, he created movements to suit the rise and fall of the notes and the mood of the song rather than a word-by-word depiction of narration of the lyrics – as evident from the two devotional dances choreographed by Shankar himself – *Swarnoborney samojjalo* and *Jo sanni sinno* – the former portraying Buddhist *sanyasinis* or Buddhist nuns and the latter depicting a passing by Buddhist *sanyasis* or Buddhist monks. The dances were composed keeping in mind the essence and the melody of the songs rather than a verbatim depiction of the lyrics through *mudras*. However, there were many instances when the music was composed after the dance had been choreographed, as was the case with Shankar's production of *Samanya Kshati* and *Udara Charitanam*, in 1961. Set to Tagore's poem of the same name, the entire choreography of the production was undertaken before the music for either *Samanya Kshati* or *Udara Charitanam* had been composed. Kamalesh Maitra, Shankar's then music director and Barun Dutta, the master drummer in Shankar's troupe, had noted down the counting and the rhythm, as well as the tempo of the choreographies. Only after completion of the dance compositions of the two ballets, the former being of almost 1 hour and 40 minutes, and the latter of 15 minutes, did Ravi Shankar set music to them. However, there were many instances where Shankar was not happy with the music as he felt it did not express what he wanted to convey or that it did not match the movements he had composed. This also happened during the production of *Prakriti Anando*, where Kamalesh Maitra had to rewrite music many a time till Shankar was satisfied that the music matched the movement and conveyed what he wanted to express. Few people apart from those who worked with Shankar, realize the amount of effort that went into Shankar's productions, reflects Bose.

A basic tenet that guided the creation of all movements in Shankar's productions and thereby his form or style is that a movement should be beautiful, powerful and above all, simple. Shankar's understanding of the terms, beauty, power and simplicity were truly unique and extremely interesting. Power according to him, in dance, did not necessarily translate into hitting or stamping the floor very hard and noisily with the feet. For Shankar, the "power" of a movement lay in how controlled the execution of it was, without stamping the feet loudly, as is the case with many *shastriya* or classical forms in India like *Kathak, Bharatnatyam* and *Odissi*. The fluid execution and transition of movements, the apparent effortless and flowing quality of the movements, can only result from a tremendous control of the mind over the body and the control of body musculature, which would result in a movement appearing beautiful and simple. The simplicity also resulted from a focus on body expression rather than on mudras and intricate complicated footwork often performed by classical artists to astound audiences.

The art of knowing the right *duration of a performance* and how much to give to the audience in order to leave them hankering for more and ensure their return to the next performance is something Shankar had mastered. According to him,

> What you want to say, you must say in as short a time as possible. I do not want to give the impression that I am showing off what I can do. The number should be short, so the audience does not get bored. The result is that before my audience really get to know what I am trying to do, my piece is finished. The image lingers in their mind. People may like some long dances, such as compositions in the classical tradition, but their mind is at times invaded by other thoughts . . . In my dances and ballets, something keeps happening all the time in quick succession to sharply engage the mind of the beholders.[15]

The possibility of the audience's focus shifting and thoughts wandering, or the audience instead of focusing on the performance, starts dissecting the performers and their negative attributes may occur if an item or a performance continues for too long.

Given the complete showman that Shankar was, apart from dance, movement, body expression and music, other aspects of a performance, be it *costume, lighting, stage* settings or stagecraft, were an equally integral part of Shankar's productions and therefore his style and form. Bose recollects that it is from Shankar that he learnt the language of headwear and the fact that they not only indicate regional distinctions but also that of socio-economic status, the faith followed, as well as political alignments. For example, the same piece of cloth can be used in different ways in terms of tying *paagdis* or turbans and that, in turn, would indicate the region of the vast and diverse country that India is, for every region has its own distinctive style of tying the head garb! The socio-economic differences become evident as even for people from the same region, the way a farmer ties the cloth around his head would be very different from that of a nobleman or that of a trader. Social occasions can even be indicated by the manner in which a turban is worn – an example of which would be, how the bridegroom wears the turban, which would be very different from an everyday tying of the *paagdi*! Similarly, the *dhoti* which is a lower body garment worn by men in India would reflect the region in terms of not only the type of cloth, colour, weave, print or colouring techniques but also the economic class. The way the dhoti is worn could also be reflective of the profession or occasion that it is being donned for. A farmer working in the fields will wear it differently from the way it would be worn during religious or social festivals, or the way the men would dress in the court, or the way they would wear it if visiting the markets.

So too would the colours, weaves, patterns and manner of wearing sarees, speak about the socio-economic divisions and regional distinctions. The manner of draping the saree by a Queen or women from the nobility, who would definitely differ from the way a fisherwoman or a woman planting saplings in knee-deep water, or a widow or a bride would don it. It is probably the painter in Shankar as well as the artistic training he received that allowed Shankar to make these minute observations on life and include them in his ballets and different items. *Samanya Kshati* is one of the prime examples of this, as the headgear of the dancers helped to take forward the various characters and roles that they were essaying. The way the ministers in the royal court tied their headwear was very different from the way the dancers tied it for the folk dance in the ballet. Similarly, not only the material but the height at which the saree was worn by the dancers during the folk dance was much higher than the way the Queen and her companions draped their sarees, which ensured that their ankles were hidden from view.

Lights were another aspect of stagecraft that played an extremely important role in Shankar's productions. Though referred from time to time throughout the course of the book while discussing various productions, it would be remiss not to discuss it when examining Shankar's form, and the way in which Shankar's dancers were trained to ensure that they used the stage lights in the best possible fashion, in order to maximize the effectiveness of the production. Given the focus of the study which is essentially the decade of the 1960s and a good part of the 1970s, the technology and equipment available for stage light was definitely not what it is today. Nonetheless, Shankar in keeping with the development in technology used lights for his performances which at that point in time were far ahead of those available in Kolkata and probably the country. Dimmers were used in *Samanya Kshati* extensively for the flashback method he chose to narrate the story and other scenes for dramatic effects. These lights were a part of Shankar's own assets and travelled with the troupe for all their performances, be it in India or internationally. In fact, after a performance of *Samanya Kshati* in Kolkata, the most renowned light man in Kolkata at that point in time, Tapas Sen, came on stage after the performance, to try and figure out the source of light in one of the scenes, which had baffled him. Strobe lights which were not available in India at that point of time were specifically imported for *Shankarscope*, which created an ambience never before witnessed by the home audiences in India. The reviewer for the English daily Statesman, after watching *Shankarscope* and the scene where strobe lights had been used, referred to it as an exotic dream, with the feel of freezing motion![16]

Given that Shankar and his troupe performed both across India and the world, stage sizes were bound to be different and therefore light fittings would also have to change accordingly. Shankar therefore adopted a method whereby this would not be necessary as the dancers would have little time to adjust to the altered light settings for each performance. A special sheet like a floor mat, with markings indicating the positions of the dancers, was part of the troupe equipment wherever the troupe travelled. The importance of the markings designating the positions of the dancers were not only important for choreography purposes, but were also aligned to the fixed lights for various sequences. The dancers had to ensure that they performed on the designated markings in order to make sure that they received the light that had been prepared and allocated for that particular sequence. The markings also ensured that the dancers would also always maintain their distances and positions, no matter which stage in which part of the world they were performing in. These markings were set during the stage rehearsal of the first production of a programme – for example, for *Prakriti Ananda*, though short on funds, nonetheless stage rehearsals were held with lights, costumes, stage sheet markings and so on, for quite a few days, before the first show of the production.

While one aspect of the lights was about the dancers taking the light on stage, the other aspect was about the control of lights. Control boards would be marked clearly to show how far the light needed to be dimmed or brightened for every sequence. Interestingly, for the production of *Samanya Kshati*, when staged in India, as the music was pre-recorded, it was the musicians of

26 Uday Shankar's Style of Creative Dance – The Form and Content

Figure 1.3 With Mamata Shankar on the extreme left, looking on in a discussion between Shanti Bose and Amala Shankar on the evolution of Uday Shankar's movements at Uday Shankar's birth centenary celebrations in New Delhi, 2001. Listening in, on the right side of the photograph, near the podium are noted dance critic and author Sunil Kothari, and at the microphone, the then Secretary of the Akademi, Jayant Kastaur.

Source: Photograph by Sangeet Natak Akademi. Courtesy, private collection of Shanti Bose

Shankar's troupe who handled the lights, as they were best versed with how the music flowed, the narrative and the musical cues.

Like all masters and great artists, Shankar's form and movements too evolved over time. However, given the challenges of demonstrating the evolution of these movements through the written word, that will have to be a separate project explored through the audio-visual media and will not be a part of this chapter.

Shankar said, "I wanted to show that there was more in life than momentary satisfaction of a craving towards beauty." Shankar's form and creativity was therefore more than just a thing of beauty. This is evidenced not only from Shankar's productions and items in the 1960s and 1970s but also from the opening scroll of Shankar's film, *Kalpana*, which states:

> *I request you all to be very alert while you watch this picture – Fantasy. Some of the events depicted here will reel off at great speed and if you miss any piece, you will really be missing a vital aspect of our country's life in its religion, politics, education, society, art and culture,*

agriculture and industry. I do not deliberately aim my criticism at any particular group of people or institutions, but if it appears to be so, it just happens to be so, that is all. It is my duty as an artist to be fully alive to all conditions of life and thought relating to our country and I present it truthfully with all the faults and merits through the medium of my art. I hope that you will be with me in our final purpose to rectify our own shortcomings and become worthy of our cultural heritage and make our motherland once again the greatest in the world.

Uday Shankar[17]

Autobiographical in nature, Shankar highlights in *Kalpana*, at times through dialogue, and at times through dance sequences, the challenges faced by modern India. Released in 1948, work on *Kalpana* had begun in the early 1940s and reflects various issues that Shankar deemed important enough to highlight in his film – be it the education system of the country, the exploitation of labour, the need to achieve food security and the plight of our farmers, and various aspects of nationalism – the positives and the negatives.

While *Kalpana* is there for everyone to view at the click of a mouse on the world wide web, items like the *Young Father* and *Chinna Bichinna* are lost to the world. Recollects Bose, the item titled the "Young Father," which though an earlier composition of Shankar, was performed by Bose during the 1966 tour of Assam, depicted a young father, struggling to manage a wailing baby – completely at a loss as to how to calm down the infant. The item portrayed the young father trying various means – be it feeding the baby, trying to put the baby to sleep, walking with the baby cradled in his arms, crooning to the baby – but all efforts proved futile. On the face of it, the item would appear to depict a challenge faced by any young inexperienced father. The twist or the statement made was through the costume and the prop used. The dancer enacting the role of the young father would enter the stage with the national flag of India, garbed in a Nehru cap and a Jawahar coat.

Context? Even after India gained independence, there were quite a few princely states which wanted to either remain independent or join Pakistan. Therefore, the new nation-state of India and its leadership faced extremely challenging times after independence to ensure that the territorial integrity of India did not fall apart. Apart from this, there were various other challenges plaguing the newly independent India which was struggling to find its feet after 200 years of colonial exploitation. This item was Shankar's way of portraying how challenged the new leadership of the nascent state was. According to Bose, when N.K. Shivashankaran used to perform the item, prior to Bose enacting the young father, he would be garbed in the manner described earlier. However, when Bose performed the item in the mid-1960s, it was enacted without the Indian flag.

The other example mentioned here, *Chinna Bichhinna*, was Shankar's artistic expression and reaction to the plight of the common man of East Pakistan before liberation and the founding of Bangladesh. While details of this have been incorporated in the chapter that explores Shankar's production of *Shankarscope*, it would be amiss if not mentioned in context of content, how *contemporary* Shankar's compositions were. *Chinna Bichhinna* performed in the late summer–monsoon period of 1971 portrayed the stories of the people of East Pakistan which resulted after Operation Searchlight was launched in March 1971, when the Pakistani administration mounted a never-before-seen assault on its own citizens, who were ethnically, culturally and linguistically different from those in West Pakistan, which was the seat of power.

Therefore, Shankar brought to stage, *content* that had never been explored before, through the medium of dance. He led the way for performing arts in India, especially dance, to play a role that was much more than what the *shastriya* or the classical forms, or the *lok* or folk forms provided for, in terms of scope. His content through his productions mirrored the challenges of India and provoked his audiences to reflect on what was being performed. Recollects Bose, when he joined the Indian People's Theatre Association (IPTA) in the mid-1950s and learnt and performed items like *Hunger and Death* which narrated the plight of poor farmers and that of an exploitative zamindar or landowner, or *Mehanati Manush*, translating to the hardworking man, little did he realize then that these were all a result of the revolution Shankar had created in the performing arts tradition in India.

Uday Shankar himself in an interview with Mohan Khokar said that the ballets he sees in India are extensions of his work, where attempts have been made to rebuild his creative form, without the choreographers having gone through the experiences that he did, which led him to create his dance and art, nor was it done with an understanding of how Shankar did it, or why he did it.[18] This book therefore, among other questions, attempts to delve into the "how" and "why" of Shankar's art form in the subsequent chapters, by exploring in detail his productions between the period of 1960 and 1977.

Notes

1 Uday Shankar, "My Love for Dance," *Souvenir of Shankarscope* (1970).
2 Mohan Khokar, *His Dance His Life – A Portrait of Uday Shankar* (New Delhi: Himalayan Books, 1983), 171.
3 Mohan Khokar, *His Dance His Life – A Portrait of Uday Shankar* (New Delhi: Himalayan Books, 1983), 171.
4 C. Kunchu Nair, *The Kathakali and the Dance Drama of India*, UNESCO, UNESDOC Digital Library, accessed January 2, 2023, url: https://unesdoc.unesco.org/ark:/48223/pf0000060001?posInSet=3&queryId=N-EXPLORE-809a6e21-dea9-4f7c-b916-aea16cfcce2f
5 Utpal K. Banerjee, *Tagore's Mystique of Dance* (New Delhi: Niyogi Books, 2011).
6 Joan L. Erdman, "Who Remembers Uday Shankar?" accessed July 10, 2017, url: https://mm-gold.azureedge.net/new_site/mukto-mona/Articles/jaffor/uday_shanka2.html
7 Ballet, The Free Dictionary, accessed July 11, 2017, url: www.thefreedictionary.com/ballet
8 Mohan Khokar, *His Dance His Life – A Portrait of Uday Shankar* (New Delhi: Himalayan Books, 1983), 167.

9 *Dada* – In the Bengali language, it is a way of addressing an older brother or someone who deserves respect.
10 Romila Thapar et al., *On Nationalism* (New Delhi: Aleph Book Company, 2016), 3.
11 Mohan Khokar, *His Dance His Life – A Portrait of Uday Shankar* (New Delhi: Himalayan Books, 1983), 96.
12 Bisakha Ghose, *Shankarnama: Smritichitre Amala Shankar* (Calcutta: Ananda Publishers Private Limited, 2019), 253–4.
13 Mohan Khokar, *His Dance His Life – A Portrait of Uday Shankar* (New Delhi: Himalayan Books, 1983), 143–4.
14 An interview of Uday Shankar by Shambhu Mitra on DD Bharati, accessed April 28, 2019, url: www.youtube.com/watch?v=JHq-uBio5vE&t=14s
15 Mohan Khokar, *His Dance His Life – A Portrait of Uday Shankar* (New Delhi: Himalayan Books, 1983), 168.
16 "Some Opinions," *Souvenir of Shankarscope* (1970).
17 *Kalpana*, accessed July 19, 2017, url: https://indiancine.ma/BKLU/player
18 Mohan Khokar, *His Dance His Life – A Portrait of Uday Shankar* (New Delhi: Himalayan Books, 1983), 171.

2 Paying Tribute to Tagore through *Samanya Kshati*

Uday Shankar's first and main production of the decade beginning in 1960 was *Samanaya Kshati*, along with a short ballet, *Udara Charitanam*. Both these ballets, based on Rabindranath Tagore's poems by the same name, were created to pay tribute to the Nobel Laureate poet on his birth centenary. Born on May 7, 1861, as per the Gregorian calendar,[1] the year 1961 saw the birth centenary year of Rabindranath Tagore. The entire country was preparing to pay tribute to the poet and celebrate the occasion, in one way or another. The year-long celebrations began in Bombay with the *Prabashi Bangiya Sanskriti Sammelan*, inaugurated by Pandit Jawaharlal Nehru, the then Prime Minister of India.[2] Among all the artists, gearing up to pay tribute to *Gurudev*[3] – the honorary title bestowed on Tagore by Mahatma Gandhi, meaning venerable teacher – in their own preferred medium, was none other than noted film director, author, illustrator Satyajit Ray, whose genius Richard Attenborough liked to Charlie Chaplin.[4] The 54-minute black and white documentary film which went on to win the Golden Seal at the Locarno Film Festival, the President's Gold Medal in 1961, as well as a Special Mention at the Montevideo World Film Festival, was titled *Rabindranath Tagore*. Though released in 1961, Ray had begun working on the documentary in 1958.[5]

When Shankar had come to India in 1933, for an interim period of four months, he was felicitated by the Mayor of Kolkata in a public reception at the Town Hall in Kolkata. Both Rabindranath Tagore and his daughter-in-law Pratima Debi were present at the reception, where the mayor had claimed Shankar to be the cultural ambassador of India, in foreign lands.[6] Following the reception, at the poet's invitation, Shankar, together with his troupe, performed in Shantiniketan. Tagore's letter to Shankar after the former's performance at Shantiniketan, which was published in the souvenir of Shankar's production of *Samanya Kshati* in 1961, reads:

> You have made the art of dancing your life's companion. Through it you have won the laurels of the West. There are no bounds to the depths or to the expansion of any art which, like dancing, is the expression of life's urge. We must never shut it within the bounds of a stagnant ideal, nor define it as either Indian or oriental or occidental,

for such finality only robs it of life's privilege which is freedom . . . . there was a time when in the heart of our country, the flow of dance followed a buoyant life. Through passage of time that is nearly choked up, leaving us bereft of the spontaneous language of joy, and exposing stagnant pools of muddy impurities. In an unfortunate country where life's vigour has waned, dancing vitiates into a catering for a diseased mind that has lost its normal appetites. It is for you to give it health and strength and richness. The spring breeze coaxes the spirit of the woodlands into multifarious forms of exuberant expression. Let your dancing too, wake up that spirit of spring in this cheerless land of ours, let her latent power of true enjoyment manifest itself in exultant language of hope and beauty.[7]

Dated as per the Bengali calendar, 29th *Ashar*, 1340 B.S. (July 1933, as per the Gregorian calendar), extracts of this letter were also published in the souvenirs of the international tours undertaken by Uday Shankar and his troupe in 1962 to the USA and Europe and in 1968 to the USA. In the write-up, "My Love for Dance," as printed in the souvenir of *Shankarscope*, in 1970, Shankar writes that Tagore's words influenced him to a great extent and thereafter, Tagore apart from William Rothenstein and Anna Pavlova, became a very important influence in his life.

Tagore and Shankar were both pioneers in their own way. They broke the traditional dualities of the classical and the folk in Indian performing arts traditions, through their creativity and genius. Be it in the field of music – in terms of melody and lyrics or literary forms like poetry, prose, novels, short stories, operas, dance dramas and even art for that matter, Tagore spurned the rigidity of classical forms and created his own genre of music which later came to be known as Rabindra-sangeet. During Tagore's lifetime, they were, however, referred to as Rabi Babur *gaan*[8] or songs of Mr. Rabi. Tagore's greatness lies in his tremendous capacity to gather the essence of a traditional raag or melody where the usage of the seven notes are set in a particular format, and give it a completely new form which would create the best setting and musical notation for his lyrics. While undoubtedly inspired by the Indian classical or *shastriya* music, be it from the Hindustani classical traditions of northern India, or the Carnatic classical traditions of southern India, Tagore was equally influenced by Indian and Western folk music. The philosophy, spirituality and the melody of the *Bauls* – the spiritual wandering bards of undivided Bengal, now listed as an Intangible Cultural Heritage of Humanity under UNESCO[9] – also had a tremendous influence on Tagore, as is evident through his music and paintings. While at times his songs remained faithful to the original melody and the rhythm to which he set his lyrics, more often than not, his music and compositions were either a blend of different ragas and rhythms, leading to the creation of a unique brand of soul touching music and emotion, that we know as Rabindra sangeet.

Like Tagore, Shankar too created a new genre in dance and gifted India, the third form – that of the creative style, which had not existed before in Indian dance traditions. Shankar's vibrant new form was a reflection of the new nation that had emerged in the twentieth century. Be it in terms of themes, movements, the associated music, the stories told, the lights and technology used, stagecraft, usage of stage space, the pan-Indian form which was Indian in essence without being provincial in nature, was a form that revolutionized dance in India.

Like Tagore's social consciousness which is reflected through his works, be they his literary compositions, or his music, operas and dance dramas, the items composed by Shankar, be it *Rhythm of Life*, *Labour and Machinery* as well as many items in *Shankarscope*, reflect Shankar's social consciousness and sense of social justice in world full of adversities for those who are not as privileged. The storyline of the item *Rhythm of Life*, for example, showcases a young man's struggle in life, as he fights against all odds that life throws his way and emerges with faith and hope for freedom and liberty. The plot of *Labour and Machinery* reflects the challenges faced by industrialized as well as developing nations where the atrocities of the mill owner solely motivated by profit maximization for self-benefit demand the labourers employed in his factory to work like machines, without ever questioning the owner's actions. This is not only shown in *Kalpana* but was also depicted in the stage performance of the item, *Khadya*. Both the dance choreographies portray how in the end, the labourers unite to break free from the shackles of enslavement. A large number of items in *Shankarscope* too were a satirical commentary on the ills of so-called modern society of the 1960s and 1970s, details of which have been captured in Chapter 6 of this book, titled "The Last Masterpiece."

As evident from the body of work which remains their legacy, both Tagore and Shankar were humanists. Referred to as the prophet of humanity,[10] Tagore writes, "This new India belongs to humanity. What right have we to say who shall and who shall not find a place therein?"[11] This was the dismayed poet's response between 1909 and 1910 in a series of essays – as translated by Surendranath Tagore – to *swadeshi*, a tool of the nationalists in their struggle to gain India's freedom. Tagore's humanism is also brought to the forefront in his dance drama *Chandalika* and the poem *Prakriti-Ananda*, with the same storyline and characters, where a thirsty and parched Buddhist monk, *Ananda*, accepts a drink of water from *Prakriti*, a young girl deemed untouchable by social norms, by virtue of her birth. Ananda's words, *Je manabo ami, shei manabo tumi kanya*,[12] roughly be translated to mean that we both belong to the same race of mankind, reflect the humanist in Tagore. Tagore's humanism also finds its way into his book *Nationalism*, where Tagore opines that one of India's primary challenges is its ethnologically diverse races, who live together as a result of the history of this land, and that the mission of India is "to face it and prove our humanity by dealing with it."[13]

Tagore's abhorrence for artificial man-made socio-economic and political divisiveness is also evident in Shankar's production, choreography, compositions and the ballets he creates based on Tagore's works, as well as his own. Shankar views children as the hope for the country's future, and there is a poignant scene in *Kalpana*, where an appeal is made to keep children away from the utterings of regionalism, and provincialism,[14] for such utterings divide Indians instead of uniting them and result in making people enemies, based on nothing but ethnic, cultural and linguistic differences. The diversity in our nation ought to be celebrated rather than used to create divisiveness. The powerful message that it is only love that can unite people and save humanity is portrayed in *Kalpana* through the words of a young girl – a representation of India's future. In *Kalpana* again, the sequence on *Labour and Machinery* showcases the disparity in circumstances between the mill owner and the labourers of the mill, as well as the inhumane treatment and exploitation of the have-nots by the haves.[15] It is therefore no surprise, that even the ballets that Shankar chooses to create, based on Tagore's works – *Samanya Kshati*, *Udara Charitanam* and *Prakriti Ananda*, all reflect the same core value – that all human beings are equal. Whether it be *Prakriti Ananda* or *Udara Charitanam*, both works of Tagore reflect the plight and disdain of society for those considered to be on the fringes of society by virtue of their birth. That this sentiment strongly resonated with Shankar is evident, as it seems to have driven him to choose to work with these two specifically, from the humongous 18 volumes of Tagore's body of work collated as *Rabindra Rachanabali*. This collation comprises the Nobel Laureate's poetry, short stories, dance dramas, dramas, operas, novels, prose, memoirs and letters based on a multitude of diverse themes and emotions. Even *Samanya Kshati*, which Shankar opted to create in a ballet format, reflects the callousness of the queen towards the villagers when she burns down their huts to warm herself after a bath in the river on a wintry morning, and how the king sets her to right by exiling her, giving her a year to rebuild the huts that she had burnt without any thought, to make her to realize the extent of loss that her one thoughtless selfish act had resulted in. Shankar's choice of Tagore's works therefore also reflects the master choreographer's strain of thought and bent of mind.

As a someone who has spent a lifetime studying, performing, teaching and researching Shankar's work, I cannot help but speculate whether it was Shankar's respect and affection for Matadin, an old man belonging to an untouchable caste, living on the fringes of society – whose movements were said to have inspired in Shankar, the desire to dance, was responsible for Shankar choosing to create ballets on these particular pieces by Tagore.

Ramchandra Guha, in the book, Makers of Modern India, writes, "Tagore was a patriot, without being a nationalist."[16] His patriotism was reflected when on May 30, 1919, Tagore returned the Knighthood that he had been awarded in 1915, to protest the massacre at Jallianwala Bagh, Amritsar, Punjab, on April 13, 1919, where 379 unarmed Indian civilians – including men, women and children – were killed, when Colonel Reginal Dyer ordered those gathered be shot at indiscriminately.[17] Tagore in his letter addressed to the British Viceroy, Lord Chelmsford, wrote,

> The time has come when badges of honour make our shame glaring in the incongruous context of humiliation, and I for my part, wish to stand, shorn, of all special distinctions, by the side of those of my countrymen who, for their so-called insignificance, are liable to suffer degradation, not fit for human beings.[18]

While lauded as being one of the greatest poets of the country, Tagore was not favoured by the anti-colonial nationalists, for the brand of nationalism that Tagore espoused, was very different from the ones being propagated by the other well-known nationalists. In his book Nationalism, Tagore writes, "conflict and conquest is at the origin and centre of Western nationalism."[19] Tagore's brand of nationalism has in fact been compared to "new" cosmopolitanism. New cosmopolitanism is an idea which is also termed "rooted" or "realistic" cosmopolitanism as it respects the various types of traditions and nationalities and believes in universal values that people and countries from all across the world should accept. Unlike "old" cosmopolitanism, new cosmopolitanism did not view it as universalism, whereby national differences were minimalized to form one universally enlightened and uniform culture.[20] Tagore believed that India had much to learn from other countries, including the West.[21] Tagore's brand of cosmopolitanism is closely linked to his idea on humanism, for he believed that the divisiveness created by nationalism leads each country and nation to become "virulent" as they are all geared towards achieving their national and thereby self-interest. It is this narrow pursual of nationalism by the countries of Europe that according to him led to the First World War.

Shankar too, whether influenced by Tagore's ideas or not, reflected in his works, a thought process, similar to the Nobel Laureate poet. In his film *Kalpana*, Shankar captures a personification of *Bharat Mata*, who is seen lamenting the hollow glorification of the motherland through calls of nationalism, as these calls did little to feed the hungry population of India, nor did this hollow cry rid the nation of the evils of communal disharmony, nor diminish regional and linguistic strife. The song *Bharata Jai Jai* is a clarion call to all Indians to unite against all evils resulting from various forms of artificial and superficial man-made divisions, so that the actual problems and issues plaguing the nation may be addressed and resolved. Shankar's *Kalpana* or dream of India was therefore one which was devoid of regional strife and provincialism, where an egalitarian society did not discriminate on the basis of race, gender, caste and creed, where education was not only available to all, but it was more than what was being provided by the then colonial powers merely to produce a category of clerks, to carry forward British administration and business. It may be noted at this point that while the film, which portrays these ideas, was released in 1948, work for the same had started in the early 1940s. Interestingly, the Indian Constitution which was adopted on January 26, 1950, by virtue of which India became a republic, encapsulates many of these ideas, which were so reflective of Shankar's dream for India as expressed in *Kalpana*. It was also for an India where the youth are gainfully employed, food security has been achieved, and India's rich and diverse cultural heritage is accepted and appreciated.

In terms of the form of dance created by Shankar – the creative genre – it too reflects this idea as the dances while undoubtedly Indian in spirit and essence were pan-Indian in nature, and not reflective of any region, or culture, unless Shankar chose to showcase the classical and folk dance forms of India in his repertoire, as he does, in his film *Kalpana*, as well. As the cultural ambassador of India, this representation of all that is best of the Indian performing arts traditions is understandable. Shankar's form incorporated the vigour of the folk forms and the finesse of the classical style as per the need of the stories to be told. With its hallmark of beauty, simplicity and power, and a focus on body expression rather than only on mudras and facial expressions, his style had a universal appeal for audiences across the globe. Shankar also essentially used instrumental music – the only exception being a few songs that he retained from Tagore's dance drama *Chandalika* for *Prakriti Ananda*, and a few songs in Bengali for *Shankarscope* – which made his performances understandable to a global audience.

Education systems in India were a concern for both Tagore and Shankar. Vishwa Bharati, now a Central University by the Act of Parliament in 1951,[22] was founded by Tagore in 1921, with Vishwa meaning global and Bharati meaning Indian. *Yatra visvam bhavatieka nidam*, a Sanskrit *shloka* which means "Where the whole world meets in a single nest,"[23] was chosen by Tagore as the motto for the University. Tagore's concerns with education even led him to create a school for children, now known as – Patha Bhavan – the House of Studies. Patha Bhavan started off as a *Brahmacharyasrama*, Tagore's school for children at Santiniketan, which was founded in 1901. Built on a seven-acre plot, Tagore's father, Debendranath Tagore, had allocated this land for the establishment of a centre for meditation and a *Bramhavidyalaya* – a school for Bramhos, as well as a library, to take forward the teachings of the *Brahmo Samaj*, a reformist movement within Hinduism which began in the late nineteenth century in Bengal. The school had only five students when it began in 1901. Vishwa Bharati, when it came into being in 1921, was premised on the unconventional approach towards academics that the school had introduced. The name Patha Bhavan was used to rename *Brahmacharyasrama* in 1925. Both the school and the university were a "conscious repudiation"[24] of the British system of education introduced in India, which according to Thomas Macaulay's *Minute on Indian Education* in 1835 was to "form a class who may be interpreters between us and the millions whom we govern; a class of persons, Indian in blood and colour, but English in taste, in opinions, in morals, and in intellect."[25] The classes for Patha Bhavan were held in the *amra kunj* or the mango grove, unhindered by the four concrete walls of a formal classroom space, conducted under the open skies, in the midst of nature. With a curriculum that focused on a holistic education, along with academics, students pursued subjects like music, painting and drama, which were an integral part of the programme. Both teachers and students shared lives that were integrated, with a focus on developing thinking and questioning individuals. Notable alumni of Tagore's education system include the Nobel Laureate economist Amartya Sen, India's ex-Prime Minister Indira Gandhi, ex-Chief Justice of India Sudhi Ranjan Das, Maharani of Jaipur Gayatri Devi, eminent sculptor Ramkinkar Baij as well as singers and scholars like Shantideb Ghosh, Suchitra Mitra and Kanika Bandopadhya, among many others.

Shankar's *Kalpana* talks about setting up a centre of education, *Kalakendra*, where the ultimate objective would be to create worthy citizens – An institution geared to help develop the body and the mind, with a gymnasium, auditorium, radio station, a library, as well as a museum. Shankar's concern regarding the education system of the country is also reflected in the sequence in *Kalpana*, when after graduating, women decry in different Indian languages that an education system and quality education unless available to all could not lead to national development and that it would simply remain as useless degrees.[26] Shankar's centre at Almora, the Uday Shankar India Cultural Centre, with a five-year programme in arts, which included training in dance, music, theatre, lighting, make-up, set and costume designing, was an experiment of sorts, designed to build a new national culture to undermine the cultural hegemony of the British, during the last years of their rule in India. Inspired by Dartington Hall model in England, which is a centre for progressive learning in arts, ecology and social justice,[27] the idea behind the centre at Almora was "to develop a spontaneous expression of the student's inner creative urge" and "to give a new interpretation" to "dancing, drama, and music."[28] While the centre at Almora, which started functioning in 1940, closed down shortly after in 1944, mainly due to the challenges of the Second World War and a whole lot of other administrative issues, nonetheless, it reflected Shankar's attempt at addressing his concerns regarding higher education in India.

Performing arts traditions in India, especially under the colonial rule, due to lack of patronage, had sunk to depths of degradation where both the artist and the art forms were demeaned and socially frowned upon. In such a situation, Tagore, even before Shankar's advent in the world of dance, worked towards uplifting the status of both the art form and the artist, through his productions in Shantiniketan. In Tagore's dance dramas, while the Kathakali style was used to portray the masculine and male characters in the dance dramas, the *lasya* or feminine style of Manipuri was used to portray the female characters. Folk dance forms like the *Kandy* dance form of Sri Lanka were also used to portray certain characters like, for example, *Kotal*, roughly translating to police officer, in the dance drama *Shyama*, named after the dance drama's lead character, a danseuse in a royal court. Interestingly, Tagore had also made arrangements to have the *Manipuri* dance form taught at Shantiniketan by a Manipuri Guru or teacher. However, the social taboo at that point in time surrounding dance and dancers, whereby the art form and its practitioners had been relegated to the kothas or houses of ill repute, the dance classes were termed fitness/exercise classes. According to Shantidev Ghosh, a Rabindrasangeet singer, dancer, actor, teacher, writer and scholar, who went to Shantiniketan, became a teacher there from 1930, and was also sent by Tagore to Java, Bali and Sri Lanka to learn their dance forms,[29] despite the desire to conduct dance classes, Gurudev could never publicly announce them as dance classes. He had to term them as "exercise" or *shorir charcha* classes, where students of the ashram would exercise in keeping with the rhythm of the *Mridunga* – one of the oldest of all drums and percussion instruments of India. These classes were suspended every time Tagore stepped outside Shantiniketan. Tagore in fact warned Shankar, albeit in his own humorous fashion, that he should be ready to face criticism like Tagore himself faced, when Tagore was blamed for corrupting youngsters from decent families by making them perform on stage for his dance dramas.[30]

Apart from Simkie, who had been Shankar's dance partner from the 1920s itself, Shankar, when he first formed his group in the early 1930s, had as his troupe members essentially his own relatives – his three brothers, Rajendra, Devendra and Ravi, his cousin Kanaklata, and his maternal uncle, whom the brothers called Mathul. Soon Zohra Sehgal, then known as Zohra Mumtaz and subsequently her sister, Uzra Mumtaz joined the troupe. Zohra had training at Mary Wigman's school.[31] Shankar and his family, who were Bramhins by birth, therefore, braved social ostracization to take up a profession that was at that point of time, not looked upon with respect in society. Thus, Shankar's contribution, like Tagore, towards social upliftment of performing arts and artists remain invaluable.

Given Shankar's fond association with Tagore, when the Government of India invited Shankar to participate in the centenary celebrations of the poet, he chose to work and build on Tagore's poem, *Samanya Kshati*. This drive in Shankar to create a ballet[32] from one of Tagore's poems, rather than work with one of Tagore's dance dramas, probably stemmed from the inspiration found in Tagore's letter to Shankar as mentioned previously, when he wrote to Shankar saying,

> I know you feel it deep within your heart that the path of the realization of your dream stretches long before you where new inspirations wait for you and where you must create in a limitless field new forms of living beauty. We hope your creations will not be a mere imitation of the past nor burdened with narrow conventions of provincialism. Greatness in all its manifestations has discontent for its guide in the path to victory where there are triumphant arches, but never to stop at, merely to pass through.[33]

1960 saw Shankar beginning his preparation for the production of *Samanya Kshati*. This was the first time that Shankar would be presenting

Tagore's poem and in true Shankar style, in a path-breaking format – in the form of a ballet. Till then, be it in Shantiniketan or in Kolkata, the performances on stage as far as Tagore's works were concerned were restricted to his dance-dramas or *nrityanatya*, dramas or *natak*, or his lyrical dramas or *geetinatya*. This was the first time that an attempt was being made to depict on stage one of Tagore's most lyrical poems, based entirely on instrumental music, without the help of any lyrics, dialogue or narration. Shankar conceptualized and depicted the entire poem through the use of creative movements, gestures, and body expression, music and other aspects of stagecraft.

Natyashastra, often attributed to be the fifth *veda*, said to be composed in the classical period between 400 and 1200 CE by Sage Bharata, enlists three types or categories of dance – *Nrutta, Nritya* and *Natya*. In *shastriya* or classical dance forms, an item is said to be *nrutta* when it is performed to a *raga* or a melody which does not have any set lyrics. Therefore, the form of dance is one where the mudras or the hand gestures are not used to depict any meaning but performed for the sake of beauty, in keeping with the melody, rhythm and tempo of the song. An example of this would be the item *Pallavi* of the Odissi dance repertoire, where the *taranas* (idiom or composition with musical syllables based on Persian and Arabic phonemes)[34] or *sargams* (sol-fas, where the actual notes are voiced instead of words or syllables) are a base on which the dance unfolds using *mudras* or hand gestures, *pada bhedas* or different foot positions, different types of head, neck and torso movements, keeping to the tune and beat, as well as increasing in tempo, as the elaboration of the melody or *raga* progresses. *Nritya* is the concept of using hand gestures, expressions and other parts of the body, to express and give meaning to the lyrics of a song, while *Natya* involves pure abhinaya or acting, and therefore a dramatic expression which may unfurl with the help of speech, lyrics and/or music.

In taking on Tagore's poem *Samanya Kshati*, Shankar brought to fore a never before explored form, where he transformed a poem of 20 verses with six lines a verse as in the original Bengali form, and converted it into a ballet of almost 1 hour 40 minutes, based purely on instrumental music, with vocal humming in a few instances, for example, to express the grief of the villagers after their huts and with it all they possessed had been burned to the ground by their callous queen. Therefore, where usually in Indian dance traditions, pure music without lyrics was only expressed through *nrutta*, Shankar used instrumental music entirely, without any lyrics to compose a complete ballet with the use of *nritya* and *natya* so to say, as they told a story that was a dramatic expression of a poem with all its characters and emotions.

Shankar, in the souvenir published for *Samanya Kshati* in 1961, wrote:

> I have long been cherishing the dream to present through dance the beauty, elegance, depth and spirit of Tagore's ideas. The theme of *Samanya Kshati* inspired me. I worked it out in the form of a full-length ballet, although I have been able to capture only a fraction of all that fired my imagination. And in order to round off the theme for the ballet

Paying Tribute to Tagore through Samanya Kshati 39

I have tried, in my humble way, to visualize what would logically follow after the poet left off.[35]

Shanti Bose speculates whether the fire that ravaged the stage in Calcutta in the late 1950s, where Shankar's troupe had been performing a couple of shows, was one of the reasons why Tagore's poem *Samanya Kshati* appealed and spoke to Uday Shankar. Recalls Bose, as it had happened at night, after a performance, luckily there was no loss of life, but led to a substantial loss in property. Fortunately, as Uday Shankar's costumes, instruments and equipment were all stored in fireproof and waterproof boxes, they had not been damaged.

The poem of *Samanya Kshati*, while originally written in Bengali by Tagore, was presented in the souvenir for the tour of the USA in 1962, in the following manner:

Samanya Kshati

The cold wintry winds blow over the clear
water of the river Varuna, away from the city,
in the quiet proximity of the village.
To the paved bank of the river, skirted by
bowers of the champa flower, proceeds for
a bath, accompanied by hundred maidens,
Karuna, the queen of Varanasi (Benaras).

The path to the river has been cleared of
people through the order of the King.
The nearby hamlets have been emptied of occupants.
Quietly flows the deep waters of the river,
save for the singing of the birds.

A turbulent northerly blows today. The
surface of the river is excited. The golden
rays of morning sun scintillate
on the wavelets like myriads of
diamonds on the scarf of a danseuse.

The gleeful cackle of the maids puts
to shame the murmur of the waves. Their
rounded arms in exquisite movements
send the waves into ecstasies. The air
throbs with their frolicsome laughter and gaiety.

After the bath the queen and maidens come
out of the water. The queen exclaims: "Oh, I die
of cold. My whole body shivers. Maids,
light a fire to drive away this chill."

Maids hurry to the nearby bowers,
to gather twigs. They rush like mad
and tug at the boughs. Suddenly the
queen calls them with a pleased smile.

"Come all of you. Look!
yonder is a hut. Set it on fire
so that I might warm my limbs."

Malati, a maid, humbly says:
"What fun is this, oh queen.
Why destroy the habitat of
some saint or some poor person
who finds shelter there."

The queen flares up and shouts
"Drive this great sympathetic soul away."
Thereupon the harried maids, in the
thoughtlessness of youth, make a mad rush
and set the hut on fire.

Thick smoke begins to swirl up and swell.
Fire leaps up crackling and throwing out
tongues of flame that appear to lick the sky.
Like tortured serpents the flames seem to gush out,
raising their hoods to the sky, with thundery sound.

The joyous song of the morning bird
turns to a plaintive wail in dread.
The crows in a group raise a raucous chorus
as the northerly gathers fury and helps the fire
to leap from hut to hut in a frenzy of relentless fury.

The small village burns down to a
mass of charred wood and ashes. Along the
emptied path, in the wintry morning,
the queen, with her hundred maids, returns happy,
clad in a red sari with a lotus in her hand.

The king was in judgement on his throne.
Grieved, shelterless poor subjects come in groups,
crouch at his feet and in hesitant, trembling voices,
narrate the rueful tale of destruction.

Flushed with shame the King leaves the throne
and enters the queen's quarters.

"Queen, what cruel sport is this?
What royal code justifies the wanton
destruction of the abodes of the poor?"

The queen, piqued, replies,
"You call them abodes, the few rickety huts.
What loss can their destruction mean.
How insignificant for an hour's joy for their queen!"

Holding his heart in distress
the king replies in rage, "As a queen
you will never know the loss of a poorman's hut to the poor.
But I will make you realize."

At the command of the King, the queen is divested
of her ornaments. Her regal red robe is pulled mercilessly
away and a torn beggar's garb was given to cover the queen's body.

Leading her to the street the King enjoins, "Beg from door to door
to raise the money to rebuild the huts you destroyed in the
thoughtless sport of an hour.

I give you a year. Return at the end of it and in the middle
of the court, in front of all, you will have to confess how
much of a loss the destruction of the
Dilapidated huts has really meant."

Rabindranath Tagore[36]

Samanya Kshati is perhaps one of the prime examples of Shankar's gift as a storyteller through his medium of art. Based on the three basic principles of his style – beauty, power and simplicity – Shankar used his own creative movements, interspersed with stylized movements of daily life, to bring to stage his interpretation of Tagore's *Samanya Kshati*.

Tagore's poem opens with an imagery of a quiet wintry morning, when the village and the path had been emptied by royal decree, as the Queen and her hundred companions would be walking down to take a dip in the river Varuna. Shankar, however, chose to present Tagore's poem in a flashback mode. The opening scene of the ballet is actually a depiction of a verse towards the latter part of the poem describing the King in his court and the arrival of the tragic stricken frightened villagers who had come to narrate to the king, their plight.

The King's Court was therefore the opening scene of the ballet. Dim lighting was used to depict the dawning of the day when the male servants would enter the stage with movements depicting the cleaning of the royal court, dusting and preparing it for the day. The *chamardharinis* or the women engaged to fan the King with special yak-tail fans known as *chamars* would then enter the stage and take their positions, flanking both sides of the throne. Then entered the guards with spears in their hands, after which, one by one, the rest of the courtiers were shown to enter the stage, using unique movements varying with their role and designation, arriving for the day in court. The first one to arrive would be an aged Minister of Finance, followed by the Minister of Defence, who would be followed by the Prime Minister. While the ministers were shown to be consulting, a guard would enter and announce the arrival of the King. The king would be welcomed to the royal court by the prime minister. Once the king entered the stage, the lights would be at their brightest, and after blessing his courtiers and his subjects, the king would then take his throne and begin the business for the day.

Figure 2.1 An image of the court scene from *Samanya Kshati* as published in the souvenir during the tour of the USA in 1962. The figures in the image include Pranati Sengupta on the extreme left as a *chamardharini*, Shankar's then Ballet Master Pappu Raghavan second from the right enacting the role of the Prime Minister, and Uday Shankar in the centre fore as the King.

Source: Courtesy, private collection of Shanti Bose

Shankar's observation of life and its reflection of it in his art is undeniable. Even in the court scene, whether it be the nuanced portrayal of all the characters in the scene or the hierarchy that is maintained between them and their communication with the king can only lead one to wonder whether he was drawing these details from his observations at the court of Jhalawar during his childhood days or from his interactions with the various Maharajas he met during his travel in India in 1930 with Alice Bonner, the Swiss painter and sculptress who provided Shankar patronage when he wanted to create a group comprising Indian dancers and musicians.[37] For example, in the court scene, as the finance minister was shown to be an aged man, his movements were in accordance with his age and hence slow and shaky. The bold and clipped movements of the defence minister – performed by Shanti Bose, reflected the regimentation and discipline that must necessarily be a part of his person. The movements of the prime minister were dignified and steady, reflective of his responsibilities, position and personality. Not only was the differentiation of the characters evident through their movements, costumes and body expression, their difference in status and importance in the court was also ensured through the positions they occupied in their distance from the king, as well as the hierarchy in communication, where only the Prime Minister would communicate directly with the King and vice versa.

The scene would continue to portray the king and his ministers continuing with the day-to-day affairs, where the king is shown to enquire of the prime minister, the state of affairs and the welfare of his people. The prime minister would report back to the king, after conferring with the other ministers present. There would be a sudden impression of a commotion from outside the court, and the defence minister after receiving the king's permission would ask the guards to find out the cause of it. The guards would return to convey to the defence minister that the poor villagers had come to meet the king. This would be conveyed to the king via the prime minister, who then on the king's order asked the defence minister to tell the guards to allow the villagers entry to the royal court.

The tempo and pitch of the music together with the overall choreography of all the artists expressing different emotions of anxiety, worry, wonder on stage – all subtle yet evident – led to the impression of taut excitement and tension that something unusual was about to unfold. The fearful and hesitant villagers, when shown in, threw themselves prostrate in the royal court. There to beg for mercy, they were at the same time afraid of the reaction of the king on hearing their complaints and pleas as it was the Queen who was responsible for their plight. The scene then unfolded with the villagers hesitant and afraid to speak in front of the king in response to the prime minister's queries, till a direct command from the king compels one of them to hesitantly approach the throne and narrate their woes.

This unfolding of the court scene was entirely Shankar's creation, as the poem only states towards the end that when the villagers approached the royal court, the king was in session:

The king was in judgement on his throne.
Grieved, shelterless poor subjects come in groups,
crouch at his feet and in hesitant, trembling voices,
narrate the rueful tale of destruction.

The court scene was then darkened, and the narrative moved into a flashback mode. Shankar's creative folk movements depicted the villagers engaged in fun and frolic, a game of dice, eating, a little flirtation which led to a fist fight between two men, with each having supporters on their side, breaking up the fight and then back to making merry. This storytelling, giving a glimpse of the life of simple yet happy villagers, cannot be identified with any region of India for the movements are Shankar's own creation. However, no one can deny that they are folk in form given their style, vigour and liveliness and quintessential representation of rural life in India. The dancing of the villagers is brought to an abrupt end with the entry of sentries, reading out a decree and ordering the villagers to clear off as the queen and her companions would be using this path on their way to bathe in the river.

The next scene moved back to the palace, with the guards standing on duty. One of the queen's companions was seen to enter the stage to ask the male guards to leave as the queen would be passing through. Shankar with his creativity and innate sense of drama added to this scene where apart from the message delivered – all through instrumental music and creative movements, a non-verbal communication between the guards and the queen's companion with a coquettish glance from the latter and the jaw-dropping reaction of the former. Tagore's poem has no mention of this.

The next scene moved on to portray the queen's maids and companions making preparation for the queen's journey to the river. This was the creation of a master storyteller, choreographer and composer at work as it is not Tagore's description of the queen and her hundred companions making their way to the river. Tagore's description of this can be found in the first four verses of the poem, as given earlier. The reason for adding on to Tagore was probably to point out the luxuries that the queen experienced and the pampering that she was privileged to. Through the use of creative movements, Shankar's choreography and composition depicted the queen's companions, maids and female guards all inspecting, cleaning, smoothening the path for the queen, spreading petals on the way so that the queen would not hurt her feet, the bodyguards preceding and then finally, the queen's entry and her walk to the river with her companions.

Again, the master creator added to Tagore's poem showcasing the queen and her companions' reactions on reaching the river and their frolicking in the waters. The initial hesitancy at the coldness of the water on a chilly winter morning, testing the waters by dipping toes, the haughtiness of the queen, yet the camaraderie that existed between her and her companions, the playfulness on the banks of the river, finally taking the plunge, and swimming in the waters of the river Varuna. Created with Shankar's own innovative movements, few of which were from an earlier composition titled *Snanam*, most of the movements were new. Once in the water, most of the movements were stylized versions of various swimming strokes – be it backstroke, freestyle, breaststroke or holding the nose, taking a dip – all choreographed and composed keeping true to the basic tenets of beauty, simplicity and power, easily understood by one and all, telling a story as only a master of his form can.

The queen and her companions then emerged from their bath. Recalls Bose, who was a troupe member at this point in time and subsequently became the Ballet Master in 1965 and was the Assistant Director for *Samanya Kshati* when it was restaged in 1972, that Dada as Shankar was fondly called, was not happy with the movements performed depicting the queen's emergence from the water, either by Amala Shankar, who played the role of the queen, or by the other dancers enacting the queen's companions. He then demonstrated the movement which left everyone mesmerized, for it was extremely feminine in nature, expressing Shankar's idea of how the queen and her companions would emerge in wet garments from the water. In this movement, there was no hierarchy between the queen and her companions as they were as women, self-conscious of their forms showing through the wet clinging garments and therefore the movement expressed innate shyness, self-consciousness and momentary discomfort. However, once they were all garbed and the queen was back in all her finery and regalia, her movements transformed into the bold and grand movements of before. The reason for mentioning this here, though this incident occurred much later during the rehearsals in Madras, before Shankar's international tour of the USA and Europe in 1962, is to showcase Shankar's eye for detail and nuanced body expression.

Once the queen and her companions emerged from the river Varuna – as described by Tagore, which is set in northern India, on the cold morning of *Magh*, a month in the Hindu calendar that would roughly translate to the months of January and February – they started shivering in the cold northerly winds, which finds the queen ordering her companions to light a fire so that they may warm themselves. While her companions go off to collect firewood in the nearby garden, the queen sights a hut and, in her impatience, asks her companions to set fire to it instead. One of her companions, Malati, pleads with the queen and implores her not to engage in such a thoughtless act. Angered at her companion's audacity to question her, the enraged queen drives away Malati, for sympathizing with the poor, instead of following her orders unquestioningly. The queen and her companions then set the hut to fire. With the northerly winds, blowing the flickering flames soon spread to the nearby huts and engulfs the entire village.

Again, the movements used were purely creative in nature – from the tugging of the boughs to gather wood, to the queen's driving out of Malati, lighting the fire and enjoying its warmth till it becomes too hot to bear; Shankar's composition and choreography to which Ravi Shankar set music is not only inimitable but easily understandable by a global audience.

The next sequence portrayed the fire dance. One of the most vigorous and rigorous compositions of the ballet, this dance interprets Tagore's verses on how the flames which slowly rose from the ground like snakeheads began their dance of destruction as they flared and moved upward, towards the sky, roaring in an uncontrollable rage. The angry flames flew from one hut to another, engulfing and devouring the entire village. In order to depict this imagery created by Tagore, the choreography saw the dancers entering the stage from both sides in slow stretched panther-like movements – quiet and unsuspecting of the peril and havoc that was about to unfold. The hint of the danger lurking in these stealthy movements at the beginning of the dance, which by the end of the dance, had progressed to a full-fledged fast-paced "horse-step" in a circle occupying the full stage with outstretched hand movements and leaps reflecting the shooting flames and the spreading fire, then went on to slow down to small tinkering steps, signifying the dying embers. This composition of Shankar depicting the rage of the fire was a never-before-seen phenomenon on the Indian stage in any dance tradition – classical or folk.

The perfectionist that Shankar was compelled him to carry on a lot of experimentation till he was satisfied with what would be finally presented – be it in terms of dance movements, music, costume, lights or other aspects of stagecraft. For example, in the fire dance itself, Shankar first tried out movements, where the dancers would be lying on their backs on the floor, with their heads towards the audience, slowly raising both their hands in shimmering movements, reflecting the rising fingers of flame. He was, however, not happy with this effect and subsequently changed it to the panther-like walk as an entry step for the dance. Recalls Bose, with respect to the costume for the fire dance, Shankar was not happy with the costume of the fire dance and on the night before their first performance, they spent almost the entire night in various costumes that Shankar felt would best express the imagery that he had visualized in his mind, inspired by Tagore's verses. Finally, the costume decided for the fire dance for the men was bare torso, red dhoti, and white square chiffon handkerchiefs about one and a half feet on the sides, which were tied to one of the fingers of the dancers on both their hands. The effect of these kerchiefs flowing with the vigorous hand movements, together with the lighting, and the projection of flames on the backdrop screen would give the effect of the flickering flames in a manner that Shankar wanted. This, along with the music on Ustad Ali Akbar's *sarod* and Ustad Alla Rakha's *tabla*, took the dance to a completely new level and managed to ingrain in the minds of the audience the colossal damage and devastation that had been caused by the fire which had charred down the entire village and left the villagers homeless.

The subsequent scene portrayed the villagers, grieving over all that they had lost. Some of the aggrieved villagers in their angst and anger at the callous act of the queen, decided to approach the king to report their tremendous loss. The humming conducted by Laxmi Shankar in this scene, which reflected the

Paying Tribute to Tagore through Samanya Kshati

Figure 2.2 Clicked at Radha Film Studio, the dancers are posing in the final costume of the fire dance, which had been finalised after a whole night's costume rehearsal. The central male figure in the image is Shanti Bose.

Source: Courtesy, private collection of Shanti Bose

lament and grief of the villagers, according to Bose, moved both the performers and the audience to tears. The flashback ended here with the heart-rending cry of the women folk, while the men folk went to meet the king.

The scene shifted back to the present where the villagers were expressing their woes to the king in the royal court. The dancers occupied the same positions as in the first court scene, when the blackout had happened. The scene would restart with the same bright lights, with the poor villager seated at the feet of the king, narrating what had happened. The king, angered and embarrassed at this thoughtless act of the queen, was seen to leave the royal court in a huff. Shankar used a single shoulder movement to express this anger, but with his focus on body expression, there was no doubt in anyone's mind among the audience, as to what the movement and the expression intended to convey. He did not deem it necessary to use *mudras* to depict anger, for he felt they often created a break in the flow of storytelling and passions. The court scene ended with the Prime Minister dissolving the court and giving leave to the courtiers, in accordance with their rank, to leave the court. This dissolution of the court also reflects Shankar's intimate knowledge of how the royal court functioned, and again an addition by Shankar, not mentioned in Tagore's poem.

The next scene moved to the queen's quarters, where the queen and her companions, completely oblivious to the terrible devastation that their thoughtless act had caused, are seen dancing and enjoying themselves.

Choreographed in Shankar's own style, the movements were lively and happy in nature as the unrepentant queen and her companions were unaware of the fallout of their action. The point to be noted here in terms of Shankar's movements and style is that while both the queen and her companions' dance was lively, so too was the folk dance performed by the villagers. However, there was no way that the audience would mistake the dance performed by the queen and her companions as a folk form – not only because of the regal costumes but also because of the finesse and sophistication of the stylized steps, in comparison to that of the movements used to choreograph the dance of the villagers. This was the genius of Shankar's neoclassical and decorative movements in this dance, created with Shankar's own creative movements.

The queen and her companions caught unawares are surprised at the sudden and untimely entrance of the king into the inner chambers of the palace. They are left wondering what may have caused it. The king's censure and questioning of the queen, as to how her royal duty could have dictated the burning of homes of the villagers', leads the angered queen to berate the abode of the villagers and question the king as to what makes him consider those huts to be homes. She also adds that the cost of the destruction caused is nothing compared to the wealth spent on her half a day's pleasure. On hearing the queen's response, the king tells her that as long as she is the queen, she will never understand the trials of the poor. He orders the queen to be stripped off of her finery and exiled from the palace, telling her that she will be given one year to gather the means necessary, to help rebuild the huts of the villagers, for only then will she realize the extent of the destruction that she had caused, and the true value of their loss – what she in her disdain considered to be *samanya kshati*, or a slight damage. She could then return to the palace and publicly acknowledge the error of her ways in the royal court.

Reminisces Bose, that Shankar used to enact the role of the King in *Samanya Kshati*, which Bose later had the privilege of performing in the re-enactment of *Samanya Kshati* in 1972 during the production of *Shankarscope*. According to Bose, Shankar's movements in this scene mirrored a dormant volcano. The restrained anger when the king hears the queen's response, or when ordering the queen's companions to strip the queen of all her finery, as well as the long walk with usage of stage space in the most imaginative way possible to the palace gates from the inner chambers, and then finally ordering the queen to beg from door to door and get enough money to rebuild the destroyed huts within a year were all very clear in their meaning despite the fact that not many mudras were used. The scene where the king stops and prevents the queen's companions from accompanying the queen for the punishment was for her alone, and she is to step out alone in the world and rebuild the huts of the villagers, is a unique illustration of how a single movement or a gesture can be used to express a complex emotion. The queen was then shown to leave the palace. What Shankar added to the scene was, through a very slow and subtle movement of the hands and turn of the head,

Paying Tribute to Tagore through Samanya Kshati 49

the torment of the king for having to take this necessary yet harsh action on the queen. There would be an interval at this juncture.

As far as Tagore's poem was concerned, the narrative ended here. Shankar, however, in his presentation and composition took off from where the poet's narrative ended and wove his own story to narrate the journey of the queen during this one year – what she endured, how she finally managed to gather the resources to rebuild the huts that she had destroyed and returned to her rightful place at the palace after rebuilding the huts destroyed by her one thoughtless act. This segment, though performed in 1961 and 1962, was not performed when *Samanya Kshati* was re-staged in 1972.

The storyline of the second part of the enactment of *Samanya Kshati* is presented in the following manner in the souvenir of the tour of the USA in 1962:

The queen passes through the market, realises the value of money.
She is stunned with pain when a thorn pricks her. She orders a passing
woman to pull it out. The woman tells the queen to do her own job and
leaves. The queen limps along.
The dark, eerie night brings experience of rising fear.
Storm, lightning, thunder. Her dread swells to panic as she sees a dead
body being carried away.
The queen, exhausted, desperately hungry, shares food with kind
travellers. She is shocked at the sight of robbers sweeping down on her
benefactors. Grieved and broken down, destiny drags her weary feet
to the site of the burnt-down village. The sight rocks her with pain and
despair, as she drops from sheer fatigue.
In her disturbed sleep, her tortured sub-conscious mind, mocks her with
gruesome visions of the past. She awakens, her soul in torment, her
assurance gone. And at the borderline of life and death, when she does
not know what to do, a sadhu is heard approaching. She throws herself
at his feet. The venerable person consoles her, gives her spiritual solace.
The queen assumes a new personality in her humility and devotion as she
begins to beg. She goes on begging from place to place.
Days pass, months roll on, the queen sticks to her mission.
Night of approaching winter. Villagers clustered near burnt-down huts.
The queen comes and observes their misery with an aching heart. They
see her and become hostile on recognizing her. An old man quietens them
and the queen reveals that she has brought money to rebuild the huts.
Huts being rebuilt. Great activity and rejoicing. As the huts rise again, it
is about the end of the year. The queen wants to go to the court. So the
villagers lead the queen to the palace.
The king and ministers receive the queen. She humbly confesses the
realisation of the great mistake she has committed in burning down the
huts of the poor. What she had lost in her selfishness and arrogance, she
now gains back hundred-fold in her humility – the warmth of love and
affection from everyone.

According to Bose, Amala Shankar's enactment and portrayal of the queen, brought to the stage, the grandeur associated with a queen. Amala Shankar's skill as a dancer, together with her graceful and powerful movements, lit the stage especially with her first entry on stage, on her way to the river. A complete artist, Bose reminisces, not only did she design the costumes for *Samanya Kshati* but she also painted the background for different slides for a few scenes which were projected on the backdrop. She also designed and painted the cover page of the souvenir of *Samanya Kshati* in 1961.

Apart from Uday Shankar's choreography of the dances of *Samanya Kshati*, and his mastery as a storyteller as well as the visual artistry he presented on stage, Bose believes that Ravi Shankar's music also played an immensely important role in making *Samanya Kshati* a success. In Ravi Shankar's own words:

> Poet Rabindranath Tagore's works have always stirred me and provided spiritual and aesthetic inspiration. And when Dada asked me to score music for the ballets based on *Gurudev's* poems, I was fully aware of the great responsibility imposed on the musical creation to maintain the dignity, grandeur and lyrical beauty of the original. The results had, furthermore, to be achieved through the abstract medium of music in the absence of words or songs, and through Indian instruments. I had, however, to employ at places melodic and rhythmic counter-points to bring out the conflicting emotional undercurrents, which should not be mistaken as usage of Harmony in the Western sense.[38]

The guest musicians for *Samanya Kshati* were the veritable who's who from the world of Indian Classical music and included maestros like Ustad Ali Akbar Khan, Ustad Alla Rakha, Smt. Laksmi Shankar. Recollects Bose, Pandit Shiv Kumar Sharma (then a young artist in the making) played the santoor for the production of *Samanya Kshati*. The guest musicians performed in addition to Uday Shankar's own troupe musicians, who also worked extremely hard to ensure the success of this production.

The immense magnitude of Shankar's productions and the respect that it garnered at the time saw many classical musicians partake in productions that were creative and experimentative in nature, and not bound by the rigidity of the classical forms. Artists like Baba Allauddin Khan, who was already a well-established and well-respected senior classical artist at that point in time, were an integral part of many of Shankar's productions, performances and tours. Bose reminisces how the then upcoming classical musician Shiv Kumar Sharma, played the santoor for *Samanya Kshati*. Though a classical artist, he later formed part of the Shiv-Hari duo delivering Hindi film music, which became classics. A few of the more renowned of them being *Silsila*, 1981; *Lamhe*, 1991; and *Darr*, 1993. Even Pandit Ravi Shankar, who shifted to Maihar to receive instruction in *Sitar* under Baba Allauddin Khan,[39] as a result of his experimenting with the creative forms of Uday Shankar, created masterpieces for Satyajit Ray's Apu Trilogy of *Panther Panchali, Aparajito* and *Apur Sansar*. Ravi Shankar's music is also eternalized in films like Richard Attenborough's *Gandhi*, Satyajit Ray's *Paras Pathar*, and Hindi films like *Anuradha, Godan* and *Meera*.[40] He not only created more than 30 new ragas in Indian Music,[41] but his *jugalbandis* or duets with Yehudi Menuhin are mesmerizing masterpieces.[42]

Given the time period and the advancement in technology and their use of it in performing arts presentations in India, the stagecraft used by Shankar in *Samanya Kshati* was a novelty. A sheet of black net, which covered the entire length and height of the stage, without any stitching or seams, was hung midway on the stage, between and parallel to the front curtain and backdrop. This sheet of net separated the stage into two halves and divided it horizontally, thereby adding depth to it. The court scenes were performed behind the net, giving it a distant surreal look. The other scenes were performed in front of the net. The setting and props for the court scene used to be ready at all times behind the net; however, the lighting was placed and conducted in such a manner that while the scenes in the front stage that is to say, in front of the net, were being performed, the court scene set up behind the net was not visible. This enabled the beginning and ending of the flashback to occur instantaneously by merely lighting up the different parts of the stage.

For his productions, Shankar used his own array of lights. The dimmers he used were not only used to fade in and out, marking the beginning and end of each scene, but the dimmer controls would be marked so that the operators would be able to replicate the exact effect required for the performance, show after show, month after month. The troupe used to rehearse with lights during the stage rehearsals, so that the dimmer controls would be marked. Interestingly, for *Samanya Kshati* in 1961, since the music was pre-recorded, the light controls and dimmers would be controlled and handled by Shankar's own team of musicians as they were best versed with the music and knew the exact musical cues on which to operate the various lights.

In fact, Tapas Sen, one of the best light men in his profession at the time, was baffled with the source of lighting in one of the scenes during the second half of the ballet. He inspected the stage on a number of occasions after the performances to understand how the light effect had been achieved. The scene in question was enacted towards the end of the ballet, where the villagers are shown huddled around a fire on a wintry night in front of their burnt-down houses. The light that glowed in the centre of the small circle of villagers and reflected a warm red glow on the faces of the villagers actually emanated from a portable light that was brought on the stage by one of the dancers. There used to be a thick, long, black cable attached to this light, but in the dim light on the stage, this cable was not visible to the audience. Once the dancers were seated in their positions on stage, the dimmers would slowly brighten up this red light. The effect created was that of the villagers warming themselves in the glow of a small fire.

Another scene that made an impression on the audience was one where the queen was tormented by her past deeds and suffered nightmares. The nightmares of the queen were enacted in the segment of the stage behind the black net under a spotlight, so that the setting for the court scene would not be visible. Shankar, who enacted the role of the king, performed a few gestures which expressed the king's displeasure with the queen – this nightmare haunted the queen for she had been pampered all her life and had never had to face the wrath of the king for devastation brought on to his subjects, who were dependent on him for their welfare.

Samanya Kshati ran continuously at Mahajati Sadan for one and a half months. During the weekdays, there was one show in the evening, while on weekends – both Saturdays and Sundays – two shows were held – one at 3 pm in the afternoon and the other at 6 pm in the evening. The purpose of adding this detail is to highlight the popularity of Shankar's art form in Kolkata at that point in time. People came in from other cities and towns and often from other states to watch him perform – such was the pull of the maestro, recalls Bose.

At Mahajati Sadan where *Samanya Kshati* was first staged in 1961, the programme used to begin with Tagore's song *Prothomo Adi Tobo Shakti*. This was followed by the song, *Hey Mor Chittyo Purno Tirtho*. The third Rabindrasangeet to be sung was *Jayo Tabo Bichitro Anando*. These songs were presented by students of the State Academy of Dance Drama and Music, under the direction of the then Dean, Faculty of Music, Ramesh Chandra Bandopadhya and Professor of *Rabindrasangeet*, Maya Sen.[43] According to Bose, given that it was Shankar's show, even the presentation of the songs was conducted in a unique manner.

The songs which were sung by the students of the State Academy of Dance Drama and Music were pre-recorded. For the presentation of the song, the singers would stand on the right and left balconies in the auditorium, flanking the two sides of the stage, lip-synching the songs. The lights would first illuminate the group on the right balcony, where the group positioned there would lip-sync the first song. Immediately after the first song, the lights would focus on the group in the left balcony, who would lip-sync the second song. The front curtains of the stage would rise towards the end of the second song, and once the second song finished all the lights would be dimmed and the third song would commence. This song was accompanied by a short film featuring Tagore and Uday Shankar, shot in Shantiniketan. This film was projected through a small projector which belonged to Uday Shankar himself, onto a standing screen in the middle of the stage. The three songs were followed by a short ballet composed by Shankar, set to music by Ravi Shankar, called *Udara Charitanam*. Based on Tagore's poem by the same name, it comprised four lines which reads:

Prachirer Chidre Ek Naam Gotra Heen,
Phutiaachhe chhoto phool atishoy deen.
Dhik – dhik kore tare kanone shobai,
Surjyo utthi bole tare bhalo aacho bhai?

Paying Tribute to Tagore through Samanya Kshati 53

Roughly translated, the poem narrates how a small and inconsequential flower had grown in a crack in the garden walls. While all the other striking and gorgeous plants and trees treated this insignificant flower in the crack of the wall with disdain, the Sun after rising in the morning, in all its glory, would greet it and ask after it.

Was the choice of this poem from the several hundred penned by Tagore, a reflection of Shankar's sympathy and empathy towards the downtrodden and marginalized, those who lived on the fringes of society? The storyline of *Samanya Kshati* too, which Shankar chose to build into a ballet, leaving aside all the existing dance dramas and *geetinatyas* penned by Tagore, empathizes with the plight of the poor masses, who are at the complete mercy of the political leadership for their welfare; and unless this leadership is a compassionate one, injustices will prevail.

The music for the ballet *Udara Charitanam* too was composed by Ravi Shankar. The dance composition for this had also been set to counting on the tabla and Ravi Shankar set music to it after the dance composition was completed. This ballet was performed only by women. The presentation of *Udara Charitanam* was followed by the staging of *Samanya Kshati*. However, this format of presentation was only adopted for the shows at Mahajati Sadan in Kolkata.

Figure 2.3 Three of India's erstwhile Prime Ministers – Rajiv Gandhi, Jawaharlal Nehru and Indira Gandhi, seated from left to right in the audience for the performance of *Samanya Kshati* at AIFACS Hall, New Delhi. The then President of India, Sarvepalli Radhakrishnan is seated between Indira Gandhi and Jawaharlal Nehru.

Source: Courtesy, private collection of Shanti Bose

54 *Paying Tribute to Tagore through* Samanya Kshati

The performance of *Samanya Kshati* on the occasion of Tagore's birth centenary celebrations was held at Rabindra Kanan on Beadon Street. Unlike present day where the poet's birth anniversary celebrations are held at Rabindra Sadan, they used to be previously held every year at Rabindra Kanan.

Shankar and his troupe went on to perform *Samanya Kshati* over seven consecutive days at All India Fine Arts and Crafts Society (AIFACS) Hall, Delhi, on request of the Indian Ministry for Scientific and Cultural Affairs, for their hosting of Tagore's birth centenary celebrations. This was held after all the performances in Kolkata. Present in the august audience, on the first evening of the performance, were none other than the then President of India, Dr. Radhakrishnan, the Prime Minister of India, Pandit Jawaharlal Nehru, along with Indira Gandhi, Rajiv Gandhi and Sanjay Gandhi, as well as several other dignitaries.

After Delhi, the troupe went on to perform in Jaipur. During one of the performances at Jaipur, the sound system stopped due to a technical snag. Such was Shankar's teamwork, which resulted from innumerable hours of rehearsals put in over a year for preparation of the production, that the entire group on stage continued performing in the same synchronized manner, without any music, until the curtains dropped. Once the snag was restored, the performance continued from where it had stopped. Not a single dancer left the stage during this mishap. They stood in their positions and resumed their dance from where the music began again. This was the level of

Figure 2.4 The cast ensemble of *Samanya Kshati* at AIFACS Hall, New Delhi, after the first day of the show.

Source: Courtesy, private collection of Shanti Bose

professionalism, proficiency and discipline among Shankar's team members – something that Shankar himself had learned from Pavlova and her team, and instilled in his troupe.

After the troupe returned to Calcutta from Jaipur, the production of *Samanya Kshati* was staged again. This time at New Empire, for seven straight days. Shankar and his troupe then began their tour of Western India. They toured for more than a month across the cities of Bombay, Pune, Nagpur and Ahmedabad. Once they returned to Calcutta, they began touring nearby places like Burdwan, Katoah, Kalna, Shiuri and others.

The reason for elaborating on these performances in terms of the cities and the days, as well as going into detail about how the dance drama was enacted, who the participants were, the performances and the technology adapted, is because of the fact that none of Shankar's performances, apart from those encased in *Kalpana*, have been recorded or documented. This was probably because recordings would have taken away from the charm of the live performances on stage, which was Shankar's primary medium. Capturing these productions on moving pictures would also have created a dent in and negatively impacted revenue generation, and detracted audience attention from the live performances. This has, however, resulted in the fact that posterity has little to go by and understand what Uday Shankar's style of dance, especially during the last two decades of his life, entailed, hence the detailed documentation.

Notes

1 Raya Ghosh, "When is Rabindranath Tagore Jayanti 2021?" *India Today*, May 7, 2021, accessed January 3, 2023, url: www.indiatoday.in/lifestyle/what's-hot/story/when-is-rabindranath-tagore-jayanti-2021-1799787-2021-05-07
2 "Tagore Centenary in Bombay," *Economic Political Weekly*, January 7, 1961, 3, accessed April 7, 2017, url: www.epw.in/system/files/pdf/1961_13/1/tagore_centenary_in_bombay.pdf
3 K. C. Mukherjee. "Tagore-Pioneer in Education," *British Journal of Educational Studies* 18, no. 1 (1970): 69–81, accessed November 22, 2021, url: https://doi.org/10.2307/3120112.
4 Sundeep Bhutoria, "Humanism and Hope: The Legacy of Film Director Satyajit Ray," *United Nations UN Chronicle*, May 2021, accessed January 3, 2023, url: www.un.org/en/un-chronicle/humanism-and-hope-legacy-filmmaker-satyajit-ray
5 Ratan Bhattacharya, "Satyajit Ray's Documentary Film Rabindranath: A saga of Creative Excellence," *European Academic Research* 1, no. 6 (2013): 901–3, accessed March 11, 2019, url: http://euacademic.org/uploadarticle/62.pdf
6 Mohan Khokar, *His Dance His Life – A Portrait of Uday Shankar* (New Delhi: Himalayan Books, 1983), 75.
7 Uday Shankar, "My Love for Dance," *Souvenir of Shankarscope* (1970).
8 Manna Dey. *Memories Come Alive: An Autobiography* (New Delhi: Penguin Books, 2007).
9 Praveen Sudevan, "Who is Baul? Documentary Delves Into the Philosophy of Bengal's Musical Mystics," *The Hindu*, April 19, 2021, accessed November 22, 2021, url: www.thehindu.com/entertainment/movies/ricky-kej-who-is-baul-documentary/article34359867.ece

10 K. C. Mukherjee. "Tagore-Pioneer in Education," *British Journal of Educational Studies* 18, no. 1 (1970): 69–81, accessed November 22, 2021, url: https://doi.org/10.2307/3120112
11 Ramachandra Guha, *Makers of Modern India* (Cambridge: The Belknap Press of Harvard University Press, 2011), 188.
12 Rabindranath Tagore, *Gitabitan* (Calcutta: Viswa-Bharati, 1997), 714.
13 Rabindranath Tagore, *Nationalism* (London: Macmillan and Co, Limited, 1918), 4.
14 *Kalpana*, accessed September 12, 2019, url: https://indiancine.ma/BKLU/player/01:18:53.761
15 *Kalpana*, accessed September 12, 2019, url: https://indiancine.ma/BKLU/player/00:50:58.667
16 Ramachandra Guha, *Makers of Modern India* (Cambridge: The Belknap Press of Harvard University Press, 2011), 186.
17 Debjani Chatterjee, "Jallianwala Bagh Massacre: Heroes of Jallianwala Bagh Remembered," *NDTV*, April 13, 2021, accessed November 24, 2021, url: www.ndtv.com/india-news/jallianwala-bagh-massacre-india-remembers-the-heroes-of-jallianwalla-bagh-2412502
18 "Tagore Renounced his Knighthood in Protest for Jallianwala Bagh Mass Killing," *The Times of India*, April 13, 2011, accessed November 24, 2021, url: https://timesofindia.indiatimes.com/india/tagore-renounced-his-knighthood-in-protest-for-jalianwalla-bagh-mass-killing/articleshow/7967616.cms
19 Rabindranath Tagore, *Nationalism* (London: Macmillan and Co, Limited, 1918), 17.
20 Louise Blakeney Williams, "Overcoming the 'Contagion of Mimicry': The Cosmopolitan Nationalism and Modernist History of Rabindranath Tagore and W. B. Yeats," *The American Historical Review* 112, no. 1 (2007): 69–100, accessed November 24, 2021, url: www.jstor.org/stable/4136007
21 Ramachandra Guha, *Makers of modern India* (Cambridge: The Belknap Press of Harvard University Press, 2011), 186.
22 Vishwabharati, accessed September 15, 2019, url: www.visvabharati.ac.in/Visva_Bharati.html
23 Vishwabharati, accessed September 15, 2019, url: www.visvabharati.ac.in/EDUCATIONAL_IDEAS.html
24 Vishwabharati, accessed September 15, 2019, url: www.visvabharati.ac.in/History.html
25 Anu Kumar, "Thomas Macaulay Won the Debate on How to Shape Indian Education. So Who Were the Losers?" *Scroll.in*, February 04, 2017, accessed October 30, 2021, url: https://scroll.in/magazine/821605/thomas-macaulay-and-the-debate-over-english-education-in-india
26 Kalpana, 1948, accessed September 15, 2019, url: https://indiancine.ma/BKLU/player/01:10:55.135
27 Dartington Trust, accessed November 25, 2021, url: www.dartington.org/
28 Sonal Khullar, "Almora Dreams: Art and Life at the Uday Shankar India Cultural Centre," *Marg: Magazine of Arts* 69, no. 4 (2018): 14–31.
29 Santidev Ghosh, Visvabharati, accessed November 25, 2021, url: www.visvabharati.ac.in/SantidevGhosh.html
30 Shanti Bose, "Adhunik Bharatiya Nritye Uday Shankar Er Prabhab," *Desh Binodan Shankhya*, (1987).
31 Mohan Khokar, *His Dance His Life – A Portrait of Uday Shankar* (New Delhi: Himalayan Books, 1983), 53.
32 The term ballet has been used here to denote a theatrical dance choreography in a specific, formalized dance technique, performed in combination with other artistic elements such as music, costume, stage scenery and other stage craft, accessed June 25, 2018, url: www.britannica.com/art/ballet
33 Uday Shankar, "My Love for Dance," *Souvenir of Shankarscope* (1970).

34 Glossary, ITC Sangeet Research Academy, accessed June 24, 2018, url: www.itcsra.org/glossary.aspx
35 Souvenir: USA Tour of 1962.
36 Rabindranath Tagore, "Samanya Kshati," *Souvenir of tour of USA* (1962).
37 Mohan Khokar, *His Dance His Life – A Portrait of Uday Shankar* (New Delhi: Himalayan Books, 1983), 45–9.
38 Ravi Shankar, *Souvenir of Samanya Kshati* (1961).
39 Music, BBC, accessed March 15, 2019, url: www.bbc.co.uk/music/artists/697f8b9f-0454-40f2-bba2-58f35668cdbe
40 Kamal Nayan Chaturvedi, Pandit Ravi Shankar as Film Music Director, Vidur's Blog, accessed March 15, 2019, url: https://mevidur.wordpress.com/2012/12/13/pandit-ravi-shankar-as-film-music-director/
41 Ravi Shankar, accessed March 15, 2019, url: www.ravishankar.org/-music.html
42 How We Met: Yehudi Menuhin and Ravi Shankar, Independent, accessed March 15, 2019, url: www.independent.co.uk/arts-entertainment/how-we-met-yehudi-menuhin-and-ravi-shankar-1575503.html
43 Souvenir: *Samanya Kshati*, 1961.

3 The Watershed Year – 1962

The year 1962 can be considered to be a watershed year not only in terms of international politics but for India's security concerns as well. The 1960s witnessed the peak of the Cold War when the world came to the brink of a nuclear war in October 1962 with the Cuban Missile Crisis. The Sino-Indian war of 1962, on the other hand, wreaked havoc in India.

Sumit Ganguly, Professor of Political Science at Indiana University, opines that India's foreign policy can be categorized into three distinct phases. The first would entail the period from 1947 to 1962 – marking India's emergence as an independent nation state to the Sino-Indian War of 1962, the second from 1962 to 1991 – marking the period from the Sino-Indian war to the liberalization of the Indian economy and the end of the Cold War; and the third phase, from 1991 to the present.[1]

India's concerns immediately after independence were manifold. Food security was the most primary concern, as by the time the British left India, the country was, as Shashi Tharoor put it, a poster child for third world poverty, with 90 per cent of the population living below the poverty line. Literacy rate was below 17 per cent, and life expectancy was at 27 years of age.[2] According to Tharoor again, India was one of the richest countries with its share in the global economy at around 23 per cent at the beginning of the eighteenth century. However, by the time the colonial powers left India, India's share in the world economy had reduced to less than 4 per cent.[3] India which gained independence in 1947 was not only struggling to survive and recover as a nation-state after nearly 200 years of British rule[4] but also needed to ensure that it did not become a pawn[5] at the hands of any major power once again, especially in the context of the politics of the post Second World War global order, which led to the creation of a bipolar world with the Eastern and Western blocs, thanks to the Cold War. India's foreign policy and its national interest was therefore determined by the international politics of the time, India's domestic needs and of course the idiosyncratic variable in terms of its then political leadership. Former Ambassador and Former Foreign Secretary of India, Muchkund Dubey writes, "The fundamental purpose of India's Foreign Policy . . . is to promote its national interest . . . but there is a hierarchy of national interests."[6] In its first phase of foreign policy, India, not

DOI: 10.4324/9781003433774-4

wanting to get drawn into Cold War Politics and become a battleground for the various proxy wars, opted for the principle of Non-Alignment, seeking to establish friendly relations with all nation states across the globe, in both the Eastern and Western blocs.

The term Non-Alignment as an integral principle of India's foreign policy was coined by V. K. Krishna Menon,[7] in the early 1950s. India's representative to the United Nations around the same time, Krishna Menon elaborated during his speech at the General Assembly of the United Nations, that the term and policy of non-alignment was intended to allow India and the other newly independent states, which had emerged from the yokes of colonialism, the third option of not aligning with either of the two blocs and thereby protecting themselves from being drawn into the battle lines of bloc politics. Getting drawn into the Cold War politics was something that these newly emergent nations could ill afford after almost 200 years of colonial rule. According to Krishna Menon, both the term and the policy were positive in nature, intent on promoting security and national interest, by extending its hand in friendship through various treaties of friendship, based on the *Panchsheel* (the five principles of peaceful co-existence)[8] as well as by creating goodwill through various cultural exchanges.

These cultural exchanges were a result of the initiatives undertaken through Cultural Diplomacy, which according to Former Ambassador and Former Foreign Secretary of India, Shyam Saran, delivers impacts that often elude traditional diplomacy.[9] Therefore, cultural diplomacy is an important aspect of a nation's soft power.[10] The cultural exchanges that India engaged in during the first phase of its foreign policy were a part of its soft power initiatives, to promote friendly relations with other nation-states, for India could ill afford hostility at this stage given that most of its resources were focused on getting the nation out of hunger, and it had become a question of grains over guns. "Soft Power," according to Joseph S. Nye, Jr, who coined the term, is the "ability to achieve desired outcomes in international affairs through attraction rather than coercion or payment,"[11] to promote its national interest, as opposed to hard military and economic power, which is capital intensive.

The Indian Council for Cultural Relations (ICCR) established in the 1950s (registered under the Societies Act in 1957) was a tool and an instrument of cultural diplomacy. The institutionalization of cultural diplomacy made evident India's dependency on soft power to help build and fortify relations with countries across the globe. The Memorandum of Association signed in 1956 states that the objective of ICCR was to foster, revive and strengthen cultural relations between India and other countries.[12]

All Shankar's performances in 1962, with his troupe, which was then known as *The Uday Shankar Hindu Dancers and Musicians*, be it at the Seattle World's Fair or in various cities of Europe, were organized by the Ministry of Scientific Research and Cultural Affairs, Government of India. The troupe's other performances in the USA and Canada in 1962 were sponsored

60 The Watershed Year – 1962

and hosted by Sol Hurok, the well-known American impresario, whom Uday Shankar had first met during his days of performance and travel of the USA with Anna Pavlova and her troupe in the 1920s.

On September 3, 1962, Uday Shankar and his troupe began their journey for the international tour of the USA, Canada and Europe. They set sail from Bombay, on a ship headed towards the port of Aden, which was to be their first stop after crossing the Arabian Sea. After leaving the port of Aden, the troupe sailed through the Red Sea and then the Suez Canal and made a stop at the Messina Islands in Italy. During this halt, the members of the troupe, many of whom were travelling out of India for the first time, got the opportunity to view the ruins of Pompeii and Mt. Vesuvius. From Messina, the ship sailed to Naples, and then on to Genoa. From Genoa, the troupe travelled to Paris by train. As the troupe had to halt in Paris for a few hours, the troupe members again got the opportunity to visit the well-known landmarks and tourist spots of Paris, including the Eiffel Tower. From Paris, they travelled by train to the English Channel. They went on to travel to London by train, after crossing the English Channel.

Figure 3.1 Uday Shankar and Amala Shankar in the course of an intercity trip break in the USA, clicked by Bose himself on his Rolleicord camera, which he had bought during this trip itself.

Source: Courtesy, private collection of Shanti Bose

The troupe's 5-day stopover in London gave the members the opportunity to visit famous tourist spots like Trafalgar Square, Madame Tussaud's Wax Museum, the British Museum, the Commonwealth Museum, Victoria and Albert Museum and other sites. London was only a stopover point for their onward journey to the USA. The troupe did not have any performances in London. The journey from London to New York was on a trans-Atlantic flight to New York, where at the New York International Airport itself, arrangements had been made for a television coverage to announce Shankar and his troupe's arrival to the USA for their performances. Present at this event were Uday Shankar, Amala Shankar, Ananda Shankar, Mamata Shankar, Lakshmi Shankar, Bhudeb Shankar, Kalpana Roy, Meena Nandi, Asoke Nandi and Shanti Bose.

After their performances in New York from September 25 to September 30, 1962, the troupe flew to Seattle, where their performance was scheduled at the Seattle World's Fair from October 2 to October 7, 1962.[13] At the Fair, Shankar and his troupe represented India, as participation in the Fair was a Government of India initiative. Hosted by Seattle City from April 21 to October 21, 1962, The Century 21 World's Fair[14] was inaugurated by President John F. Kennedy through a speech delivered via telephone.[15] The fair saw 24 participating countries exhibit across the five theme areas of The World of Science, The World of Tomorrow, The World of Commerce and Industry, The World of Art and The World of Entertainment.[16]

The next stop after Seattle was Vancouver. From Vancouver, the troupe flew to Montreal. From Montreal, to New York. From New York to Detroit, Chicago, Kansas City, Denver, Los Angeles – Hollywood, San Francisco, Las Vegas, Oklahoma City, San Antonio, Houston, New Orleans, Atlanta, Washington, DC, Baltimore, Boston, Cleveland, before the troupe again flew back into New York.

After their last performance in New York, Shankar and his troupe returned to London via flight. This too was for a layover, as now the troupe was on their way to Amsterdam in the Netherlands, for their first performance in Europe in 1962. From the Netherlands, Uday Shankar and his troupe went on to perform in quite a few cities in Germany – Bonn, Frankfurt, Stuttgart, Munich and Berlin. The troupe's next destination was Yugoslavia. From Yugoslavia, they went to perform in Poland, from Poland to Copenhagen in Denmark and Stockholm in Sweden. The Norwegian capital of Oslo saw the last performance of Shankar's troupe in Europe, before they returned to India. This turned out to be Shankar's last tour of Europe with his troupe.

All the performances in the various cities and countries across Europe were, as mentioned previously, organized by the Ministry of Scientific Research and Cultural Affairs, Government of India; and therefore, Shankar and his troupe performed in these countries by virtue of representing the Indian government, and thereby was a means of taking forward India's cultural diplomacy through soft power. The troupe then set sail to return to India from Europe once again by ship. Uday Shankar, Amala Shankar, Mamata

62 The Watershed Year – 1962

Figure 3.2 The cover page of the souvenir of the tour of the USA and Canada in 1962, as presented by Hurok.

Source: Courtesy, private collection of Shanti Bose

Shankar, Asoke Nandi – Amala Shankar's younger brother, and Asoke Nandi's daughter, Nandita, returned to India by flight directly from Oslo, as Amala Shankar's father had taken ill. As winter had set in by the time the troupe set sail from Europe, the first ship that they boarded on their return journey was equipped to travel on icy waters. A novel experience on the

Figure 3.3 The cast of *Samanya Kshati*, after their performance in Hollywood.
Source: Courtesy, private collection of Shanti Bose

return journey Bose recollects was the celebration of India's Republic Day on January 26, 1963, on board the ship. The troupe members sang one of India's most popular patriotic songs *Saare Jahaan Se Achha*, penned by the Urdu poet Mohammad Iqbal in 1904,[17] who interestingly later went on to became one of the spiritual and founding fathers of Pakistan along with Sir Syed and Jinnah.[18] Lakshmi Shankar had taught this song to the troupe members. The ship finally docked at Bombay on February 3, 1963, completing the troupe's tour of five months – of which nearly two months were spent in the USA and almost three months in Europe.

While Shankar and his troupe were touring the USA, Canada and Europe, the world nearly went to the brink of destruction and back, with the Cuban Missile Crisis. Termed the most dangerous crisis that the world has ever seen, when the two superpowers came eyeball to eyeball,[19] this 13-day crisis from October 16 to 28 in 1962 is what kept President John F. Kennedy from addressing the closing session of the Seattle World's Fair on October 21, 1962. Though the official reason for his inability to address the closing session stated that he was down with a bad cold, a cheeky headline in the American press read, "President Kennedy's Cold War 'cold' supersedes Seattle World's Fair closing ceremonies on October 21, 1962."[20]

India too, during this period suffered its own devastation, when on October 20, 1962, Chinese forces launched a massive attack at several points on Indian outposts, along the northern frontier of India.[21] Though journalist Neville Maxwell, in his book, *India's China War*, squarely places the blame on India's shoulders as the aggressor in the Sino-Indian war of 1962,[22] others consider China to be the aggressor as the military preparedness of China vis-à-vis the military unpreparedness of India tells its own story.[23] Nonetheless, one of the after-effects of the Sino-Indian war, which proved to be a watershed

64 The Watershed Year – 1962

Figure 3.4 Souvenir cover of the tour of 1962 in Europe.
Source: Courtesy, private collection of Shanti Bose

in India's foreign policy, was that there was now a distinct shift from the use of soft power to hard power in India's foreign policy considerations. With the Sino-Indian war, the need to develop India's military capability to defend its borders became evident. It also became evident that treaties of friendship and cultural exchanges and other soft power initiatives were not enough to

Figure 3.5 Bose with Lakshmi Shankar and Rajendra Shankar's daughter Viji on the left, Asoke Nandi's (Amala Shankar's brother's) daughter, Nandita in the centre and Mamata Shankar on the extreme right, in front of Universal Studios. Ananda Shankar can be seen standing on the extreme left.

Source: Courtesy, private collection of Shanti Bose

ensure India's national security and territorial integrity. Therefore, India was compelled to move away considerably from its primary reliance on the use of soft power to generate goodwill, to a more hard stance, as it now became a question of guns over grains.[24] This was therefore Shankar's last international tour where he and his troupe performed in programmes organized by the Government of India.

The preparation of the five-month tour of the USA, Canada and Europe which the troupe had set off for, in the first week of September 1962, began quite a few months earlier. After the production of *Samanya Kshati* in Kolkata in 1961 and various tours and performances across India, Shankar gave the troupe members a month's vacation. Preparations for the international tour began in 1962, after this break with continued rehearsals for *Samanya Kshati* and another production, *Dances of India*. The troupe had also prepared for a shadow play based on the Life of Buddha. However, Hurok's son-in-law, who had visited India prior to the tour, to finalize arrangements, was

66 *The Watershed Year – 1962*

not very keen on it being performed during the tour. The Great Renunciation, also based on the life of Buddha, was however, a part of the repertoire. It depicted the story of Prince Siddharth till he renunciated his worldly life. This was not performed on stage and not as a shadow play, and was shorter in duration compared to the ballet on the Life of Buddha.

The rehearsals for the international tour of 1962 began at Shankar's Golf Club Road home in Kolkata, where the troupe members attended the General Class held by Uday Shankar. With a two-fold goal in mind, these classes were held with the intent of helping focus the mind on achieving coordination and synchronization of the body and mind; as well as to maximize the dexterity of the performers. The exercises taught and practised during these general classes required the dancers to exercise all the joints and limbs together with various other body parts. Improvisation classes were also conducted during this time to enable the dancers to be conscious of how to harness expressions, react to various actions, as well as hone creativity, in contrast to only being performers of the dances taught. These improvisation classes saw Shankar pair off dancers and give them a subject. The dancers would be given some time to decide how to express their thoughts on the given topics through their imagination and creatively express them through dance movements.

Shankar transported the entire team to Madras after a month of these general and improvisation classes. Rehearsals were conducted for over four months at Shankar's home in Madras on 14, Bog Road, which was situated next to the house of Shivaji Ganesan – an iconic figure in Tamil cinema. The move to Madras and the four months of dedicated preparation were conducted with the intention of removing the performers from any personal and family distractions. While Shankar's family members – both immediate and extended – stayed at Shankar's home, the other troupe members housed together in a rented property and thereby, bonded well – a basic necessity for any successful team activity. Rehearsals were conducted for almost seven hours a day – from 1 pm to 8 pm, with a break for lunch and tea, six days a week, with Sunday being a rest day. However, as the day of travel neared, rehearsals were conducted every day, including Sunday. Since many of the troupe members did not return home to Kolkata from Madras, but went on directly to Bombay to board the ship, they were away from their homes for almost nine months during this stretch.

Among the items that the troupe learned and prepared to perform in *Dances of India* were The Great Renunciation – based on the life of Buddha, *Astrapuja*, *Brahmaputra*, *Khadya* – which included Shankar's much appreciated composition of *Labour and Machinery*, glimpses of which audiences had already received in the film *Kalpana*, and *Panthadi*. There were some items that the troupe had also prepared for, but which did not find place in the final repertoire like the *Harvest Dance*. Aside from these items, Amala Shankar performed the well-known and popular song *Krishna Ni Begame Baro*, created by Carnatic Composer, Sri Vyasaraja Tirtha,[25] around the fifteenth to sixteenth century CE.[26] Shankar also performed his renowned item, *Indra*, composed by him in the 1930s. Shankar and his wife, Amala, apart from these solo appearances in various items under *Dances of India* also performed together in the short ballets of *Brahmaputra*, *Khadya* and *The Great Renunciation*.

Though the troupe had been prepared with the two performances of *Samanya Kshati* and the *Dances of India*, they performed the latter for most of their performances in the USA, Canada and Europe. As all the performances in Europe and one in the USA at the Seattle World Fair were at the behest of the Indian government, Shankar in his role as the cultural ambassador of India presented to the audiences of the USA and Europe, India's rich cultural heritage. Given in the following is a write-up on the items that were performed as a part of *Dances of India*, as published in the souvenirs during the tour of 1962. The reason for showcasing these in detail is to give an idea of how Shankar used his style to create a narrative that was beyond pure entertainment and presented the idea of India to the West.

Khadya

In days of yore, happy peasants lived in a village rich in nature's bounty. Farming was their only livelihood. The machine age had not come their way. One of the village boys was educated in a large city and learned the techniques of the machine world. He returned to the village and took into confidence the son of the old village Headman. The old Headman and his son's newly wedded bride disapproved of their ideas of exploiting the villagers. The girls became modern and disregarded their elders. Gradually all were reduced to automations. The villagers realized their error and revolted. They were arrested and forced to work but managed eventually to escape and return to their happy life in the fields. The Headman and the exploiters reached a compromise, and all realized that the help of machinery in the form of tractors aided their agricultural pursuits and a new harmony between the dignity of labour and the contribution of machinery was attained.

Astrapuja

Worshipping their arms, the warriors boast of their weapons and flourish them. They earn the approbation and good wishes of their women as they leave for battle.

Krishna Ni Begame Baro

Yashoda calls out to her son Krishna, and in her overwhelming love for him, sees in him the whole Universe.

Panthadi

The item used to begin with two girls entering the stage with an imaginary ball, which they would play with. Finally, while playing, one of the girls would throw the ball so forcefully, that it would seem as if the ball had disappeared among the audience, and that is how the item ended.

Indra

According to Vedic tradition, Indra is the Lord of the Heavens, the Stars, the Clouds, Thunder, Lightning and Rain. As the Supreme, he is here represented in the act of initiating the lesser gods in the perfect art of dance.

Brahmaputra

The mighty river Brahmaputra flows in serene majesty and life in the fields and in the village goes on smoothly. But trouble arises: there are whispers. Two lovers are seen in suspicious circumstances. They are madly in love and know not what is right and what is wrong. Suddenly the river overflows its banks and in its mighty fury and floods cause havoc. The people attribute it to the sin of the lovers. The lovers themselves are caught in the floods, drowned and washed away in the rolling waters. The floods recede and life goes on as usual in the fields and in the village. The Brahmaputra flows again in serene majesty; only a scarf was left on the bank of the river.

The Great Renunciation

"Regard the world as an empty trifle," said Lord Buddha, "only then will the world yield to happiness, enabling you to live blissfully in all life's vicissitudes." At his birth holy men predicted that Prince Siddharth (as Lord Buddha was known before the renunciation) shall either be the King of Kings – trampling on the necks of enemies – or he shall tread the path of self-denial and deliver the world from ignorance. To prevent the Prince from following the path of self-denial, his father Suddhodana, put him in a palace, with his Queen Yashodhara, where he could not come face to face with woe, want, pain, plague, age or death.

One day Prince Siddharth wanted to see what lay beyond the palace. While passing through the streets, the prince saw a sick man on the road. He asked his charioteer, "Why is it that he pants and moans and gasps?" His charioteer replies that it is because of illness that "comes like a sly snake and stings unseen?" "Then all men live in fear?" asked the Prince, "and none can say I shall sleep happy and so I shall wake?"

The Prince passed along and an old man crept forth. The Prince asked, "What thing is this who seems a man, so miserable, so horrible and so sad?" Channa, his charioteer answered that he was an aged man, who was like them years before but the thievish years had pillaged him of his strength and form. Then spoke the Prince, "But shall this come to me should I live so long, and to my sweet Yashodhara, my lovely Queen?"

The prince passed further and saw people carrying a dead man. The Prince pointed to them and Channa replied, "Those men are carrying the dead." The Prince asked, "Is this the end which comes to all who live?"

The Prince passed further and saw a holy man lifting his hands in prayer to Heaven. Channa said, "This is the man who prays for the well-being of himself and all the people, having left the world and its pleasures."

The Prince returned to the palace with a heavy heart. That night, Queen Yashodhara dreamt a frightful dream, which ended with a voice crying, "The time is come," and in her tears, she slept again. That night, the stars in the sky ranged together and appeared to ask the Prince, "this is the Night, choose the way of greatness or the way of God – to reign as King of Kings or wander alone." Prince Siddharth chose the latter. "I will depart; I shall seek the truth for all men's sake. The kingdom I crave is more than all things which change to death." He lay aside his youth, his joys and his Queen Yashodhara and softly stepped out with his hands clasped on his heart.

For any production in performing arts, and especially for dance, music, lighting and costumes play a very important role in the production process. Therefore, each of Shankar's troupe members were intrinsically linked to these in some way or the other, and had to train in these aspects under Shankar's guidance, in order to understand what showmanship was about. Since it was a set group of dancers who were performing in either different roles or different items, costumes were stitched and kept ready in a manner which permitted quick changes so that the audience was not even able to make out that it was the same dancer performing again. These quick changes required a change in costume right from the headgear, to jewellery, to the garment being worn. Each dancer had to bear the responsibility for their own costumes in the sense that they had to ensure that all their costumes for their different performances were placed in order of the sequence of the items. For this tour, most of the costumes were newly made. A few old ones were altered for a couple of items and in a few cases rearranged with new patterns on them. The men had to learn how to tie different types of *paagdis* – which are a traditional Indian head-dress consisting of a long piece of cloth, tied around the head – with different styles indicating regions, class, social occasions and so on. Some of the *paagdis* which were more elaborate and rather time-consuming to tie were stitched to allow quick changes. The hair ornaments used by women dancers, which were also intricate, were stitched together and joined so that they could be worn quickly as an individual piece instead of having to spend time wearing them as separate pieces. This was necessary because each item performed required a different set of ornaments, in keeping with the scene to be enacted or the demands of the dances performed.

Large waterproof and fireproof boxes were used to carry all that the troupe required for their performances, be it lights, musical instruments, props, costumes and ornaments and all other associated paraphernalia. The waterproof and fireproof boxes for the costumes used to contain 5–6 wooden trays of costumes for the dancers. Each tray measured about 3 feet in length × 2 feet in breadth and was about 5 inches in depth. Each individual tray had all the costumes a dancer needed to wear, along with their ornaments. In case a dancer had fewer items to perform, or male dancers, whose costumes were not as elaborate, the dancers shared one tray between two dancers. While there was someone employed with the troupe to press the costumes before each performance, it was up to the dancers to rearrange their costumes that they had worn, and required for the next performance, in their respective trays along with the ornaments and other pieces used by them for the performance.

The troupe members were also given prince coats and overcoats to wear, which were like uniforms, to help identify the group members and give them a common identity. The members had to wear them when travelling from one city to another, or during the formal occasions that they were required to attend. As mentioned by Uday Shankar in a televised interview on Kolkata Doordarshan Kendra with the thespian Shambhu Mitra, soft skills and etiquette was also a part of the training that was imparted to all the troupe members before commencing on international tours.[27] This is a practice that many corporate organizations continue to practice in the present day.

The dancers in the troupe for the tour of 1962 to the USA, Canada and Europe included Pappu Raghavan, who was the Troupe Coach and Ballet Master, Asoke Nandi, who was the Ballet Registrar, together with Asit Chatterjee, Raman Nair Vasudevan, Animesh Bakshi, Ganesh Dutta and Shanti Bose. As Shanti Bose was yet to adopt his stage name at this point, his given name Amarendra Bose is printed in the souvenir of 1962. It was only from the international tour in 1968; on Uday Shankar's suggestion, Shanti Bose adopted the name that he was commonly known by, as his stage name. Meena Nandi, Kabita Bakshi, N. Jayashree, P.S. Vasantha, Kalpana Roy and Purnima Bose were the women dancers on this tour, apart from Uday Shankar and Amala Shankar.

Lakshmi Shankar was the Music Director and Conductor for the tour, for both *Dances of India* and *Samanya Kshati*. The music during the international tour was performed live, unlike the performances of *Samanya Kshati* in India. Lakshmi Shankar was also the vocalist for this tour. Recalls Bose, in one of their performances in Europe, when some of the musical instruments had failed to arrive in time for a performance due to airline issues, Lakshmi Shankar, single-handedly vocally carried through the entire ballet of *Samanya Kshati* for almost 1 hour and 40 minutes with a few supporting instruments. Married to Uday Shankar's younger brother, Rajendra Shankar, Lakshmi Shankar was Uday Shankar's sister-in-law. The other musicians who accompanied the troupe for this tour were Rabin Das on the *Sarod*, Soumen Dey on the Flute, Tarun Ganguly on the Drums, Ranjan Mazumdar on the *Sitar* and Sambhunath Mukherjee on Percussion. Uday Shankar's son, Ananda Shankar, played the *Sitar* and percussion instruments.

Amala Shankar designed the costumes for both *Samanya Kshati* and *Dances of India*. Bhudeb Shankar, Uday Shankar's cousin, was his Personal Manager. Chiranjilal Shah, who had been with Shankar from the days of the Uday Shankar Culture Centre at Almora, deserves special mention as Shankar had complete confidence in him and Shahji, as he was called by everyone with affection and respect, was the one responsible for checking out the suitability of the stage, the backstage and the greenrooms before every performance.

A five month international tour by Shankar and his troupe, of which three months were spent performing in Europe as India's representative and thereby taking forward India's foreign policy initiative of cultural diplomacy and soft power, does not find detailed discussion in any hitherto existing literature on Shankar, and hence the detailed documentation in this chapter.

Notes

1 Sumit Ganguly, ed, *India's Foreign Policy: Retrospect and Prospect* (New Delhi: Oxford University Press, 2010).
2 "India Missed the Bus for They Threw us Under Its Wheels: Shashi Tharoor on British Rule of India," *Scroll.in*, September 10, 2017, accessed November 28, 2021, url: https://scroll.in/video/850022/india-missed-the-bus-for-they-threw-us-under-its-wheels-shashi-tharoor-on-british-rule-of-india
3 "Viewpoint: Britain Must Pay Reparations to India," *BBC News*, July 22, 2015, accessed November 28, 2021, url: www.bbc.com/news/world-asia-india-33618621
4 Amartya Sen, "Illusions of Empire: Amartya Sen on what British Rule Really did for India," *theguardian.com*, June 29, 2021, accessed December 30, 2021, www.theguardian.com/world/2021/jun/29/british-empire-india-amartya-sen
5 Norman D. Palmer, "India's Position in Asia," *Journal of International Affairs* 17, no. 2 (1963): 126–41, accessed November 28, 2021, url: www.jstor.org/stable/24381368
6 Muchkund Dubey, *India's Foreign Policy: Coping with the Changing World* (New Delhi: Orient Black Swan Private Limited, 2016), 1.
7 Mani Shankar Aiyar, "The Non-Alignment Man," *The Indian Express*, January 5, 2020, accessed November 28, 2021, url: https://indianexpress.com/article/books-and-literature/historian-jairam-ramesh-v-k-krishna-menon-a-chequered-brilliance-the-many-lives-of-v-k-krishna-menon-jawaharlal-nehru-6199932/
8 Panchsheel, Ministry of External Affairs, Government of India, accessed April 10, 2017, url: www.mea.gov.in/Uploads/PublicationDocs/191_panchsheel.pdf
9 Eighth Pupul Jayakar Memorial Lecture, *Cultural Diplomacy Leveraging India's Soft Power by Shri Shyam Saran*, INTACH, April 18, 2016, accessed November 28, 2021, url: http://intangibleheritage.intach.org/eighth-pupul-jayakar-memorial-lecture-cultural-diplomacy-leveraging-indias-soft-power-by-shri-shyam-saran/
10 India's Culture Diplomacy and Soft Power, Former Ambassador Bhaswati Mukherjee, Ministry of External Affairs, Government of India, October 18, 2019, Accessed November 28, 2021, url: www.mea.gov.in/distinguished-lectures-detail.htm?855
11 Joseph S. Nye, "Public Diplomacy and Soft Power," *The Annals of the American Academy of Political and Social Science* 616 (2008): 94–109, accessed May 21, 2023, url: http://www.jstor.org/stable/25097996
12 Indian Council for Cultural Relations, accessed May 5, 2019, url: www.iccr.gov.in/content/constitution

72   The Watershed Year – 1962

13 The Seattle Public Library, Special Collections Online, accessed June 27, 2018, url: http://cdm15015.contentdm.oclc.org/cdm/compoundobject/collection/p15015coll3/id/2588/rec/7
14 Century 21 World's Fair, Seattle Municipal Archives, accessed June 27, 2018, url: www.seattle.gov/cityarchives/exhibits-and-education/digital-document-libraries/century-21-worlds-fair
15 Seattle World's Fair – 1962 – Century 21 Exposition, accessed June 27, 2018, url: www.62worldsfair.com/
16 Alan J. Stein, "Century 21 – The 1962 Seattle World's Fair, Part 2," *History Link. Org*, April 19, 2000, accessed January 8, 2023, url: http://historylink.org/File/2291
17 Ifrah Mufti, "Allama Iqbal: Pakistan's National Poet & The Man Who Gave India 'Saare jahan se achha,'" *The Print*, November 9, 2018, accessed December 30, 2021, url: https://theprint.in/features/allama-iqbal-pakistans-national-poet-the-man-who-gave-india-saare-jahan-se-achha/147155/
18 Najmul Hoda, "Mohammad Iqbal, Who Wrote 'Saare Jahan se achha', Made Modernity a Dirty Word for Muslims," *The Print*, November 9, 2021, accessed December 30, 2021, url: https://theprint.in/opinion/mohammad-iqbal-who-wrote-saare-jahan-se-achha-made-modernity-a-dirty-word-for-muslims/763165/
19 James G. Blight, Joseph S. Nye and David A. Welch. "The Cuban Missile Crisis Revisited," *Foreign Affairs* 66, no. 1 (1987): 170–88, accessed November 28, 2021, url: https://doi.org/10.2307/20043297
20 Greg Lange, "President Kennedy's Cold War cold supersedes Seattle World's Fair Closing Ceremonies on October 21, 1962," *History Link. Org*, March 15, 1999, accessed June 27, 2018, url: www.historylink.org/File/967
21 Joseph R. Stauffer, "Sino-Indian Border Dispute-1962," *Naval War College Review* 19, no. 9 (1967): 81–117, accessed September 16, 2021, url: www.jstor.org/stable/44640979
22 Neville Maxwell, "Sino-Indian Border Dispute Reconsidered," *Economic and Political Weekly* 34, no. 15 (1999): 905–18, accessed September 16, 2021, url: www.jstor.org/stable/4407848
23 Joseph R. Stauffer, "Sino-Indian Border Dispute-1962," *Naval War College Review* 19, no. 9 (1967): 81–117, accessed September 16, 2021, url: www.jstor.org/stable/44640979
24 P. Terhal, "Guns or Grain: Macro-Economic Costs of Indian Defence, 1960–70," *Economic and Political Weekly* 16, no. 49 (1981): 1995–2004, accessed March 15, 2019, url: www.jstor.org/stable/4370452
25 KarnATik, accessed November 29, 2021, url: https://web.archive.org/web/20071104111756/www.geocities.com/promiserani2/c1298.html
26 KarnATik, accessed November 29, 2021, url: https://web.archive.org/web/20071227054028/www.geocities.com/promiserani2/co1083.html
27 An Interview of Uday Shankar by Shambhu Mitra on DD Bharati, accessed April 28, 2019, url: www.youtube.com/watch?v=JHq-uBio5vE&t=14s

4 Revisiting Tagore

After the tour of 1962, once the troupe returned to India on February 3, 1963, Uday Shankar disbanded the troupe. Barun Dutta, Dhurjati Sen and Kamalesh Maitra, who had not been a part of the 1962 tour of the USA, Canada and Europe, had already in the meantime joined Yogendra Sunder Desai's troupe, the Indian Revival Group (IRG).

The IRG, as the name suggests, was akin to a revival movement in Indian dance traditions. Formed in 1948, the year after India gained independence, the founder-director of the group, Yogendra Sunder Desai, made it IRG's mission to revive India's lost cultural traditions and immersed himself in collecting folk dances from the remotest corners of India, as well as costumes, music, mythology and literature; and then presenting them to the Indian masses, army jawans in the frontier areas, prisoners in jails, industrial workers, farmers in the remote interiors of India, as well as to students, with the idea of awakening them to India's rich heritage. Son of Darbar Gopaldas Desai, the first Indian prince to abdicate his throne and join the freedom movement, Yogendra, as he was called by his associates, not only participated in the freedom struggle as a member of the *Vanar Sena*[1] but also later joined the *Satyagraha*[2] in Rajkot;[3] he was also a part of the Quit India Movement. His association with both Mahatma Gandhi and Sardar Vallabhbhai Patel left a strong mark on him. A student at Tagore's Shantiniketan, he had also learned Kathakali, Manipuri and Kathak, before he founded the IRG in 1948.[4]

After touring with the IRG for a couple of years, some of the troupe members, who had been previously associated with Uday Shankar in different capacities, decided to form a troupe of their own. The Indian Ballet Troupe (IBT) came into being towards the end of 1963 as a result of the enthusiasm of Uday Shankar's associates like Kamalesh Maitra, Barun Dutta, Dhurjati Sen and Shanti Bose. Apart from this core group, for their performances, IBT inducted a few dancers from outside as well. Timir Baran, who was the music director of Uday Shankar's troupe in the 1930s, also joined the IBT for their tour of Assam. N.K. Shivashankaran who had been a part of Shankar's troupe previously, also joined the tour, as did Pappu Raghavan, Shankar's erstwhile Ballet Master. The troupe with Shanti Bose as the Ballet Master, performed their own choreographed pieces which were inspired by

DOI: 10.4324/9781003433774-5

74 Revisiting Tagore

Figure 4.1 The performers of IRG with King Mahendra of Nepal, at the palace, on occasion of celebrations of India's Independence Day when IRG had performed there. King Mahendra is at the centre in a white coat. He is flanked by Yogendra Sunder Desai in a dark prince coat/sherwani, on the right, while Shanti Bose, in costume, is on the left of King Mahendra.

Source: Courtesy, private collection of Shanti Bose

Uday Shankar's creative style, the folk forms learned under Yogendra Sunder Desai, along with the classical styles of Kathakali and Manipuri learned by Bose at the Academy of Dance, Drama and Music.

IBT's repertoire saw them performing items like *Sari* – a dance item from the Kathakali style of Indian classical dance, *Tarja* – a folk form of Bengal, the inspiration for the latter was from the dance *dhinak natin tina* in Shankar's film *Kalpana*.[5] The other items that IBT performed included *Madia*, a tribal dance form from central India, Fishermen's Dance, folk dances from Gujrat, Punjab, a Manipuri Dance – *nila kamala dala shyam*, a *Tabla Taranga* by Kamalesh Maitra and a short ballet titled *Kirat Arjun*. Depicting a story from the third parva of the Mahabharata – the Vana Parva or the Aranyaka Parva, *Kirat Arjun* narrates an encounter between Lord Shiva in the form of a *Kirat* – a mountain dwelling hunter, and Arjun.

Shankar in the meantime, after the tour of 1962, together with Amala Shankar opened the Uday Shankar India Culture Centre in Kolkata in 1965. The institute was a reminiscence of his centre at Almora, though on a much smaller scale. It became a centre for learning not only Uday Shankar's style of creative dance but various classical styles of India as well. Pappu Raghavan was engaged at the centre for teaching Kathakali. The creative artist in Shankar, however, soon became restless for a new production. By the end of 1965 itself, he contacted Kamalesh Maitra and Barun Dutta and informed them of his plans. As Uday Shankar was well acquainted with the work that IBT had been doing, he asked Maitra and Dutta to gather the troupe members of IBT at his residence on Golf Club Road for his new production.

Shanti Bose at this point in time was on a tour of Assam with IRG, and therefore unable to attend the meeting on the first day that Uday Shankar met the artists of IBT. During this meeting, Shankar told everyone present that he needed to get in touch with Bose for his new production. After much difficulty given that communication is not what it is today, and the fact that the IRG was on the move as it was touring with its productions, Bose was contacted and arrangements were made for another dancer – Ramgopal Bhattacharya, to join the IRG in place of Bose, for the troupe's subsequent performances.

On returning to Kolkata, Bose went to meet Uday Shankar immediately. Rehearsals had already begun in Film Services studios which were situated on the ground floor of Shankar's house. Within a few days of the rehearsals, Shankar appointed Bose as the Ballet Master of his troupe. Bose's responsibilities included coaching the troupe and perfecting their movements, as well as composing and choreographing a few of the dances for the new production.

The production this time round was to be *Prakriti – Ananda*, based on Tagore's poem of the same name and his dance drama *Chandalika*, which were thematically and story wise, similar, with the same characters. It has been contended that Uday Shankar had seen a production of *Chandalika* a few days ago[6] and felt that this piece of Tagore's work could be best interpreted through his own unique style. However, given Shankar's past work, I cannot help but speculate if this was indeed the only reason, for productions of Tagore's other dance dramas, like *Shyama* and *Chitrangada* were also quite popular and regularly staged in Kolkata at that point in time. Outside of Shantiniketan, the person responsible for popularizing Tagore's dance dramas the most was the notable Rabindra sangeet singer, Santosh Sengupta. In fact, all the HMV now Sa Re Ga Ma records of Tagore's dance dramas around that time were recorded under his direction. Of the various Tagore's dance dramas performed under Santosh Sengupta's aegis, the most popular of them was *Shyama*. The primary roles of *Shyama* and *Bajrasen* were performed by different dancers at different points in time in the 1960s, such as Chitra Sen, Arati Gupta, Manjushree Chaki Sarkar for the portrayal of the title character and Balkrishna Menon, Shakti Nag and Himangshu Goswami for the portrayal of the male lead, Bajrasen. *Ashramik Sangha*, which was an organization comprising artists who had been associated with Shantiniketan, under noted Rabindra sangeet singer and teacher, Shailajaranjan Majumdar, primarily staged Tagore's *Balmiki Pratibha* and *Bhanusingher Padabali*, where prominent Rabindra sangeet singer Ashoketaru Bandopadhyay used to play the role of *Balmiki* – the dacoit turned poet in Tagore's work of the same name. Ruma Guha Thakurta led Calcutta Youth Choir, was also well known for its enactment of *Balmiki Pratibha* played by Arup Guhathaurta. Therefore, the question that arises is why did Shankar not choose to work with Tagore's other works, but instead, chose to work with *Chandalika* and *Prakriti Ananda*.

That Uday Shankar was quite taken with Buddhism and Buddhist philosophy is evident in the choice of his productions on the *Life of Buddha*, in shadow and *The Great Renunciation*, which was presented on stage.[7] As discussed in the *Introduction* of this book, the importance of Matadin in Shankar's life in terms of his inspiration to dance was so much so that when Shankar returned to India in 1930, he went and fell straight at Matadin's feet – an unimaginable act as Shankar was a Brahmin by birth and Matadin from a so-called untouchable caste of Chamars,[8] living on the fringes of society. Could Matadin and the ostracization of the community as witnessed by Shankar also have been a reason for Shankar's inspiration to create *Prakriti Ananda*? Keeping in mind the fact that Uday Shankar as an artist firmly believed in expressing his ideas and thoughts through his own medium, which reflected the contemporary socio-political and economic scenario, I cannot help but speculate whether any major incident around this time may have impacted Shankar and inspired him to choose to work with Tagore's *Chandalika* to create *Prakriti-Ananda* as opposed to the other works of Tagore, which were being performed regularly in Kolkata at that point in time.

The major incident alluded to in the previous paragraph had occurred in India's socio-political canvas in the mid-1950s, about ten years before the production of *Prakriti Ananda*. Though the Constitution of India abolished the practice of untouchability in all forms, the practice of it unfortunately still continued[9] and continues in certain pockets of the country.[10] On October 14, 1956, Dr. B. R. Ambedkar embraced Buddhism in a mass conversion in Nagpur with almost five lakh Dalits. The term "Dalit" (literally meaning "crushed," "downtrodden" or "oppressed") refers to the so-called untouchables of the Hindu caste system – who are at the very bottom of the social, cultural, economic strata.[11] *Acchyuts* (untouchables), *Harijans* (Children of God) and Scheduled Castes are some of the other terms used to describe the community. Dalit deprivations include extremely low ritual status, generally wretched economic conditions, and a denial of access to many common cultural and political resources. According to the National Census of 2011, the Scheduled Caste population of India constituted 201,378,372 people, which is more than twenty crore people.[12] Ambedkar chose Buddhism as the religion for conversion as he believed it to be a religion based on ethics and morality, which had no place for the caste system.[13] Could this mass conversion also have brought to fore in Shankar's mind, the plight of the people from the lower castes in India? After all, Shankar's previous ballet based on Tagore's poem *Udara Charitanam* had also hinted at the ill treatment of the marginalized by the society at large. This was a 15-minute ballet based on a four-line poem that was performed in addition to *Samanya Kshati*. What was the need for this ballet, if not a sense of sympathy and empathy on the predicament of the ostracized community in the country?

Therefore, I firmly believe that it was not just watching a performance of *Chandalika* that led Shankar to create *Prakriti Ananda* but a confluence of the three other factors, namely his admiration towards Buddhist philosophy and its teachings, his childhood memories of the *Chamars*, especially his affection and respect for Matadin; and the mass conversion by the Dalits to Buddhism, led by Dr. Ambedkar, to overcome the ostracization faced by Dalit the community in India – that led him to create the production of *Prakriti Ananda*.

I use the term "create" with reference to *Prakriti Ananda* as Uday Shankar combined elements from both Tagore's dance drama *Chandalika* and Tagore's poem *Prakriti-Ananda*, for this production. His creation was modelled, as always, keeping the global audience in mind, and therefore he reworked to replace many a song and dialogue with instrumental music. He also made additions and chose to emphasize certain segments of both the dance drama and the poem, which he felt would best express his perception of these two works by Tagore.

Tagore's *Chandalika* and *Prakriti Ananda* are based on a Buddhist *Jataka* tale. The term *Jataka*, in Pali and Sanskrit, the two languages prevalent in ancient India, means "Birth." These stories are based on the former lives of Lord Buddha, essentially used for didactic purposes. There are over 550 *Jataka* tales, many of which have parallels in non-Buddhist literature as well, including the *Panchatantra*[14] and Aesops's fables.[15] The *Shardulakarna Avadana*, which is the original Jataka tale on which Tagore's *Chandalika* and *Prakriti Ananda* are based, tells the story of *Prakriti*, a young girl belonging to the untouchable caste and *Ananda*, a Buddhist monk who tired and thirsty asks her for a drink of water.[16]

The outline of *Prakriti Ananda* as printed in the brochure of the 1968 tour of the USA is as follows.

Prakriti – Ananda

The ballet opens with young girls and boys dancing to welcome spring. Prakriti, a girl of untouchable caste, wants to join them but is spurned. The curd seller and bangle seller are also warned not to sell their goods to her as she is an untouchable. Broken-hearted, Prakriti refuses to offer flowers to a God who has made her an untouchable. Prakriti is drawing water from a well when Ananda, a disciple of Lord Buddha appears and asks her for water. Prakriti reveals her caste and tells him that she is an untouchable. Ananda changes her life completely when he tells her that they are both human beings and accepts water from her.

Prakriti falls in love with Ananda and asks her mother who practices witchcraft, to use her magical powers and bring back Ananda. Prakriti's mother calls her disciples to join her rituals and strengthen it. She requests one of them to bring a magic mirror to observe the effects of magic upon Ananda. Prakriti looks into the mirror and sees the agony that the magic is causing Ananda.

The mother's witchcraft brings wind, rain, storm and thunder, and finally Ananda appears. The mother, exhausted by her magic rituals dies. Ananda is on the verge of losing himself to Prakriti when the mighty power of Lord Buddha recalls him to his spiritual life.

The dance drama used to begin with the three main characters appearing on stage one at a time, under the centre spotlight to different sets of music which defined their characters. First came *Prakriti's* mother, then *Ananda* and finally *Prakriti* herself. This gave way to the first dance of the dance drama, *Nabo bashontero danero daali*, celebrating the joyous ambience of spring. It was composed in a unique way. However, as the details of the way this was composed through each individual dancer's improvised movements has been elaborated on while discussing the form and content of Uday Shankar's style of creative dance in Chapter 1, I will not go into the details of it at this stage, except to say that Shankar extracted from his dancers, their creative best.

As far as the choreography was concerned in terms of usage of space, the dancers used to sit on the stage, facing each other in vertically parallel lines from the audience. The women would sit on one side near the wings, while the men sat on the other side near the opposite set of wings. The first part of the song would be performed by the women alone, where each individual dancer would perform their own separate compositions together, in tandem with the song. The impression that this created on stage was that everyone, inspired by the beauty of spring, was expressing their joy through dance in their own special way. The second half of the song was performed in pairs. There were four pairs in this dance. A male and a female dancer would get up from their respective sides, perform a duet to a verse and then go back and sit in their respective places. In the third and final part of the song, the men exited the stage, and only the women performed on the stage to a defined choreography which was the same for everyone.

The next group dance was *Mati toder daak diyeche*. Apart from a few new movements, this dance, choreographed by Bose, comprised folk movements of Shankar's own style, which he had previously used in *Harvest Dance, Grass Cutter, Khadya* and *Brahmaputra*, and the folk dance in *Samanya Kshati*. In addition to the dance based on Tagore's song, Shankar also added another piece of folk dance based purely on instrumental music, which preceded the song. Here again the vigour and the liveliness of the movements set it apart and gave it a distinct rural flavour and sense of "folk," as compared to the joyful dance of the first scene and the rigorous and vigorous movements incorporated in the dances in the "*mantra*" scenes in the latter part of the dance drama.

However, the most unique composition of this dance drama, according to Bose, was probably the two dances that Shankar himself had composed for the songs of the Buddhist monks and the Buddhist nuns. He used decorative and devotional movements for this composition keeping in mind while composing, the melody, spirituality, the essence and purpose of the songs, *Jo sannisinno barabodhimule* and *Swarnobarne samujjalo nabo champadole*.

The last major group dance sequence was the *mantra* portion which portrays *Prakriti's* mother using her *maya* or special powers to bring *Ananda* to *Prakriti*, in order to fulfil her daughter's unrequited love. This is because, while for Ananda, Prakriti had just been someone who had been kind enough

Figure 4.2 Folk dance scene *Mati toder daak diyechey* from *Prakriti Ananda*.
Source: Courtesy, private collection of Shanti Bose

to give him a drink of water when he was thirsty, for Prakriti his accepting of a drink of water from her was an unbelievable act of kindness. This was all the more so as *Prakriti's* previous interactions with the flower girls, the curd seller and bangle seller had all left her feeling hurt, unwanted and angered, leading her to curse her mother for bringing her into this world knowing the unjust and unfair society that awaited her. Distraught, *Prakriti* also questions why she should offer flowers and prayers to a God who has obviously chosen to keep her amidst societal hatred; and had seemingly tricked her whereby she was destined to live in this darkness forever. Therefore, a drink of water, while for Ananda, was an act of kindness from Prakriti, as she gave him water when he was parched and thirsty, for Prakriti, Ananda accepting a drink of water from her, led her to fall in love with Ananda, whereby she wanted him with her at any cost. For this, she turns to her mother, who was known to be well versed in the art of "maya," or "illusion,"[17] to bring *Ananda* to her. To reflect the power of the magic, Shankar created and added to Tagore's creativity. In a few instances, he did away with the songs and the lyrics of *Chandalika* and sought to depict the strength of the sorcery through the vigorous and intoxicating movements of *Madia*, a tribal dance form from central India.

One of the probable reasons for doing away with the lyrics may have stemmed from the fact that Shankar always had a global audience in mind.

80 *Revisiting Tagore*

Figure 4.3 A pose from the folk dance *Madia*, as performed by Shankar's troupe on the tour of the USA in 1968. The dancers from left to right are Sunanda Bose, Dhurjati Sen and Srimati Dutta.

Source: Courtesy, private collection of Shanti Bose

Doing away with the lyrics was one of the ways of ensuring that the story had universal appeal and was not lost to an audience due to language barriers. He sought to interpret the heightened trance created by the magic through bewitching swaying movements, which I cannot help but wonder may have been an inspiration from his childhood days in Nasrathpur where he witnessed the dances of the chamars, who lived on the fringes of town, inebriated on country liquor, dancing frenzied movements to the resounding beat of drums. This was in fact where he saw Matadin dance and is said to have been inspired by him.[18]

While in *Chandalika*, Prakriti's mother tells her that she has a *maya darpana* or a magic mirror, which will reflect the effects of her *maya*. Shankar built on this element substantially to showcase the power of the mirror which reflected a tormented *Ananda* as he was being slowly but irrevocably pulled towards *Prakriti*, away from his vows of a monk, by the force of Prakriti's mother's *maya*. Any mirror that had the power to reflect this torment was undoubtedly extraordinarily powerful. To convey the strength of this mirror, Shankar created a separate dance around it.

Shanti Bose, who was Shankar's Ballet Master at this point in time, incorporated many of Shankar's own movements, while composing the dance for the *mantra* scenes, like, for example, movements from *Labour and Machinery*, as well as Kathakali. In a few instances, Shankar asked Bose to change the sequence of the steps, in order to enhance the build-up of the dance. This was the hallmark of Shankar's choreography – small movements should precede larger movements or else the impact created by the big movement would be lost. The use of movements from Kathakali, while composing the scene where Prakriti's mother dances with her disciples, especially the sequence for the song *Jage ni ekhono jage ni* was incorporated to add to the inherent boldness of the movements to reflect the powerful impact of the *maya*. Shankar of course was the final voice in approving of these compositions, which were finally staged.

Shankar also added a new dimension to the dance drama, through his interpretation of two relatively minor roles – the characters of the Curd Seller and the Bangle Seller. Neither of them sold their wares to *Prakriti* once they realized that she was an untouchable. However, Shankar portrayed through his composition, a difference in their reactions, which is not there in Tagore's dance drama. The Curd Seller was shown to react by cursing her, while the Bangle Seller was depicted to be compassionate and expressed his sympathy for her. These small touches leading to a nuanced portrayal of the personality of these characters, in turn, reflected the diversity of social behaviour and provoked the audience to reflect on what was the desirable form of behaviour towards the downtrodden.

Shankar used to inspire and encourage his dancers to perform their best in various ways. Bose used to play the role of the Bangle Seller. The entry step for the character was a step from a *Naga dance* from Northeast India. Though Shankar had an earlier composition called *Naga Chief*,[19] this

82 *Revisiting Tagore*

Figure 4.4 A scene from *Prakriti Ananda* with Shanti Bose as the Bangle Seller, Jharna Dutta as *Prakriti*. The other dancers from left to right are, Polly Guha, Sunanda Sengupta and Bani Bandana, at Mahajati Sadan, 1966.

Source: Courtesy, private collection of Shanti Bose

step that Bose performed had been learned by him from his Manipuri dance teacher during his days at the State Academy of Dance, Drama and Music. Shankar used to love watching Bose perform this step. Recollects Bose, "Dada used to say, Shanti, you float in the air – your feet don't seem to touch the stage when you perform that step." So much so that despite the fact that Shankar used to enact the role of Lord Buddha at the end of the ballet, he used to sit in the front row of the audience till Bose had exited the stage in his role as the Bangle Seller. This kind of encouragement and the knowledge that the maestro was out there in the audience inspired his dancers to put in better than their best.

Another addition that Shankar made to the original version of Tagore's *Chandalika* was that Prakriti's mother's disciples were shown to drag Ananda, enchained in the forces of black magic and temptation to her and her daughter. The movement of this enchained dragging was similar to the one showcased in *Kalpana* in the scene[20] where the mill owner is shown dragging the workers of the mill and their leader enacted by Shankar, for daring to raise voice and protest against the mill owner's inhuman policies, after paying off the police. Another novel interpretation of the dance drama was the appearance of Lord Buddha at the end, recalling *Ananda* to his spiritual life. While

Figure 4.5 Uday Shankar as Lord Buddha in the last scene of *Prakriti Ananda*.
Source: Courtesy, private collection of Shanti Bose.

Tagore's dance drama *Chandalika* mentions that everyone offers prayers to Buddha, the various performances staged till then had never shown Buddha's appearance on the stage.

The IBT dancers, who joined Shankar's troupe for *Prakriti Ananda*, apart from Shanti Bose, included Dhurjati Sen, N.K. Shivashankaran, Jharna Dutta, Shubhra Ghosh, Bani Bandana and Sunanda Sen Gupta. Other dancers who were not a part of IBT, but joined the troupe for this production, were Sadhan Guha, Polly Guha, Chandranath and Pranati Sen Gupta. Pranati Sengupta had been a part of Uday Shankar's troupe during *Samanya Kshati*. A magnificent dancer, with a strong base in Kathakali, and also an alumnus of the Academy of Dance, Drama and Music, Shankar had sent for Pranati especially to enact the role of Prakriti's mother.

About a year before *Prakriti Ananda*, renowned *Rabindrasangeet* artist Subinoy Roy had presented *Chandalika*. Shanti Bose had been in charge of the dance direction for this production. Jharna Dutta had played the role of Prakriti in this presentation of *Chandalika*. On Bose's recommendation, Jharna Dutta was accepted to enact the role of Prakriti in Shankar's production. Rehearsals for the production continued for almost three months. During this period, Shankar was financially not strong enough to maintain a troupe as he had earlier. Nonetheless, the troupe members dedicated themselves to the production without any salary unlike Shankar's previous productions. The troupe members for this production only received a very nominal sum by way of conveyance fare. However, a daily allowance was given to everyone after the production started playing to the audience.

Like for *Samanya Kshati* and *Udara Charitanam*, the instrumental music for the *Prakriti Ananda* too was composed after the dance compositions had been completed. The emphasis on music was laid not only to give a free flow to dance as compared to the limitations that can be faced due to the lyrics of the song but also because, as mentioned earlier, Shankar always kept an international audience in mind. The lyrics of the song could not be understood by a non-Bengali-speaking audience. For the same reason, Shankar shortened many of *Prakriti's* songs as well, without altering the basic outline of the story of *Chandalika*.

Before composing the music for *Prakriti Ananda*, Kamalesh Maitra noted down the counting and the repetitions for each movement. He would then compose the music and play it for Shankar. Sometimes Shankar made him rewrite the music even thrice if he did not get what he had in mind, or felt that it did not suit the movements of the dance. This was evident all the more so in the *mantra* scene, where Shankar wanted various kinds of effect music. A perfectionist to the core, he never compromised or settled for anything less than what he considered to be perfect for his production and that applied to music as well. Apart from extracting the exact music that he wanted from Kamalesh Maitra, Shankar would also extract different rhythms from Barun Dutta. Dutta not only played the *tabla* but various other percussion items in Shankar's collection all arranged around him as per his convenience.

The musicians for *Prakriti Ananda* included Kamalesh Maitra on the *sarod*, Barun Dutta on the *tabla* and percussion instruments, Vishnudas Sadhukhan on the flute, Soumen Ghosh on the *taarsanai* and Kishore Ghosh on the *sitar*. As far as the vocals were concerned, Arghya Sen used to render the part of *Ananda* and the Bangle Seller, Krishna Gupta used to sing the part of *Prakriti's* mother, Papia Bagchi used to impart her voice for *Prakriti*, and Kamal Gupta – the Curd Seller. These artists, apart from singing for their respective characters, also sang in unison for the group songs.

Partly due to financial reasons and partly due to the novelty it would cause, the troupe did not have any costumes in the true sense of the term like they did in the previous productions. The women would be donned in everyday colourful cotton saris, while the men would wear white dhoti kurtas in the first sequence and continue in the same dress for the folk dance – all of which they carried from their homes. Only the Buddhist monks and *Ananda* would be dressed in saffron robes. Of course, later in the *mantra* scene, the dancers changed into a particular set of costumes. The effect therefore was that the audience was privy to and witnessing an informal presentation which began with men and women celebrating spring and all of a sudden without noticing would be plunged into an intense, passionate drama and be caught in its throes.

To elaborate on how Uday Shankar took inspiration in creating movements from daily life events, Shanti Bose narrated the following anecdote. However, what is noteworthy is that, while his ideas may be inspired by very simple everyday events, when incorporated on stage, they added on a whole new dimension. Sunanda Bose, nee Sengupta, used to have thick, long and curly hair. One day, during the rehearsals of the *mantra* scene, her hairdo opened. Sunanda continued dancing without stopping to redo her hair. At the end of the dance, Shankar said that for the *mantra* scene, all the women would dance with their hair left open as it gave an additional sway to their movements, and ultimately on stage, it enhanced the impact of the dance. Of course, it implied more rehearsals, for now the head movements too had to be coordinated minutely, so that swaying of the hair was also completely synchronized!

Stage rehearsals started at Mahajati Sadan three or four days before the performance of *Prakriti Anando*, with full costume and stage lights. Unlike *Samanya Kshati*, where the musicians handled the lights, for *Prakriti Ananda*, that was not the case as the music was not recorded for the performances in India. The musicians would be seated inside the wings, leaving the full stage for the dancers. The lights, which were Shankar's own, were handled by Golok Seal, who also played certain percussion instruments. Shambhu Mukherjee was in charge of the sound system. Of course, supervising them all was Shankar's own trusted Shahji (Chiranjilal Shah) who was Shankar's stage manager. As mentioned earlier, hailing from the days of the Almora centre, Shahji had been with Shankar through the days of *Kalpana* and even the production of *Samanya Kshati* and the international tour of 1962.

Prakriti Ananda was staged in Mahajati Sadan for almost three months at a stretch. Like with *Samanya Kshati*, performances were scheduled for one show every evening during the weekdays and two shows during weekends – on both Saturdays and Sundays. After performing continuously for almost three months, Shankar gave his troupe a break for about a month. The members returned from their break and started rehearsing *Prakriti Ananda* again at Birla Academy, but this time for a tour of Assam. Before they left for their tour of Assam, they also performed in a few places like Ranchi and Burnpur. In Ranchi, for a couple of shows, Uday Shankar performed his solo, *Indra*. During these shows, the group also joined Shankar in his performance but in a unique manner. The back curtain used to have slits in it. The dancers would stand hidden behind the curtains with only their arms visible, which would be spread through the slits during a particular movement, which involved the wave of the arms. It was reminiscent of a scene from *Kalpana*,[21] except that this was executed on stage and not on screen.

The troupe's first show in Assam was held in the city of Guwahati, and their last performance in Dimapur. After touring Assam for almost two and a half months, Shankar fell ill after the performance at Dimapur. He had suffered a mild stroke. The troupe returned to Calcutta by train. Shankar flew in after a few days once he had recovered enough to travel. This was in December 1966.

Just a note, Amala Shankar who had been an integral part of Shankar's productions earlier had ceased to be a part of Shankar's productions after the tour of USA, Canada and Europe in 1962. She was not a part of *Prakriti Ananda* in 1966, nor was she a part of the tour of the USA in 1968, or the productions of *Shankarscope* in 1970, 1971 and 1972.

Notes

1 Literal translation implies 'monkey brigade', a resistance movement against British colonialism, led by a young Indira Gandhi, which grew to 60,000 young revolutionaries, accessed December 30, 2021, url: https://inshorts.com/en/news/indira-gandhi-formed-vanar-sena-as-child-to-fight-british-1479565283086
2 *Satyagraha* or the force that is generated by the adherence to truth was conceived and used by Mahatma Gandhi as a framework for his non-violent method of resistance, accessed December 30, 2021, url: www.mkgandhi.org/faq/q17.htm
3 The *Satyagraha* movement in the princely state of Rajkot in western India occurred between 1938–1939. H. Raghunath, "Rajkot Episode of 1938–39: Indian Nationalism in the Princely Context," *Proceedings of the Indian History Congress* 40 (1979): 670–80, accessed December 30, 2021, url: www.jstor.org/stable/44142008
4 Indian Revival Group, accessed July 15, 2019, url: http://indianrevivalgroup.com/?page_id=33
5 Kalpana, 1948, accessed December 30, 2021, url: https://indiancine.ma/BKLU/player/00:40:18.976
6 Mohan Khokar, *His Dance His Life – A Portrait of Uday Shankar* (New Delhi: Himalayan Books, 1983), 136.
7 Mohan Khokar, *His Dance His Life – A Portrait of Uday Shankar* (New Delhi: Himalayan Books, 1983), 126–7.

8 Mohan Khokar, *His Dance His Life – A Portrait of Uday Shankar* (New Delhi: Himalayan Books, 1983), 49.
9 Janki Nath Bhat, "Untouchability in India," *Civilisations* 4, no. 4 (1954): 565–70, accessed January 4, 2023, url: www.jstor.org/stable/41377660.
10 Indulata Prasad, "Caste-Ing Space: Mapping the Dynamics of Untouchability in Rural Bihar, India," *CASTE: A Global Journal on Social Exclusion* 2, no. 1 (2021): 132–52, accessed January 4, 2023, url: www.jstor.org/stable/48643389.
11 Gyanendra Pandey, "The Time of the Dalit Conversion," *Economic and Political Weekly* 41, no. 18 (2006): 1779–78, accessed March 16, 2019, url: www.jstor.org/stable/4418177
12 Scheduled Castes Population – Census 2011, accessed March 16, 2019, url: www.census2011.co.in/scheduled-castes.php
13 Meena Bardia, "Dr. B.R. Ambedkar His Ideas About Religion and Conversion to Buddhism," *The Indian Journal of Political Science* 70, no. 3 (2009): 737–49, accessed March 16, 2019, url: www.jstor.org/stable/42742756.
14 A collection of animal fables which originated in India attributed to Sage Vidyapati, often referred in Europe as the Fables of Bidpai, accessed December 30, 2021, url: www.britannica.com/topic/Panchatantra-Indian-literature
15 Jataka, accessed June 28, 2018, url: www.britannica.com/topic/Jataka
16 Gushtaspshah Kaikhushro Nariman, Moriz Winternitz, Sylvain Lévi, Eduard Huber, *Literary History of Sanskrit Buddhism*, accessed March 16, 2019, url: https://books.google.co.in
17 Illusion, especially the material world of senses, accessed December 1, 2021, url: www.collinsdictionary.com/dictionary/english/maya
18 Mohan Khokar, *His Dance His Life – A Portrait of Uday Shankar* (New Delhi: Himalayan Books, 1983), 19.
19 Mohan Khokar, *His Dance His Life – A Portrait of Uday Shankar* (New Delhi: Himalayan Books, 1983), 127.
20 Kalpana, 1948, accessed December 12, 2021, url: https://indiancine.ma/BKLU/player/00:58:38.081
21 Kalpana, 1948, accessed December 2, 2021, url: https://indiancine.ma/BKLU/player/00:16:42.086

5 Revisiting the USA and Looking Forward

A dynamic shift in India's foreign policy occurred with the advent of Indira Gandhi, who took over the reins of the government in January 1966.[1] India had by then been through three wars – the Indo-Pak war of 1947, the Sino-Indian war of October 1962[2] and the Indo-Pak war of 1965.[3] The first two wars took place during the tenure of Prime Minister, Pandit Jawaharlal Nehru, while the third war occurred during the time of Prime Minister, Lal Bahadur Shastri. As mentioned earlier in the book, during Nehru's tenure, soft power was emphasized on, as with the legacy of poverty, left behind by the British, India was not really in a position to invest in hard power, and Nehru sought to develop relations between India and other nations essentially through various treaties of friendship.

However, this drastically changed when Indira Gandhi came to power. "Where Nehru had articulated India's national interests in high-flown phrases of world peace and cooperation, Indira stressed security, territory, and prestige . . . In contrast to her father's alleged "moralism," Indira Gandhi's actions are described as pragmatic."[4] Given this shift in outlook and policy, Uday Shankar, whose troupe had received the patronage from the Government of India on numerous occasions during Nehru's tenure, now ceased to enjoy the same support. The focus of the Indian Government now shifted to increasing its hard power essentially in terms of its defence capability. What before the Sino-Indian war of 1962 had been a question of guns or grains, post the war, became guns at the cost of grains.[5] In such a scenario, performing arts naturally took a back seat in India's foreign policy considerations. Therefore, unlike the previous tour of the USA, Canada and Europe in 1962, where the Government of India had sponsored the troupe's performance in the Seattle World's Fair, and for three months in different cities and countries across Europe, this time around in 1968, it was only Sol Hurok who sponsored Shankar's trip to the USA, with his troupe.

Ill health suffered by Shankar in December 1966 could not keep the showman in Shankar subdued for long. After a year's rest, towards the beginning of 1968, he sent for all his troupe members again. He had already started preparations for what would turn out to be his last tour of the USA in 1968. With his troupe gathered around him, he told them that he would take them

DOI: 10.4324/9781003433774-6

Revisiting the USA and Looking Forward 89

across the USA with shows from the East Coast to the West Coast. He had already toured there seven times. This would be his eighth tour. Recollects Sunanda Bose, God willing, he said, he also hoped to take them to Europe someday. After all, it was the seat of Western culture and unless they saw it for themselves, they would not be able to imagine it.

Apart from the troupe members who were there with Shankar, for *Prakriti Ananda*, Shikha Mukherjee along with Ramgopal Bhattacharya also joined Shankar's troupe for the tour of 1968. Seven girls from the Uday Shankar India Culture Centre, Kolkata, also joined the tour. They included Anupama Das, Pali Sanyal, Shikha Mitra, Shefali Ghosh, Anju Nath, Tapati Mukherjee and Jana Gupta Bhaya. This was perhaps the youngest group of dancers that Uday Shankar had ever toured with.

This time, the rehearsals were held at Indrapuri studios from 11 am in the morning to 5 pm in the evening, with a break of an hour for lunch. The troupe rehearsed for almost four months. Although the rehearsals were held during peak summer in Kolkata, Shankar always arrived punctually at the rehearsals. Because the troupe members numbered more than in the previous years, it meant more rehearsals. Given the perfectionist that Shankar was, he could never settle for anything else, no matter how much time it took to attain. If anyone failed to execute any movement correctly, he would immediately stop the dance and ask where and why the dancer faced a problem. If the dancer failed to answer, Bose was given the responsibility of correcting their movements.

Figure 5.1 The troupe members outside Indrapuri Studio after rehearsal, in preparation for the 1968 tour. Seen in the centre is Shirley, who had come down from USA for a couple of months to train with Shankar.

Source: Courtesy, private collection of Shanti Bose

This perfection was not only limited to the dancers, even the musicians had to rehearse regularly as Shankar did not approve of musicians following notation sheets while playing on stage. As a result, after four months of continuous rehearsals, the musicians too would play both the musical interlude at the beginning of the show and during the performance of the dances, without referring to any written notations. Another aspect of Shankar's showmanship was reflected in the way the dances and the music presented, were coordinated on stage for this international performance. A black net as used in *Samanya Kshati* covered the entire stage, running parallel to the front curtain and the back screen dividing the stage horizontally in two parts. The musicians used to be seated in the section behind the black net. During the music piece played at the beginning of the performance, the lights would be focused on the musicians. After that and during the rest of the performance, the lights would be restricted to and focused on the front portion of the stage where the dancers were performing. The musicians would play along more or less in the dark except for the slight light that may have filtered through from the front of the stage. Hence, it was absolutely necessary for the musicians to know the music by heart.

Like *Samanya Kshati*, which despite being recorded, was performed to live music during the international tour of 1962, so too was the case with *Prakriti Ananda* during the tour of the USA in 1968. The music for *Prakriti Ananda* was recorded in 1968, before the trip to the USA by HMV (presently Sa Re Ga Ma) Record Company at their recording studio in Dum Dum. The dancers in the troupe had also lent their voices to the group songs. This recording was sold in long-playing format during the troupe's performances in the USA. Nonetheless, the stage performances saw live music accompanying the dancers.

The performances during the tour of 1968 used to begin with a musical piece, based on an evening melody – *Raag Mohan-Kosh*. The musicians apart from Shankar's music director Kamalesh Maitra who played the sarod, included Barun Dutta on the *tabla*, Kishore Ghosh on the *sitar*, Vishnu Das Sadhukhan on the flute and Ramesh Chandra on the *esraj*.

This was followed by the first item, *Deva Dasis* – a dance based on Bharatanatyam. The second dance item was *Madia* – a tribal dance from Central India. After this came *Kartikeya*. During the tour of 1968, Bose performed this item, which had been a favourite of Shankar's – dressed in the maestro's own costume. *Laiharoba* – based on the Manipuri form, was the next item that was performed. The item that followed *Laiharobe* was *Astra Puja*. There would then be an interval of ten minutes.

The main ballet of the programme – *Prakriti Ananda* – was performed in the second half after the break. With an innate understanding of his audience, Shankar re-evaluated the length of *Prakriti Ananda* for an all-American audience. As a result, many songs were replaced with music so that the theme of the story could be universally understood without having to resort to lyrics in any particular language. The main storyline as written by Rabindranath Tagore, however, remained intact.

Figure 5.2 The troupe members at the HMV studio in Dum Dum during the music recording of *Prakriti Ananda* in 1968, before the tour of the USA. While professional singers sang the songs for the lead characters, the dancers lent voice to the group songs, along with the professional singers.

Source: Courtesy, private collection of Shanti Bose

The need for this arose mainly because Shankar's performances usually comprised an all-American audience. There would only be an odd couple of people of Indian origin here and there. According to Bose, there was a stark difference in the audience demography when Bose and other dancers toured the USA later, with stalwarts in the field of music like Santosh Sengupta and Suchitra Mitra. In these subsequent visits, the audience was always primarily Indian or people of Indian origin, especially the Bengali community, with a few non-Indians scattered here and there. It is this that led Bose to reflect that when performing with Shankar, there was a sense that they were representing India to the Western world! This experience of the performers reiterates the contention that Shankar was a representative of India and Indian culture to the West, a harbinger of the cultural revolution in modern India.

The third part of the programme used to commence with a performance of *Tabla Taranga* by Kamalesh Maitra. It used to be again performed in the latter segment of the stage, behind the net. This was followed by a folk dance from Gujarat, after which Uday Shankar used to present *Indra*. This would be followed by *Sari* – a traditional dance in Kathakali style; and the last item of the show would be *Punjabi* – a folk dance from Punjab.

The items, *Deva-Dasis*, *Laiharoba* and *Sari*, were performed by the girls of The Uday Shankar India Culture Centre, Kolkata. The rest of the items and *Prakriti Ananda* were performed by Shankar's own troupe members. The necessity of denoting this lies in the fact that at this point in time, Shankar was not involved with the running of the Centre. Amala Shankar was in charge of it, and ran it with the support of Uday Shankar's erstwhile troupe members like Pappu Raghavan, Robin Das (Sarod), Soumen Dey (Flute). They were not a part of the tour of 1968.

During the tour of the USA, Shankar presented items in his own inimitable style, as well as many items that were based on folk and classical styles. Some of the items presented during this tour were what his team members, who were essentially from IBT, used to perform as part of the repertoire of IBT. This was mainly due to shortage of time. The phrase "shortage in time" does not reflect the number of months the troupe had to prepare, for they had almost four months to rehearse. But given the fact that the number of dancers for this trip was much more than in previous years, together with the fact that most of the troupe members were new, led Shankar to include only a few items from his old repertoire – for Shankar could never compromise or settle for anything that did not match his idea of perfection. This has in existing literature been pointed out as an indication of bane of Shankar's creativity.[6] There however, does not seem to be any anomaly in this, for as India's cultural representative, showcasing India's folk and classical forms is something Shankar had undertaken even in his film, *Kalpana*. Thus, for Shankar, the identity of being Indian remained the foremost throughout his career. And as is evident from his productions during this period, as well as before, his productions were a celebration of the ethno-cultural diversity that India represented. In fact, it is probably because of this, though Shankar's form did not focus as much on mudras, compared to body expression, nonetheless, the souvenirs of the tour of the USA in 1962 as well as 1968, carried a segment on *mudras* and their significance.

The time shortage also resulted from the fact that in 1968, Uday Shankar had been selected to direct the dances for the Olympic game ceremonies to be held in the Mexico Olympics of 1968. Shanti Bose was to be his assistant in this project. However, India boycotted the games by way of protest over South Africa's inclusion in the Games. The protest stemmed from the fact that the South African government had allowed the malpractice of Apartheid to be carried with regard to their team selection. The world community soon joined in the protest and finally South Africa was ousted from the games. India rejoined, but by then, Shankar had already confirmed the tour of the USA with Hurok, and so the Olympic project could not be undertaken.

Once the troupe was ready for their performance, they had to extend their focus to costumes as well. Shankar already had the costumes required for the folk dances and the classical dances. However, a few others had to be stitched. A tailor used to come to Indrapuri studio to take measurements and stitch the costumes. The dancers had to try them on and inform Shankar whether they would allow or hamper swift costume changes. Besides, it was not just the garments that the dancers had to change for every item, but as mentioned before, their *paagdis*, head adornments, as well as all their ornaments. The women also had to change their hairstyles for each item. Unlike their performance of *Prakriti Ananda* in India, where they performed the first half in simple everyday clothes, the dancers wore specified costumes for the presentation of the dance drama in the USA.

Shanti Bose recalls, that for *Kartikeya*, Shankar had told him that Bose would be performing the item during this tour, in Shankar's own costume. The first dance item in the programme that Bose had to prepare for was Kartikeya. So naturally, on the first day of the dress rehearsals at Indrapuri studio, Bose dressed in the costume of *Kartikeya*, crown in hand, approached Shankar to get his approval of whether all was as it should be. Others were also ready in their costumes, all prepared to go on stage. In front of everyone, Shankar took the crown from Bose's hand and placed it on his head saying, "My Guru taught me this dance and now I am handing it over to you." Shares Bose, for him, this was the most precious and rewarding moment of his life till date.

Unlike Shankar's other items, which were purely his own creation, *Kartikeya* was the only item composed in Kathakali by Guru Shankaran Namboodri that Shankar used to perform. The item was not only a favourite of his but was loved by the audience all over the globe. The item portrays *Kartikeya*, the golden son of *Shiva* and *Parvati*, preparing to battle the demon *Taraka*. He seeks blessings from his Mother and Father – *Parvati* and *Shiva*, respectively, and all other Gods and Goddesses. He accepts his armour from *Indra* – the King of Gods – and sets out on his chariot to challenge the demon. So dear was this item to Shankar, and given the fact that this was the first time that someone else apart from him would be performing it, that even before the first show at Montreal, Shankar asked the troupe to reach the auditorium four hours ahead of the show. They usually went in two hours before every performance. Even after four months of rehearsal in Kolkata, Shankar spent almost two hours perfecting every movement, look and gesture that Bose executed in the item. Recollects Bose, that by the end of that practice session with Shankar, Bose became so stressed that he came down with fever and had to take paracetamol and sleep for about half an hour before he could prepare himself for the performance.

A few days prior to the tour, Shankar's Personal Manager, Bhudeb Shankar, who was also Uday Shankar's cousin, handed the troupe members their relevant travel papers. Along with these was a detailed itinerary of the tour. It contained details of travel arrangements, a list of the 34 cities where they would be performing, the dates of the performances, the days when the troupe would be resting, as well as contact numbers in each of the cities that they would be touring, for emergency purposes. The purpose of going into these little details is to highlight the kind of professionalism and level of organization that was associated with Shankar's tours.

94 Revisiting the USA and Looking Forward

On September 28, 1968, the troupe embarked on their tour by Air India, from Dum Dum Airport. They reached New York after halting at Cairo, Rome and London. They were put up at Paramount Hotel on the Fifth Avenue in New York City. They stayed in New York for a week. During the course of the week, they rehearsed for three days in the auditorium of Hunter College. Shankar's impresario Sol Hurok threw a party for The Uday Shankar Hindu Dancers and Musicians during their stay at New York on the 48th floor of Times Building. Apart from the troupe members, and the staff of Hurok's company, other guests were also present. During these seven days in New York, time aside from their rehearsals, the troupe members also got a chance to tour New York and visit some must-see tourist sites. After this, they flew to Montreal where they were to perform the first show of this tour. They performed in Montreal for two consecutive days at the grand Place Des Art – Montreal's Centre for Performing Arts.

Back in New York, they were again put up in the same hotel for about another week. They performed at a stretch for six days at Hunter College in the heart of Manhattan, New York. After New York, the troupe toured different cities of the USA mostly in a huge air-conditioned luxury bus. This helped as the bus would also take the troupe sightseeing around the city in which they performed. Sometimes if the distance was more than could be comfortably travelled by bus, the troupe would fly to their destination, but their costumes, instruments, lights and other paraphernalia would be transported by the bus, which would arrive at the designated city in time for the performance.

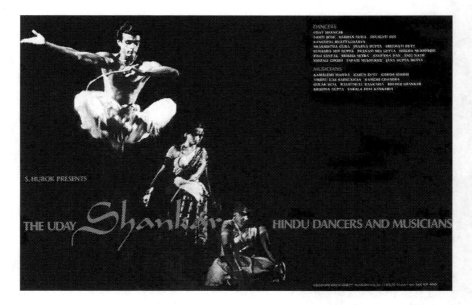

Figure 5.3 The centerspread of the souvenir of the tour of 1968 in the USA. From left to right, Shanti Bose, Jharna Dutta nee Basak and Pranati Sengupta.

Source: Courtesy, private collection of Shanti Bose

Revisiting the USA and Looking Forward 95

Figure 5.4 The troupe members sightseeing with Shankar at an American Indian reservation in Indiana. Bose himself is the photographer for this image. From left to right, Uday Shankar with Sunanda Sengupta, Polly Guha peeking in between Shankar and Sunanda Bose, along with other troupe members.

Source: Courtesy, private collection of Shanti Bose

Washington DC, Baltimore, New Haven, Boston, Wellesley, Pittsburgh, Cleveland, Indianapolis, Detroit, Chicago, Ann-Arbor, Lafayette in Indiana, Oxford in Ohio, Cincinnati, Kansas City, St. Louis, Tulsa, Oklahoma City, Stillwater, Wichita Falls, Houston, Corpus Christi, San Antonio, New Orleans, Florence, Lafitte, Beaumont, Phoenix in Arizona and San Diego were the cities that the troupe not only performed in but also got the opportunity to go sightseeing. Of course, there was a golden rule. The members could go sightseeing only after their first performance in that particular city, not before. Receptions were also organized in a few cities in honour of Shankar and his troupe.

The performances were greatly appreciated in the USA. So much so that not only did they perform to packed houses, there would be people standing in every nook and corner of the auditorium to view the performances. Sometimes they even performed two shows on the same day to meet the demands of the ticket sales. Newspapers of every city that they performed in showered them with praise, and so it became a part of the troupe members' practice to collect newspapers after their performances from every city, before they departed from it.

96 *Revisiting the USA and Looking Forward*

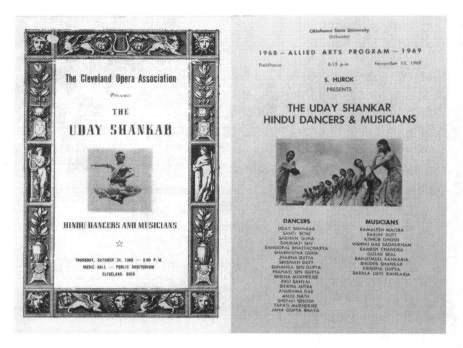

Figure 5.5 Promotional material used at Cleveland and Oklahoma. The promo on the left for Cleveland depicts Bose in his jump posture from *Prakriti Ananda*, while the image on the right portrays Bose instructing the women dancers of the troupe in his capacity as the Ballet Master Shankar's troupe.

Source: Courtesy, private collection of Shanti Bose

According to Bose, Shankar had an ardent fan following in the West. A memorable incident occurred during one of the shows in the USA. Shankar introduced his team to an elderly lady. She had an album of Shankar's photographs, pamphlets and autographs for all his previous seven visits to the USA, along with pictures of herself at these various stages of her life. She had collected her first autograph of Shankar as a young girl. She may or may not have realized that this would be the last time she would be collecting his autograph. Shankar had a special relationship with his audience in the USA. The troupe witnessed many elderly people come up and embrace him. They would wait for Shankar's next tour of the USA after every tour. Sometimes, if the troupe did not perform in the city of their residence, they would travel to the nearest city to watch him perform. In the televised interview on ABP Ananda, with Suman Dey, Ravi Shankar said that Uday Shankar was probably India's first superstar, much before the concept became popular in India.[7]

After performing for two days in San Diego, the troupe was supposed to travel to Los Angeles. But Shankar fell ill. The news of Shankar's illness was initially restricted to his Personal Manager, Bhudeb Shankar, his Manager,

Chiranjilal Shah and his Ballet Master, Shanti Bose. The doctors had at first diagnosed Shankar's complaint of an ache in the neck as muscular pain. Nonetheless, they decided to take him to the hospital for further investigation. Bhudeb Shankar and Chiranjilal Shah accompanied Shankar to the hospital. They returned with the news that he had suffered a cerebral attack. This information too was restricted to Kamalesh Maitra and Shanti Bose. They were given the responsibility to proceed to Los Angeles with the entire troupe as planned, as another 2 weeks of the tour was still left, before the troupe was supposed to return to India. In Los Angeles, the rest of the troupe, unaware of this turn of events, visited Disneyland as had been planned. Maitra and Bose stayed back at the hotel, awaiting news of Shankar. Only once the troupe returned, were they informed about Shankar's attack and the fact that the last couple of performances of the trip had been cancelled. The troupe moved on to Seattle as planned, as their departure from the USA had been planned from Seattle. While waiting at the Seattle Airport, they met Amala Shankar, who on hearing about Shankar's attack had flown in from India. Shankar stayed on in the USA till he was declared fit to fly back to India.

Notes

1 Smt. Indira Gandhi, PM India, accessed March 15, 2019, url: www.pmindia.gov.in/en/former_pm/smt-indira-gandhi/
2 Joseph R. Stauffer, "Sino-Indian Border Dispute – 1962," *Naval War College Review* 19, no. 9 (1967): 81–117, accessed March 15, 2019, url: www.jstor.org/stable/44640979
3 Bharat Verma, "The Indo – Pak War of 1965," *Indian Defence Review*, January 4, 2021, accessed January 8, 2023, url: www.indiandefencereview.com/spotlights/indo-pak-war-of-1965/
4 Arthur G. Rubinoff, "India's Search for Power: Indira Gandhi's Foreign Policy, 1966–1982. By Surjit Mansingh," *The Journal of Asian Studies* 44, no. 3 (1985): 643–44, accessed March 15, 2019, url: www.jstor.org/stable/2056319
5 P. Terhal, "Guns or Grain: Macro-Economic Costs of Indian Defence, 1960–70," *Economic and Political Weekly* 16, no. 49 (1981): 1995–2004, accessed March 15, 2019, url: www.jstor.org/stable/4370452
6 Mohan Khokar, *His Dance His Life – A Portrait of Uday Shankar* (New Delhi: Himalayan Books, 1983), 13.
7 An interview with Pt. Ravi Shankar on ABP Ananda, accessed April 28, 2019, url: www.youtube.com/watch?v=gS4a875tXlg&t=21s

6 The Last Masterpiece

Shankarscope was Shankar's last masterpiece. Once Uday Shankar returned to India after the tour of 1968, he spent a few months in recuperation. However, towards the beginning of 1970, he sent word to a few of his close associates that he wanted to embark on a new production. In the souvenir of *Shankarscope*, in 1970, he wrote,

> For the past 20 years or more I have been thinking of preparing a most unusual type of variety show which no one could ever imagine . . . .. due to acute financial stringency, I could not take up this project in hand earlier – although during the recent past some of the countries, I understand, have successfully come out with similar entertainments which I have never seen. Whatever it may be, I am now happy that my dream has come true at last. This is a unique variety show on the stage with the help of the film. It combines stage and screen together with magical effects, and is highly developed technically which I am sure will create a new channel for a great industry in this country.[1]

In the same write-up, he also wrote "From the very beginning of my artistic career, I never wanted to go on with mere repetitions, but always tried to produce something new and exclusive, strictly based on Indian traditions and culture."

With Ranjit Mull Kankaria as the producer, this final production of Shankar's was a culmination of all his lived experiences, and mirrored some of the socio-economic–political challenges faced by India in the 1960s and 1970s. Technologically, it was way ahead of its time, as it was the first time that such an experiment had been undertaken in India, which used both the stage and the screen concurrently. Through his creativity and innovation, Shankar posed pertinent questions and even critiqued various aspects of Indian society. The themes varied from that of unemployment, to the then current trend of Bollywood movies, to questioning what comprises true beauty. The 1971 production of *Shankarscope* also witnessed the inclusion of the item *Chinna Bichinna*, based on the havoc created by West Pakistan in East Pakistan through Operation Searchlight. The horrors followed and finally

DOI: 10.4324/9781003433774-7

The Last Masterpiece 99

culminated in the war of liberation in East Pakistan, leading to the formation of Bangladesh. This chapter details the items performed in *Shankarscope*, the stories they told, how they were performed, the technology used, the music recordings and the re-staging of it in 1971 and 1972. In the 1972 restaging, a one-hour reworked version of *Samanya Kshati* was also staged with Shanti Bose as the Assistant Director, and in the lead role of the King, which Shankar himself used to previously portray. Bose was also still the Ballet Master for Shankar's troupe.

As far as the title of the production is concerned, Uday Shankar wrote,

> my beloved friend, the distinguished journalist Royjee (Late Manashi Roy) . . . former Patrika columnist . . . after seeing my earlier creations of Shadow Play . . . remarked, "Well, Mr. Shankar, the show is unique, but you have probably made a mistake by not naming it *Shankar scope*." That is why this production is titled Shankarscope.[2]

After his recuperation, towards the beginning of 1970, Shankar sent word to a few of his close associates that he wanted to meet them to begin working on a new production. Bose, along with a few others, gathered at his house on Golf Club Road. Shankar sat them down and described his novel idea of merging both the film and stage performance for this new production. The idea being that the show would create a visual illusion that characters from screen would come alive on stage. The assembled groups were all at a loss, for it was beyond their comprehension as to how such a merging could be achieved.

By the time the group had been assembled, Shankar had already started working on the music of *Shankarscope* with his Music Director, Kamalesh Maitra, who not only composed the music but also penned the lyrics for the introductory song. Maitra had begun working on the lyrics for other songs as well, with Gouri Prasanna Mazumdar. Mazumdar had penned the dialogues used in the item "Eternal Song." Shankar had begun discussing his plans in detail with cinematographer, Mahindra Kumar, as this was to be a unique film which would require tremendous synchronization for the scenes which would combine both film and live performances on stage. Although the dancers did not have much of a role to play during this period of the production, nonetheless, Shanti Bose as Shankar's Ballet Master was present for these sessions along with a few other members, to better understand what Shankar had envisaged.

Shankar had always been fascinated by magic and the art of illusion. His fascination with this had probably developed from the days he spent in Ambika Charan's darkroom, developing the photographs he had shot. He devised his own tricks, baffling the teacher who had introduced him to a few tricks in magic. Shankar also explored the fascinating world of daubing colours on pieces of glass and watching their magnified reflections on the wall with the help of Ambika Charan's magic lantern.[3] His fascination with light and shadow is evident from the shadow play productions he had created on *Ram*

Leela[4] and the life of Lord Buddha.[5] Recollects Bose, both *Ram Leela* and *Life of Buddha* had been staged at Eden Gardens, where the audience used to be seated in the gallery while the performance could be seen on a huge white screen. The shadow play of *Ram Leela* was in black and white, and used to attract thousands of people from neighbouring states and shouts of "Jai Shri Ram" could be heard as the audience exited the stadium in hordes. Life of Buddha, also a shadow play, was in colour. Bose, who was yet to be associated with Shankar back then, had been invited for the performance by Hirendranath Kundu, a member of Shankar's troupe at that point in time – who had enacted the role of a young Buddha. Seeing the Life of Buddha as a colour shadow play, according to Bose, was mesmerizing, it was like being in a dreamland! While both Uday Shankar and Amala Shankar performed in Life of Buddha, they did not perform in *Ram Leela*. Use of light and shadow is also evident in Shankar's film *Kalpana*, which Satyajit Ray is said to have watched 11 times, so enamoured of it, was he.[6] This was the first time that Shankar could give rein to his dreams for a multimedia production, with the aid of technology as available in the 1970s, and of course the financial support of Ranjit Mull Kankaria. Ranjit Mull Kankaria, a noted film producer and distributor, presented the production of *Shankarscope*. Like the rest of the troupe, he too was initially not very clear on Shankar's concept of merging the stage and the screen, and how it could be achieved for any performance.

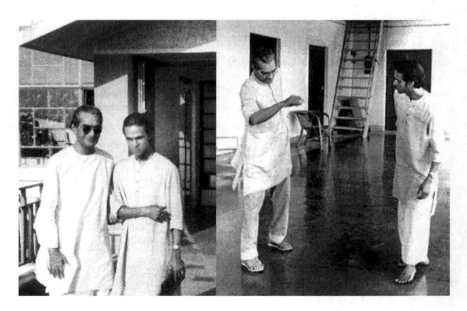

Figure 6.1 Uday Shankar with Shanti Bose. The image on the left is from the time that the shooting location for *Shankarscope* was being scouted. The image on the right depicts Shankar demonstrating a movement to Bose.

Source: Courtesy, private collection of Shanti Bose

After a few days, to help his associates understand exactly what he had in mind, Shankar displayed his hand-made three-dimensional model of about two feet in length, one foot in height and one and a half feet in width. He had made this model using boxes of various sizes, including matchboxes, all set on a tray. Given here is an illustration by Shanti Bose of how the screen, the stage and the backdrop were set up for the production of *Shankarscope*, to enable the merging of the live performance on stage and the recorded film on screen, technically feasible.

There was also a staircase behind the cage like cuboid structure, to enable the artists to climb up to the platform E. As far as the technical aspect was

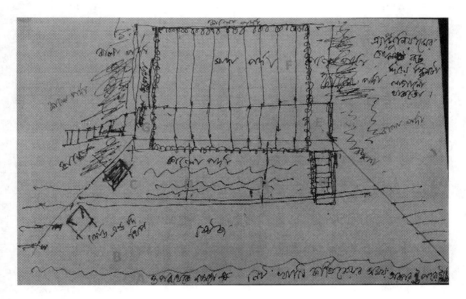

Figure 6.2 This image is a rough hand sketch of the stage and screen for *Shankarscope* sketched by Bose himself, while explaining how the performances took place, and the merging of the stage and screen was made possible. I took a photograph of it – digitally added the alphabet key in grey, to the image, to help identify the sections described.

Key for the picture:

A – Audience

B – Stage

C – Black curtain covering a cuboid-shaped cage-like structure

D – Two overlapping flaps used as entrance and exit by dancers, which was not visible to the audience

E – A platform, of about 4 feet in width, on top of C where the dancers would stand, the entrance to which was point G

F – White projection screen comprising eight overlapping flaps encased in a frame of aluminium piping, suspended on three suspenders, which could lower and raise the screen as necessary

G – Entrance point for dancers on the platform, marked as E

H – A staircase with eight steps which would lead the dancer to the stage

concerned, the merging of the screen characters with the same characters in life on stage was achieved by gently diminishing the size of the character on screen in the film, to the actual height of the person in real life. The character on screen would move to the right-hand side of the screen towards the point G. Through careful synchronization, not only was the height matched but a simultaneous switching off of the screen projection and the switching on of a dim light at entrance point G would make it appear as if the character had suddenly stepped out from the screen come alive on stage. The performer would then use the eight steps – which were wide enough to allow a single person to move comfortably – to come down on stage and perform their item. This was the technique that was used for all the items except for the item *Beauty Competition*, the details of which has been discussed later in this chapter.

The first item performed in *Shankarscope* was based on the title song *Scope Scope Shankar scope*, in which all the dancers used to perform on stage, together. The lyrics and music of this introductory song were written by Shankar's music director, Kamalesh Maitra. Like many of Shankar's works, most of the items in *Shankarscope* were a commentary on the existing socio-economic–political scenario. While some were a spoof, others a satire. So, despite providing a good deal of humour, the items also provided food for thought on many a social norm. The introductory song was like a call to a *tamasha*, or a grand show held at fun fairs in rural and semi-urban areas, where usually a variety of items are performed. This song gave a glimpse through the lyrics, the items and issues that would be presented and focused on in *Shankarscope*.

Various clips from the film *Kalpana* were included in *Shankar scope* in 1970. They comprised the song *Bharat Jai Jan* – written by the poet Sumitranandan Panth, *Dance of Shiva*, *Dream of Rhythm*, *Kartikeya*, *Drum Dance* and *Naga*.

Among the longer items, a portion of *Prakriti Ananda* was shown on film through dialogues, which would give an overview of the storyline, while the *mantra* sequence was depicted on stage through live performances. What is interesting to note is that while Pranati Sengupta played the role of the mother on screen, Polly Guha enacted the role of the mother on stage in 1970. The role of the mother was portrayed by Anupama Das on stage in 1972.

The item *Eternal Song* portrayed a young couple, newly engaged and very much in love. They met with a fatal accident on the way back from their engagement party. Before meeting their end, like all young lovers, they had been committed to each other. But after death, they realized that nothing that they had believed to exist was real. The earth, the sky, the wind, forests, oceans, vice or virtue, man or woman, fear or envy, caste or religion – nothing existed, for nothing is eternal. There is only God, the one Supreme Power. Was this a reflection of Shankar's own experience and realization? One can only wonder.

Both film and stage were used to execute this item. The first half was shown on screen. It was only when the young couple found themselves in the realm of the unknown after death did the performers step onto the stage. One of the most appreciated acts in this item was the young couple vanishing from the stage at the end of their performance. Like all illusionary tricks, this too was a simple yet well-conceived and a well-executed one. So much so that the audience was never able to guess the trick behind it. Bose and another dancer used to be dressed entirely in black – black socks, black slacks, black full-sleeved T-shirts, black gloves and finally a black mask which would cover their entire head till the shoulders. Only the space for their eyes would be left uncovered. These too were covered with two patches of black net at the twin openings. Two white sheets of cloth would be kept lying on the stage. The young couple, after exploring life after death, would pick up the two sheets, hold it behind themselves, above their heads and walk towards the black screen C, as shown in Image no. 13. Bose's partner and he, dressed completely in black, standing very close to the black screen C, near the openings marked as D, would take the sheets from the performers' hands and hold it in close proximity in the same manner momentarily before letting the sheets go, while the young couple would swiftly exit through the opening D. Bose and his partner being dressed in black would be invisible in the dim light, and so the illusion was that the young couple had suddenly vanished from the stage.

The items titled *Announcer and Belly Rolling* (Parts I and II) were a satire on the bleak problem of unemployment as well as the lack of a skilled and employable workforce. According to the archived website of the Planning Commission of India, the body was set up by a Resolution of the Government of India in March 1950, in order to promote the "standard of living of the people by efficient exploitation of the resources of the country, increasing production and offering opportunities to all for employment in the service of the community."[7] When the first five-year plan was launched in 1951, although employment featured as an important agenda for the development of the country, it was not expected to pose a major challenge, as the commission believed it had taken measures to generate employment of reasonable magnitude to productively employ the growing labour force. An economic growth rate of five per cent was targeted, with an emphasis on labour-intensive consumer goods sectors. This was expected to generate enough employment to prevent any increase in unemployment. These assumptions and expectations formed the basis of the five-year plans during the first two decades after India gained independence – that is, the 1950s and 1960s. But despite these projections, the on-ground reality was that the magnitude and rate of unemployment in India increased significantly. Economy grew at a rate of around 3.5 per cent per annum as against the planned and projected rate of 5 per cent per annum. Employment grew at a rate of 2 per cent per annum. However, the growth in the Indian labour force during this period was at 2.5 per cent per annum, and this resulted in an increase in unemployment. Between 1952 and 1972, the magnitude of unemployment had almost doubled from around 5 to 10 million, while the rate of unemployment had jumped from 2.6 to 3.8 per cent.[8]

This problem of unemployment, very interestingly, was also captured by Satyajit Ray in his film *Pratidwandi*, the first film of the Calcutta Trilogy in 1970 itself, the other two being *Seemabadhha (1971)* and *Jana Aranaya (1975)*.

In the item *Announcer and Belly Rolling* in *Shankar scope*, Shankar not only addressed the problem of unemployment but also critiqued the capability of the Indian system in terms of capacity building. Part I of the sequence portrayed an interviewee, who had gone for a job interview but did not possess any qualification or the required skill set, which would be pertinent to the demands of the job that he had applied for. The only skill he excelled at was belly rolling, which though at that moment set him apart, did not make him employable. The interviewee was asked to come back again, and when the interviewee did come back (as is portrayed in the item Announcer and Belly Rolling Part II), the interviewer informs the candidate that, now, he too has learned the art of belly rolling and therefore the candidate will not be required. The piece therefore reflects that India, as a nation-state, has not been able to create an employable workforce, who are equipped to deal with the demands of the job market; and that the skill sets that they do possess are easily replaceable.

Another humorous piece was *Lady and the Thief*. A short spoof on the life of a modern society lady through stage and screen, it generated much laughter from the audience. Shankar's abhorrence for the shallow so-called society ladies had already been expressed in some sequences of *Kalpana* where they are depicted to be couch critics and express false sympathies, while not doing anything effective on the ground, to resolve the problems of society. This item began with the lady in question, being out, attending a dinner party, leaving her old mother-in-law at home in the care of a trusted and faithful *darwan* or guard. During her absence, a thief entered her house (Bose used to enact the role of the thief) and tried to escape with valuable ornaments. But the thief could not escape as he was trapped and caught by the old lady herself, much to the surprise of the thief himself as well as the audience.

Shankar's disdain for potboiler films of the film industry had already found expression in his film *Kalpana*, where the film showcases how producers are only interested in backing set formulas in the movie-making business, which would ensure box office success. These so-called assured box office hit formulas did not lack producers. In *Shankarscope*, Shankar, through the item *Dance Mad*, mocks the so-called box office hit plot formula of eve-teasing Romeos falling in love with the heroines, followed by over-the-top melodramatic love affairs. This modus operandi was popularized by the then-existing popular cinemas of the 1960s. The use of film, which is such a powerful medium for cheap thrills, was obviously something that Shankar did not appreciate. The entire sequence was expressed through instrumental music and mime, without any dialogue.

According to the souvenir, the item *Beauty Competition* was a colourful, entertaining satire on beauty competitions in the country. Given that most of the items which had been created specifically for *Shankarscope* was a comment on the then-contemporary Indian society, it cannot be but speculated whether the fact that 1966 was the year when India first won at an International Beauty Pageant, led to the creation of this item, in which Shankar questions what is true beauty. Indrani Rehman had represented India in the Miss Universe Contest of 1952; however, there was no representation from India again for another 12 years. Meher Castelino Mistri and Persis Khambatta represented India at the same contest in 1964 and 1965, respectively.[9] But it was only in 1966 that Yasmin Daji was declared the third runner-up at the Miss Universe Pageant. 1966 was also the year when Reita Faria Powell was crowned Miss World at the Miss World Contest.[10] Indian participation in the Miss World pageant had commenced in 1959, though there was no representation for the years 1963 to 1965. Indian representation at the Miss International contest was something which also began in 1960. What is interesting is the fact that in November 1970, a group of feminist activists stormed the stage at the Royal Albert Hall, London, to disrupt the Miss World Beauty contest,[11] and it was only in the 1980s that the contest added the tagline of "Beauty with a purpose." But in the early 1970s itself, as is evident in *Shankarscope*, Shankar questions what is true beauty and focuses on the temporary nature and shallowness of external beauty; and the fact that true beauty lies within, and it is this beauty that makes a person truly beautiful.

In this item, the *Beauty Competition*, which was the second last item of the show, both the white screen F as referred to in Image no. 12 and the projection on the screen would be slowly lowered in front of the black screen C. This was possible because the white projection screen F used to be suspended with three near-invisible suspenders from the top. This action required a tremendous amount of coordination as the speed of the descent of both the screen and the projection had to be the same to ensure that the audience did not even realize that there had been a change in the level of the projection and the screen. Given that technology back in the 1970s was not what it is today, this was indeed a wonder! There was about 1 foot space between the two screens – F in front and C directly behind it – that is, the white screen on which the film was being projected, and the black one, which would now be behind the projection screen, which was the backdrop. In the last shot of this item, six beauty queens were projected on the screen. They used to suddenly burst out of the screen and start performing live on stage. This was achieved by the use of the six overlapping flaps in the white screen. Once the screen had been lowered, the six dancers, who were being shown on the screen, would enter through the flap D in the black screen C and position themselves against their respective flaps and images. Then again with remarkable synchronization, the projection would be switched off and the stage lights would be switched on simultaneously, and the six dancers who were being shown on the screen would come alive on stage and perform by entering through the six flaps, all at the same time. This was the only sequence where the dancers would come directly onto the stage rather than first on the platform

106 *The Last Masterpiece*

E and then onto the stage B. Shankar had during one of the shows used this technique to come on stage directly at the end of the show. The film would show Uday Shankar drive up in a car and then open the door and step out onto the stage using the same technique described earlier. However, he did not continue with the act.

The last item of *Shankarscope* was titled *Epilogue*. This was a joyous dance, where all the dancers of the troupe participated. The souvenir of *Shankarscope* mentions it as an unusual group dance introduced for the first time in India. The "unusual" and "introduced for the first time in India" referred to the striking aspect of this dance, which was the use of strobe lights or stroboscopic lamps.

In the spring of 1966, New York filmmaker Jonas Mekas in his regular column for Village Voice magazine wrote about the emerging trend of using strobe lights for art happenings.[12] Harold Edgerton came to be introduced to stroboscopy as a doctoral student at the Massachusetts Institute of Technology in the 1930s. An electrical engineer by training, he discovered that stroboscopic lights enabled him to visually observe many a motion in motors, which was otherwise not possible. This breakthrough brought to the forefront the realization of the tremendous potential of strobe lights in allowing the human eye to view high-speed motion that had never been observed before. By 1937, Edgerton utilized this technology not only for research, and photography in uncontrolled weather conditions and undersea, but for other artistic applications outside the laboratory. The final test came in 1939, and when during the Second World War this technology was used to capture images at night for reconnaissance purposes.[13] The 1960s was a time when Light Art or Luminism as a movement took over the world of Art by storm. The term Light Art is generally used to describe works of art in which artificial light, usually electric, plays a very important role. Although artists had experimented with this since the eighteenth century, it was only in the 1960s that it acquired the proportions of a movement across the USA and Europe.

Lighting had always played a very important role in Shankar's productions. Such was its importance that he had his own light equipment with state-of-the-art technology, many of which were not available in India during the time that he was using them in his productions. Often on occasion, he had his musicians and stage manager handle the lights. His usage of lighting techniques had confounded the best technicians in India at the time. He took this further in 1970 with *Shankarscope*, when he introduced the technology of strobe lights on the Indian stage. The strobe lights could be adjusted to whatever tempo was required and as per the review of the show in Statesman, a leading English daily of the times, this "final dance with the light throwing flickering shadows on the backdrop looked like an exotic dream."[14] This was augmented by the fact that strobe lights give the feel of freezing motion at rhythmic intervals. Quite clichéd now, they were nonetheless, in the early 1970s quite a path-breaking and an innovative enterprise.

However, the item that stole the show in *Shankarscope* according to one and all was *Kartikeya*. This item was the first item after the interval. This was necessary as the stage had to be readied with a black net, which did not have a single stitch on it, covering the entire stage. It was dropped towards the front of the stage, behind the front curtains. This black net had been used in most of Shankar's productions, be they *Samanya Kshati*, *Prakriti Ananda*, or during his tours, for various purposes. In *Shankarscope*, once the interval was over and the front curtains had been opened, a clipping of Kartikeya from the film *Kalpana* used to be projected on the netted screen. Simultaneously, all the dancers of the troupe – the men dressed in cream-coloured *dhotis* and the women clad in sarees – would dance in a dim light behind this projection on the stage. Statesman opined, "Mr. Shankar secured a unique effect by projecting the *Kartikeya* sequence on a transparent screen behind which the cast was dancing. Careful synchronization between the screen images and the movements on the stage was evident in all the sketches."[15]

So grand, impressive and novel was this production that the press critic from Cine Advance not only termed it "An Unforgettable Evening," but also wrote, "Even 'unique' seems to be a mild term to describe what I have seen that evening."[16] Such was the demand, for *Shankarscope*, that it ran with two daily shows at the Academy of Fine Arts for two whole months, with matinee and evening shows at 3 pm and 6 pm, respectively, and on two occasions with three shows on Sundays, when a morning show was added for school children.

The opening day of *Shankarscope* on December 11, 1970, saw Mamata Shankar present a Bharatanatyam recital under the direction of Guru Gyan Prakashan.

After 1970, Shankar and his troupe again staged *Shankarscope* during the summer of 1971 in Kolkata, for one and a half months at Mahajati Sadan. A few new items were introduced in the performance this time round, one of them being *Chinna Bichhinna*. Among other things, the legacy left behind by the British Raj in 1947 was a divided sub-continent with the two nation-states of India and Pakistan formed on the basis of which religious majority occupied which segment of the region – the Hindus and Muslims, respectively. The logistics of this divide based on religious demography, however, left Pakistan with two territories – West Pakistan and East Pakistan – with more than 1600 kilometres of Indian territory between the two segments. Not only did this geographical distance impact the economic and political separation of the two regions, this separation was further compounded by the ethnic distinctions between the two regions. West Pakistan was chosen to be the nation-state's political centre as most of the ruling elite had migrated to West Pakistan. This divide between the two territories of Pakistan can be brought to the fore by the fact that between 1947 and 1970, East Pakistan, received only 25 per cent of the country's industrial investments and 30 per cent of its imports, despite contributing to more than 59 per cent of

108 *The Last Masterpiece*

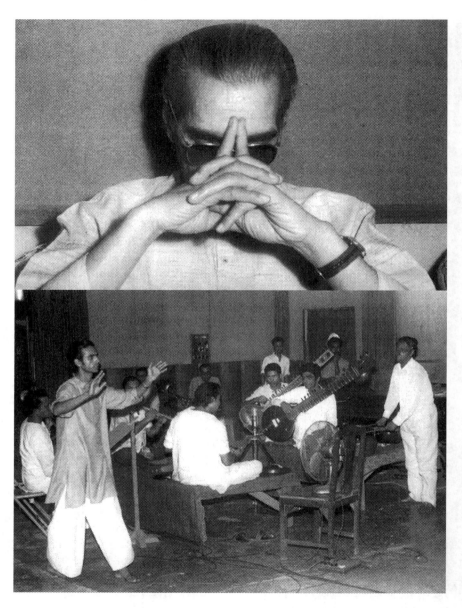

Figure 6.3 The music recording for *Shankarscope* was conducted at Technicians Studio, while the film recording was held at New Theatres Studio No. 2. The image on the top portrays Uday Shankar in a focused and reflective mood in the control room of the studio during the music recording of *Shankarscope*; while the lower image depicts the scene in the recording room, with Shanti Bose, on the extreme left, instructing the musicians during the recording of *Shankarscope*. Kamalesh Maitra is on the extreme right.

Source: Courtesy, private collection of Shanti Bose

The Last Masterpiece 109

Figure 6.4 Shankar and Bose, visiting an exhibition on the voyage of Apollo 11 by Neil Armstrong and Buzz Aldrin in 1969. The exhibition held at Eden Gardens, Kolkata, in 1970, included a stone brought back from the moon. This photograph of Shankar and Bose was clicked in front of that stone exhibit. The reason for including this image is to bring to the fore that even at the age of 70, Shankar was enthusiastic enough to go and visit this exhibition, reflecting his eagerness to know about anything and everything that was happening around the world.

Source: Courtesy, private collection of Shanti Bose

Pakistan's exports. Elites of West Pakistan viewed the inhabitants of East Pakistan as being culturally and ethnically inferior. The attempt to impose Urdu as the national language, in a region, where less than 10 per cent of the population had a working knowledge of it, was a further attempt to suppress East Pakistan's interests. A geographically cyclone-prone area, East Pakistan was hit by Cyclone Bhola in late 1970, leading to a loss of 300,000 lives. The sluggish response of West Pakistan to the crisis, despite having the necessary resources being available, further angered the Bengalis of East Pakistan. According to French journalist Paul Dreyfus, "Over the years, West Pakistan behaved like a poorly raised, egotistical guest, devouring the best dishes and leaving nothing but scraps and leftovers for East Pakistan."[17]

In 1970, West Pakistan announced its first general elections, which would be held for the first time in the country, since it had gained independence. However, General Agha Khan Mohammad Yahya Khan, the third President of Pakistan, placed limits on the voters' choice on the basis of the fact that the integrity of the country was more important than the results of the election. It was decided that 138 seats would be allotted to representatives of West Pakistan and 162 seats would go to East Pakistan which had about 20 million more inhabitants. The surprise winner of the elections was Sheikh Mujibur Rehman from East Pakistan, whose campaign platform had been that of Bengali nationalism and autonomy of East Pakistan. This overwhelming majority resulted all the more from the fact that the votes of West Pakistan were split between different parties. Shocked by the results, the President delayed calling the first meeting of the assembly, and instead instituted martial law in the country. East Pakistan witnessed strikes and riots erupted as a response to this measure. A civil disobedience movement was announced by Mujibur Rahman in the presence of a gathering of 50,000 people in Dhaka on March 7, 1971. A last attempt to resolve the issue across the table was made when Rahman and Khan met between March 16 and March 24, 1971. An agreement of sorts seemed to have been reached, but on the night of March 25, 1971, Mujibur Rahman was arrested and 60,000 to 80,000 West Pakistani soldiers who had already infiltrated East Pakistan, began what would be come to known as Operation Searchlight, which involved the systematic massacre and rape of Bengali civilians by Pakistani soldiers.[18] Hundreds of students were slaughtered at Dhaka University, offices of various Bengali dailies were also burned down, and journalists and newspaper staff were charred to death. Apart from Dhaka, operations were also launched simultaneously in Peelkhana and Rajarbagh. According to the report of the Dhaka Tribune, while Khan left for Lahore before the massacre began, Zulfikar Ali Bhutto, the leader of the Pakistan People's Party was there at the Hotel Intercontinental in Dhaka during the operation and appreciated the role of the Pakistani army.[19]

The then Prime Minister of India, Indira Gandhi termed Operation Searchlight a "genocide" within a week of its commencement, as early as March 31, 1971. Estimates of the total number of dead ranged from five hundred thousand to three million according to different sources. By May 1971, one and a half million refugees sought asylum in India.[20] According to an appeal made – by the Public Diplomacy Wing, Ministry of Foreign Affairs, Government of the People's Republic of Bangladesh, for rendering justice and recognizing the Bangladesh genocide, 200,000–400,000 Bengali women had also been raped by the personnel of the Pakistani armed forces.[21]

The impact on West Bengal, which bordered East Pakistan, was the most pronounced not only in terms of the huge influx of refugees, but the horrifying narratives they brought with them. *Chinna Bichhinna* in *Shankarscope*, presented in the late summer–monsoon of 1971, was a portrayal of the horrors and the sufferings of the Bengalis of East Pakistan in face of the brutality carried out by the Pakistani administration.

In 1971, *Shankarscope* was originally scheduled to run for one month, but given the demand for it, the performances ran for one and a half months at Mahajati Sadan. The hot and humid summer–monsoon season in Kolkata made it very taxing for the dancers as they were performing two shows daily. They had approached Shankar by the end of one month to reduce the number of shows to one show daily instead of two shows a day, and continue with two shows during weekends. However, this was not to be, instead, given the demand for the show; it was extended on the same schedule to run for another 2 weeks. Week-long shows in New Delhi and on return, in Kolkata, were also accepted. While the other dancers acquiesced, Bose together with Dhurjati Sen, after completing the Kolkata schedule of one and a half months, did not travel with the troupe to Delhi, nor did they participate in the staging of the production when the troupe returned to Kolkata and performed the show for a week at Kalamandir.

Shankarscope was again restaged in 1972. Shankar sent word to Bose through Anil Chatterjee to rejoin the troupe, and according to Bose, he found it difficult to respond in the negative to Shankar, after being associated with the maestro for such a long time, and so Bose rejoined Shankar's troupe again for *Shankarscope* in 1972, as the Ballet Master, as well as the Assistant Director for the production of *Samanya Kshati*. As the Assistant Director of the 1972 production of *Samanya Kshati*, Bose rearranged and, in a few instances, re-choreographed a few of the dances for the ballet. The show ran with one show daily and two shows on weekends.

When *Shankarscope* was restaged in 1972, *Samanya Kshati* was staged for one hour, after which *Shankarscope* was presented for another hour. A few movie clips from *Kalpana* previously shown during *Shankarscope* were discarded at this point. *Samanya Kshati* was presented in a shortened version as originally depicted in Tagore's poem. The principal characters of Queen Karuna and the King were played by Anupama Das and Bose, respectively. The roles had previously been performed by Amala Shankar and Uday Shankar himself. Both *Prakriti Ananda* and *Shankarscope* were staged under the banner of Uday Shankar Ballet Troupe.

Shankar's magnum opus, *Shankarscope*, which merged film with live performers engaged in dance, music, acts of illusion and mime, use of innovative lighting, apart from other aspects of stagecraft, became a trendsetter and paved the way for multimedia productions, which is what most of the current performances in India, follow.

Shankarscope in 1972 was Shankar's last production. By now, at the age of 72, Shankar was not in the best of health. He had also broken down emotionally and become very lonely. But as fate would have it, he found a reason to live life anew. His renewed vigour led him to formulate in his mind, a new production. He wanted to name it *Stagnant and Flow*. The story that he shared with his close associates at the time, including Bose, was to be set in the background of a mountain by the sea. The ballet would depict the story of an enclosed, stagnant pool of water, in a small depression on the side of the mountain. Time had led to the pool to become muddy and filthy. Suddenly, one day, a huge wave lashed against the mountainside. The fathomless sea washed away all the dirt and filth from the pool, and gave it a new life.

112 *The Last Masterpiece*

Figure 6.5 From the first scene of *Samanya Kshati*, as staged during 1972, with Bose in the role of the King, in Shankar's own costume.

Source: Courtesy, private collection of Shanti Bose

The pool, with its new-found youth, was once again inspired to start living with renewed verve. However, despite having formulated this idea for a new production, Shankar was unable to give form to it. Death snatched away this creative genius on September 26, 1977.

Notes

1 Souvenir: Shankarscope (1971).
2 Ibid.
3 Mohan Khokar, *His Dance His Life – A Portrait of Uday Shankar* (New Delhi: Himalayan Books, 1983), 19.
4 Fernau Hall, "Honoring Uday Shankar," *Dance Chronicle* 7, no. 3 (1984): 326–44, accessed July 9, 2017, url: www.jstor.org/stable/1567655
5 Ibid.
6 Priyanka Dasgupta, "Satyajit Ray was Obsessed with Kalpana and Loved Amala Shankar's Dance Pieces," *Times of India*, July 24, 2020, accessed December 4, 2021, url: https://timesofindia.indiatimes.com/city/kolkata/satyajit-ray-was-obsessed-with-kalpana-and-loved-amala-shankars-dance-pieces/articleshow/77157103.cms
7 Planning Commission, accessed June 21, 2018, url: http://planningcommission.gov.in/aboutus/history/index.php?about=aboutbdy.htm
8 Papola, Trilok S. and Gerry Rodgers, eds, *Labour Institutions and Economic Development in India*. Vol. 97 (Geneva: International Institute for Labour Studies, 1992).

9 India at the Big Four International Beauty Pageants, accessed June 21, 2018, url: https://en.wikipedia.org/wiki/India_at_Big_Four_international_beauty_pageants
10 Winners, Miss World, accessed June 21, 2018, url: www.missworld.com/#/past_winners
11 Miss World: My protest at 1970 beauty pageant, accessed June 21, 2018, url: www.bbc.com/news/av/magazine-26437815/miss-world-my-protest-at-1970-beauty-pageant
12 "A Digital Trip: Strobe Light and the Birth of New Media Art (Trends in Contemporary Art Lecture Series)," *Department of Art, Art History and Design, University of Notre Dame*, accessed June 21, 2018, url: https://artdept.nd.edu/news-and-events/events/2016/11/07/dr-tina-rivers-ryan-talk-a-digital-trip-strobe-light-and-the-birth-of-new-media-art-trends-in-contemporary-art-lecture-series/
13 Harold "Doc" Edgerton, MIT, accessed June 21, 2018, url: http://web.mit.edu/6.933/www/Fall2000/edgerton/www/intro.html
14 Souvenir: *Shankarscope*, 1971.
15 Souvenir: *Shankarscope*, 1971.
16 Ibid.
17 Lorraine Boissoneault, "The Genocide the U.S. Can't Remember, But Bangladesh Can't Forget," *Smithsonian Magazine*, December 16, 2016, accessed June 22, 2018, url: www.smithsonianmag.com/history/genocide-us-cant-remember-bangladesh-cant-forget-180961490/
18 Ibid.
19 Mekhala Saran, "Operation Searchlight: All That Bangladesh Lost on 25 March 1971," *The Quint*, March 25, 2018, accessed June 22, 2018, url: www.thequint.com/videos/operation-searchlight-began-on-25-march-1971
20 Lorraine Boissoneault, "The Genocide the U.S. Can't Remember, But Bangladesh Can't Forget," *Smithsonian Magazine*, December 16, 2016, accessed June 22, 2018, url: www.smithsonianmag.com/history/genocide-us-cant-remember-bangladesh-cant-forget-180961490/
21 Imtiaz Ahmed, "Recognising the 1971 Bangladesh Genocide: An Appeal for Rendering Justice," *Ministry of Foreign Affairs, Government of the People's Republic of Bangladesh*, February, 2022, accessed January 8, 2023, url: www.ucl.ac.uk/risk-disaster-reduction/sites/risk_disaster_reduction/files/bd_genocide_booklet.pdf

7 Uday Shankar's Style of Creative Dance – Its Impact and the Legacy

The vibrant new form of dance that Uday Shankar created, breaking away from the duality of the classical and folk forms in Indian dance traditions, was a corollary of modern India. Shankar introduced new movements in dance and formulated the basic tenets of his technique and style, thereby creating a revolution of sorts. He categorised the movements he created – at times, inspired by movements of daily life, and at times, inspired by music – according to different themes. With its basic tenets of beauty, power and simplicity, the form and technique of Shankar's art was not only for the purposes of entertainment but a window to India's problems, and a platform for creativity and innovation. Shankar moved away from the strictures posed by the *Natyashastra*, to emphasize body expression, as he felt that *mudras* not only often break the flow of storytelling if used as a tool of translation of lyrics but are also not clearly visible to the audience seated in the last row of the auditorium. He developed basic exercises to ensure the suppleness of limbs and fluidity of movement which he deemed important enough to be conducted by himself alone, at the centre in Almora, where everyone had to participate in the General Class. He strongly believed in the connection between the mind and the body, which he felt was vital for any dancer or performer for that matter. Improvisation was another element he sought to teach to help harness creativity among his students and troupe members. This was to arouse the artist in the performers and provoke them not only to perform but also to reflect, react and create.

Creativity for Shankar, however, was not only restricted to the creation of new movements, usage of stage space and the manner of storytelling. His creativity also extended to the way in which Shankar harnessed technological advancements and innovations from across the world and more often than not introduced them in the arena of performing arts, thereby giving form to his ideas in a manner never before conceived or seen in India. As discussed before, dimmers were something that Uday Shankar brought to India as far as stage lighting was concerned, as were stroboscopic lights. The most interesting part is that whenever the performance was performed to recorded music, it was the musicians who handled the lights as they were best attuned to the sequence and the musical cues of the ballet being performed. This was the case with the productions of *Samanya Kshati* performed in India.

DOI: 10.4324/9781003433774-8

Shankarscope was a production which combined stage and screen together to achieve illusionary effects. Uday Shankar felt that this production which was "highly developed technically . . . will create a new channel for a great industry in this country."[1] The first show of its kind in India, the trend for combining audio-visual media and stage performance, which has become quite the norm in most prestigious events in performing arts, was established by Uday Shankar. According to Shanti Bose, his then Ballet Master for the production of *Shankarscope* and the Assistant Director and Ballet Master for the production of *Samanya Kshati*, as far as the technical aspect was concerned, the merging of the screen characters with the same characters enacting live on stage was a major challenge in *Shankarscope*. What is awe-inspiring is that this was achieved with technology not what we are used to in the twenty-first century, but more than half a century ago, in 1970.

As discussed in the last chapter, the use of strobe lights or stroboscopic lamps for the first time in India, in the last item of *Shankarscope* titled *Epilogue*, was a striking feature of the production. The lights could be adjusted to whatever tempo was required and according to the English daily, *The Statesman*, this "final dance with the light throwing flickering shadows on the backdrop looked like an exotic dream." This was augmented by the fact that strobe lights give the feel of freezing motion at rhythmic intervals. Quite clichéd now, they were nonetheless, in the early 1970s quite a path-breaking and innovative enterprise.

Uday Shankar introduced India to other never before seen or utilized technology for stagecraft. During the tours that the troupe undertook not only internationally but in various parts of India, one of the challenges faced by them was the fact that the size of the stage varied from one auditorium to another. This implied that it would result in a change of position of the lights and dancers. Given the perfectionist that Shankar was, he eliminated this problem through the use of a sheet that was laid out on stage before every performance. The positions of the dancers used to be marked on this sheet, so that even if the size of the stage differed, the dancers would always perform in their designated positions. The lights were also fixed on stands which were placed in prefixed positions. During the stage rehearsals of first performance of the production, the dancers had to position themselves and mark their positions in order to ensure that they not only maintained their distances accurately but also aligned to the lights as required for different sequences.

Therefore, whether it was the usage of dimmers, portable lights, strobe lights, the multi-media production of *Shankarscope*, the use of recorded music, the use of a seamless-net to divide the stage, or other aspects of stagecraft – all of which are commonplace now in the field of performing arts – were first introduced by Uday Shankar in the performing arts traditions of India.

Shankar used his dance to present an alternate portal to view the challenges of modern India and the socio-political and economic turmoil that it faced after gaining independence in 1947. His thought-provoking productions on the plight of marginalized communities in society, his social awareness and his sense of social responsibility ensured that he did not use his style purely for the purpose of entertainment but to provoke his audience to reflect on the world they inhabited. This is reflected through Shankar's compositions which brought these issues to the fore and presented them to his audiences across the globe – whether it was through his compositions of *Rhythm of Life*, *Labour and Machinery*, or various items in *Kalpana*. *Rhythm of Life* portrayed the struggle of a young man who battled various adversities of life to emerge with new faith and hope for freedom. *Labour and Machinery* illustrated the problems faced by industrialized nations, the economic atrocities of capitalist societies, and how men and women mechanically pursue their daily lives. But in the end, the victory of truth, justice and humankind is inevitable. Many of the items of *Shankarscope* were also either a satirical or socio-political commentary on issues that plagued India in the late 1960s and 1970s, as has been discussed in detail when describing the items in the chapter titled "The Last Masterpiece."[2]

The shift in his compositions from representing the mythology of India, to telling tales of the struggle of the newly independent nation, and the dynamics of a resurgent India, represents a shift in his dynamism as a creator, as well as the perception of India by the Occident. His tremendous ability to observe daily life and represent it through his dance makes him a visual chronicler of the life and times of the common man and therefore the history of the period.

The legacy of Shankar, and his impact on society and performing arts in India, also extends to his role as the harbinger of social upliftment. He helped remove the social stigma attached to dance and dancers, thereby elevating the status of performing arts to the respect that it demands. With his troupe, not only in the formative years but also subsequently, Uday Shankar heralded another important social change. He brought the upper caste Brahmins and the Indian upper middle class and middle class on stage at a time when this was frowned upon. With his foray into dance when his troupe initially consisted primarily of his family members, Uday Shankar denounced the social stigma attached to the art form as he hailed from a *Brahmin* family. He also brought on stage dancers, Indian women from respectable families, like his cousin Kanaklata and others like Zohra Sehgal and her sister Uzra, Amala Nandi, as well as Ragini, Padmini and Lalitha. This was in direct contradiction to the traditional dance forms where the norm was that men portrayed the roles of women on stage. This was the case, for example, in *Kathakali*. In the *Gotipua* tradition of *Odissi*, young boys dressed as women would perform in the courtyards of the temples of Odisha. Women dancers were essentially from the devadasi tradition, or a *rajnartaki* or *tawaif*, a dancer in the royal courts. Exceptions were of course there, like Balasaraswati, who though from the devadasi tradition broke boundaries and forged a path of her own in the field of Bharatnatyam. She too admired and respected Shankar, and as Shanti Bose recollects came to visit him at his home in Madras in 1962, when preparations were going on for Shankar's tour of the USA, Canada and Europe. Tagore too, as discussed in Chapter 2, had already started staging dance dramas with women performers in Shantiniketan. He had taken measures to ensure that Manipuri dance classes were conducted in Shantiniketan, though they were termed "fitness" or *sharir charcha* classes and were suspended whenever Tagore was not in Shantiniketan. Shankar therefore questioned the established social structures and hierarchy including the stereotypes attributed to the tradition of Indian performing arts traditions. Through Uday Shankar, dance in India found a new respectability. Men and women from respectable families, for whom performing on stage had been unthinkable, now came forward and started taking up dance professionally.

At a time, as written in the souvenir of 1962, when women conductors or musical directors were rare even in the Western world, he had appointed Lakshmi Shankar as the Music Director of his troupe, Uday Shankar Hindu Dancers and Musicians, during a tour as important as the one in 1962, spanning five months across the USA, Canada and innumerable countries of Europe. A perfectionist for whom work was God, he paid the highest tribute to talent and hard work, irrespective of gender norms as dictated by society.

With Shankar, we also see many classical musicians and dancers delving into the world of what came to be known as the creative form. Apart from Ravi Shankar, who was Shankar's youngest brother and grew to become a sitar maestro in his own right, senior artists like Baba Allauddin Khan, whom Shankar respected tremendously and addressed as Baba and his wife as Ma (recollects Shanti Bose), other artists like Ustad Alla Rakkha, Lakshmi Shankar, Timir Baran, Vishnudas Shirali and Pandit Shiv Kumar Sharma, were all involved with Shankar's productions at some point or the other. That was the kind of respect that his productions garnered. His film *Kalpana* also saw many classical artists, and Gurus participate and treat the space with as much dedication and faith, as they did when performing in the classical sphere. Most of the dancers for the film were also trained Kathakali dancers. Even during the period 1960–1977, when Shankar was based in Calcutta, many of his dancers were trained either in Kathakali, Manipuri and Bharatnatyam or even all the three forms at the Academy of Dance, Drama and Music.

Uday Shankar brought to Indian performing arts a level of professionalism that had not existed before. Based on the experience of his association with the professionally managed dance troupe of Anna Pavlova, Shankar brought together a team of dancers "The Uday Shankar Hindu Dancers and Musicians" with the aim of professional stage performances. This was a direct shift from the traditional *guru-shishya parampara*[3] of training in performing arts in India. The quest for perfection and the intensive and extensive dedication to achieve that perfection remained common, however. Punctuality, professionalism in behaviour within the troupe as well as when they were on tour, paying his artists for their time and effort, ensuring that his troupe had the best of comfort in terms of travel and stay while on tours elevated the respect given to performers to a great extent.

Therefore, the impact that Uday Shankar had during the time he lived and performed in, was immense. In an age when the leaders of modern India were trying to unite India in their struggle for independence, Shankar's dance form contributed to this nationalistic endeavour by overcoming the provincial dimensions and being quintessentially Indian in nature. The impact of Shankar's art form on performing arts traditions of modern India places him in the position of one of the architects of modern India, whose contribution is no less valuable and important than many other oft-mentioned names. Unfortunately, non-textual works and their contribution often remain unacknowledged in their role of nation-building.

Ramchandra Guha, in the prologue of his edited book, the Makers of Modern India,[4] opines that he considers Mahatma Gandhi, Jawaharlal Nehru and Dr. B.R. Ambedkar as being the architects of modern India in the sense that with Gandhi in the 1920s and 1930s, emerged the concept of an united India; Ambedkar was the father of the Indian Constitution, the legal framework within which India would function; and Nehru in the 1950s and 1960s was the architect of modern India in terms of its role as a newly independent nation state. But apart from this trinity, Guha also includes makers of modern India, social reformers like Ram Mohan Roy, Jotirao Phule, feminists like Tarabai Shinde and Kamaladevi Chattopadhya. Their commentaries on modern India had a profound impact on the intellectual and liberal population of India. Uday Shankar's works too are a commentary on the India that he witnessed closely during his growing up years till the 1920s. He witnessed India closely again, when he came back to India for an extended visit and toured the country with Alice Boner in the 1930s and finally returned from the West and stayed back in India from the 1940s. He was witness to the tremendous change that India underwent right from an oppressed India to an independent India, as well as the challenges faced by modern India. On the one hand, while Shankar uses his choreographies as a critique of modern India, based on his perception, he also explores the ways and means that may be adopted and explored to move ahead. Shankar is a path breaker when it comes to the form and techniques of his style, together with the creation of the third genre – that of the creative style in Indian dance; the usage of technology, stagecraft, professionalism, championing women's position based on their capability and was not dictated by gender norms.

Shankar's legacy was carried forward by his direct disciples in various ways in keeping with their own interests and forte. Although dissatisfied with the way Uday Shankar Culture Centre, Kolkata, was being run, which was expressed by Shankar in his letters to the various committee members of the institute,[5] and although Amala Shankar herself states in her memoirs that she did not teach Shankar's style for almost a decade due to personal reasons, nonetheless, she started recreating Shankar's productions at a later date for the purpose of creating records so to say. I distinctly remember accompanying my mother, Sunanda Bose to see *Mahamanav* in the early 1990s, based on the life of Buddha, and my mother telling my father, Shanti Bose, on returning home, *Boudi ekhono ki shanghatik movements korchen!* which would roughly translate to, it is unbelievable how wonderfully Amala Shankar is performing movements even at this age! *Boudi* being the term that Amala Shankar was addressed by the members of Shankar's troupe – meaning the wife of *Dada* – as Shankar had come to be universally known.

As Mamata Shankar writes, her mission and purpose in life is to take forward her father, Uday Shankar's unique and inimitable dance style, which she learned from her mother, Amala Shankar.[6] Recollects Shanti Bose, during the tour of 1962, although Mamata Shankar was then a young girl, nonetheless, she knew by heart all the dances that were being performed during the shows, and would dance backstage, inside the wings, all the steps in sequence, in her childlike fashion of course, while the dancers were performing on stage, to the audience.

Narendra Sharma, Shankar's student from the Uday Shankar Culture Centre at Almora, carried Shankar's legacy forward through his troupe, *Bhoomika* in New Delhi. *Flying Cranes*, one of Bhoomika's most mesmerizing presentations (which I had the privilege of viewing as an audience member, along with other presentations staged sometime in the early 1990s in Kolkata), was originally choreographed by Narendra Sharma during his days at Shankar's Almora centre.[7] Another composition which touched me so much that I can vividly recall it even after almost 30 years, told the story of a conference held on children in the Year of the Child. After heated debates,

Figure 7.1 Shanti Bose and Mamata Shankar, enacting the lead roles of Shyama and Bajrasen in 1978, in a production of Tagore's dance drama, *Shyama*.

Source: Courtesy, private collection of Shanti Bose

Figure 7.2 Bose paying homage to Uday Shankar on his birth centenary celebrations at the *Uday Shankar Shatabdi Samaroh* in New Delhi, organized by Sangeet Natak Akademi (SNA) in 2001. From left to right are Shyamanand Jalan, Jayant Kastaur – the then Secretary of SNA, Narendra Sharma, Sachin Shankar and Shanti Bose. Picture credit – Sangeet Natak Akademi.

Source: Courtesy, private collection of Shanti Bose

discussions and consumption of food and drinks, the conference ultimately did not resolve anything. The last scene depicted the irony of it all when a child rag picker was seen picking up the waste papers and clearing the room after the conference.

Shanti Bardhan who was associated with the Almora centre,[8] after his association with Uday Shankar, worked with the IPTA – Indian People's Theatre Association which was formed in 1943, and was also known as *Bharatiya Jan Natya Sangh*, *Bharatiya Gana Natya Sangh* or the *Praja Natya Mandali*.[9] A revolutionary and freedom fighter at heart, he created a dance on the Bengal famine of 1943, attributed as a man-made famine and often termed the worst economic disaster in South Asia in the twentieth century. Along with his wife, Gul Bardhan, Shanti Bardhan co-founded the Little Ballet Troupe, later known as the Ranga Shri Little Ballet Group, now based out of Bhopal. One of the troupe's renowned performances is the puppetry dance format, through which they narrate the story of *Ramayana*. With puppet-like movements, many of which were seemingly based on Kathakali, reminisces Bose, after seeing the troupe's staging of the *Ramayana*, in Kolkata. This was, however, after Shanti Bardhan's demise in 1954. Interestingly, Shankar's *Kalpana* also had a sequence on how human beings were being made to dance like puppets following the edicts and diktats stemming from age-old traditions, and people were following them, without questioning them.[10]

Prabhat Ganguly who had married Simkie in the early 1940s at Almora[11] played an important role in the Little Ballet Group as a choreographer and a teacher who taught exercises and improvisation[12] as devised by Shankar. The method devised by Uday Shankar, in his own words, was based on the realization that,

> After all this experience in the world of dancing, that dancing as beautiful as it is, passes, (and) dies with the disappearance of the interpreter. So, I created a new method which could be applied to any kind of dance to the world – and not only that this method can be used in schools and colleges without making students dancers. It may be called a new school of dancing altogether which I very strongly feel is going to stay.[13]

He believed that this would help no matter which profession a person chose to follow, lawyer, teacher, politician, actor as the control of the mind over the body is an essential element in any form of communication. Uday Shankar had applied to the Government of India under Indira Gandhi's aegis for funding to make this work; but unfortunately, he did not receive it.

Simkie, Shankar's dance partner of almost two decades till the 1940s choreographed the dream sequence for Raj Kapoor's film *Awaara* released in 1951. Raj Kapoor the noted film actor, director and producer of Indian cinema played the beloved tramp in this film where the dream sequence poses a point when the hero is torn between the choices offered by life. Simkie – the film credits state her name as Madame Simkie[14] – composed the sequence in Shankar's trademark style of beauty, simplicity and power.

Sachin Shankar, Uday Shankar's cousin, who was a student at the Almora Centre, and laments the closure of the Uday Shankar Culture Centre at Almora; and goes on to blame Amala Shankar squarely for her inaction in holding the centre and Shankar's associates like Simkie, Zohra Sehgal, Shanti Bardhan, Rajendra Shankar and Lakshmi Shankar together, in a letter written to Amala Shankar on July 7, 1970,[15] carried forward Shankar's style through his choreography in films like Nagin (1954), *Madhumati* (1958) and *Johny Mera Naam* (1970).[16] Sachin Shankar put in a performance himself in the film *Munimji* (1955).[17] Sachin Shankar with his troupe had performed on more than one occasion at The Academy of Fine Arts, Kolkata. According to Bose, Sachin Shankar's composition on train, to Salil Chowdhury's music, was what intrigued and touched him the most. It told the story of the various passengers who boarded the train and got off when they had reached their respective destinations, various vendors and their calls selling different food and beverages and so on. This one single item managed to portray the diversity that India is in every respect.

Shanti Bose's contribution in terms of taking Shankar's legacy forward has unfolded in a two-pronged manner. The first is in recreating Shankar's productions that he had been associated with as a dancer, and subsequently as the Ballet Master from 1965 and the Assistant Director for *Samanya Kshati* in 1972. The second is in the field of synthesizing the world of Rabindranath Tagore's works with Shankar's style, movements and techniques.[18] With his foray into Shankar's troupe at a time when the maestro was paying tribute to the Nobel Laureate on his birth centenary, Bose's first exposure was to a synthesized world of Tagore and Shankar through *Samanya Kshati* in 1960. Uday Shankar's other productions of *Udara Charitanam* and *Prakriti Ananda* were also based on Tagore's work, with which Bose was intrinsically involved. Bose went on to work with stalwarts in Tagore's music with productions of Shyamasree Tagore, Santosh Sengupta, Suchitra Mitra and his own dance institution Nrityangan, which he co-founded with Sunanda Bose, with Uday Shankar's blessings in 1969.[19] Bose's compositions portray not only Shankar's style most prominently, as he was associated with the maestro

Figure 7.3 Sulakshana Sen had the privilege of performing Kartikeya with Shanti Bose. Apart from the challenge and honour of performing this item with a perfectionist like him, her moment of crowning glory was when Mamata Shankar came backstage after seeing the performance, and with a warm hug praised Sen, saying that she had been curious to see how Sulakshana would perform this beloved item of her father's.

Source: Courtesy, private collection of Shanti Bose

Uday Shankar's Style of Creative Dance 123

Figure 7.4 Shanti Bose and Sunanda Bose as *Arjun* and *Bir Chitrangada* in Nrityangan's first production of Tagore's dance drama *Chitrangada* in 1969.

Source: Courtesy, private collection of Shanti Bose

for 17 long years, but also the folk forms learned with Yogendra Sunder Desai as well as the classical styles of Kathakali, Manipuri and to a certain extent Bharatnatyam learned at the Academy of Dance, Drama and Music. Bose was also associated in the 1950s with the IPTA in West Bengal, known as the *Bharatiya Gana Natya Sangh*, before he joined either the Academy or Uday Shankar or the Indian Revival Group. Sunanda Bose who was associated with Shankar from 1965 to 1968, and with the IBT before that, brings in her compositions, not only Shankar's style but elements of Manipuri which she trained in under Guru Bipin Singh and Kalavati Devi at Manipuri Nartanalaya, Kolkata.

However, despite Uday Shankar's tremendous contribution to Indian dance and the impact that it had and continues to have, it is hardly acknowledged today. In her article titled "Who remembers Uday Shankar?" Dr. Erdman writes,

> Why, I asked myself, did no one talk of Shankar in India today? Wasn't he the forerunner of India's great dance renaissance in the 1930s? Why did one of Delhi's major presenters claim that her ballets owed nothing to Shankar, when it was clear to me that they did?[23]

124 Uday Shankar's Style of Creative Dance

Figure 7.5 Uday Shankar with the cast and crew of *Chitrangada* after Nrityangan's first performance. Second from the left is the noted poet, author, journalist and litterateur, Narendranath Mitra[20] who was the then President of Nrityangan. *Rabindra sangeet* singer, Arghya Sen,[21] who also participated in the production, can be seen standing in the second row to the right of Shankar.

Source: Courtesy, private collection of Shanti Bose

This is hauntingly reminiscent of Shankar's own words that, "The ballets I see in India are no doubt an extension of my work. I feel that strongly."[24]

Another aspect that irked Dr. Erdman, as mentioned earlier in this book, is the "smug dismissal of Uday Shankar which characterized his (Uday Shankar's) latter years."[25] The last two decades of Shankar's life – the 1960s and the 1970s – have usually been depicted in literature on the maestro as a very depressing grey phase, one of degeneration, where he worked himself into despair and that it was generally an unsuccessful period. However, the period 1960–1977 continued to be one where Shankar was at his creative best, when even ill health could not deter the artist in him, and he went on to create three new original productions of *Samanya Kshati* (1961), *Prakriti Ananda* (1966), *Shankar scope* (1970, 1971 and 1972 – together with an abridged version of *Samanya Kshati*) and two international tours with his troupe in 1962 and 1968.

The period undoubtedly witnessed Shankar's transition from being a performer and a choreographer to that of solely becoming a creator, but his art only evolved to new heights, continuing to forge new paths, breaking

Uday Shankar's Style of Creative Dance 125

Figure 7.6 Noted dance scholar, Dr. Sunil Kothari,[22] felicitating Shanti Bose after Nrityangan's staging of the recreation of *Samanya Kshati*, at the *Uday Shankar Shatabdi Samaroh* in 2001, organized by Sangeet Natak Akademi in New Delhi. The re-creation was in the format as presented in 1972, when Bose was the Assistant Director for the production of *Samanya Kshati*, as well as the Ballet Master of Shankar's troupe.

Source: Picture credit – Sangeet Natak Akademi. Courtesy, private collection of Shanti Bose

technological barriers and introducing to India, never before seen spectacles. Therefore, far from being a grey phase, Shankar's work during the mature years of his life reflects that just as autumn manages to dazzle the earth in all its maturity and presents itself in warm and glorious hues, so too did the maestro's style mature and unfold itself in the autumn years of his life.

Notes

1 Souvenir: Shankarscope (1970).
2 From the souvenirs of Uday Shankar's productions in the 1960s and 1970s.
3 *Guru-shishya parampara* – The traditional teacher-student way of learning in India.
4 Ramachandra Guha, *Makers of Modern India* (Cambridge: The Belknap Press of Harvard University Press, 2011).
5 Bisakha Ghose, *Shankarnama: Smritichitre Amalashankar* (Calcutta: Ananda Publishers Private Limited, 2019).
6 Mamata Shankar, transcribed by Madhumanti Poito Chowdhury, "Uday Shankarer Ananya Dhara," *Anandabazar Patrika*, December 29, 2021.
7 Joan L. Erdman with Zohra Sehgal, *Stages: The Art and Adventures of Zohra Sehgal* (New Delhi: Pauls Press, 1997).

8 Incredible Choreographer Shanti Bardhan, accessed April 17, 2021, url: www.youtube.com/watch?v=Lbh12Ni8ln0
9 Indian People's Theatre Association, accessed December 15, 2021, url: https://ipta.in/
10 Kalpana, 1948, accessed September 15, 2019, url: https://Indiancine.Ma/Bklu/Player/01:05:47.669
11 Indian Sun: The Life and Music of Ravi Shankar, Oliver Craske, Google Books, accessed December 30, 2021, url: https://books.google.co.in/books?id=KSuzDwAAQBAJ&pg=PP64&lpg=PP64&dq=prabhat+ganguly+and+simkie&source=bl&ots=qtm83bXqy6&sig=ACfU3U3DdNoBdrGBrPBWseCF_SfNotCskg&hl=en&sa=X&ved=2ahUKEwjDsMfUmIz1AhUPxzgGHf3dCCsQ6AF6BAgnEAM#v=onepage&q=prabhat%20ganguly%20and%20simkie&f=false
12 Anjana Rajan, "Body of Work," *The Hindu*, December 15, 2016, accessed December 20, 2021, url: www.thehindu.com/features/friday-review/theatre/body-of-work/article16300483.ece
13 Uday Shankar, "My Love for Dance," *Souvenir of Shankarscope* (1970).
14 *Awaara*, accessed December 28, 2021, url: www.youtube.com/watch?v=u4mjCJaJe-g
15 Bisakha Ghose, *Shankarnama: Smritichitre Amalashankar* (Calcutta: Ananda Publishers Private Limited, 2019), 100–5.
16 Sachin Shankar, IMDb, accessed April 28, 2019, url: https://Www.Imdb.Com/Name/Nm1281193/
17 Munimji – O Shivji Bihane Chale, accessed January 8, 2023, url: www.youtube.com/watch?v=bIGJymRn5tQ
18 Sen, Sulakshana, "Shanti Bose's Synthesis of the Two Worlds of Tagore and Shankar," *Nartanam*, XII, no. 2 (2012): 63–9.
19 Sen, Sulakshana. "Shanti Bose: The Journey Continues," *Loud Applause*, (2017): 5–7.
20 Narendranath Mitra, accessed December 30, 2021, url: www.goodreads.com/author/show/4859098.Narendranath_Mitra
21 Arghya Sen, Oxford Reference, accessed December 30, 2021, url: www.oxfordreference.com/view/10.1093/oi/authority.20110803095423224
22 Anuj Kumar, "Eminent Dance Scholar and Critic Sunil Kothari Passes Away at 87," *The Hindu*, December 27, 2020, accessed December 30, 2021, url: www.thehindu.com/news/national/dance-historian-sunil-kothari-dies-of-cardiac-arrest/article33429773.ece
23 Joan L. Erdman, "Who Remembers Uday Shankar?" accessed July 10, 2017, url: https://mm-gold.azureedge.net/new_site/mukto-mona/Articles/jaffor/uday_shanka2.html
24 Mohan Khokar, *His Dance His Life – A Portrait of Uday Shankar* (New Delhi: Himalayan Books, 1983), 171.
25 Joan L. Erdman, "Who Remembers Uday Shankar?" accessed July 10, 2017, url: https://mm-gold.azureedge.net/new_site/mukto-mona/Articles/jaffor/uday_shanka2.html

Bibliography

Primary Sources

Souvenirs

(Courtesy, private collection of Shanti Bose)
Souvenir: *Samanya Kshati* (1961)
Souvenir: *Shankar scope* (1970, 1971 and 1972)
Souvenir: Tour of USA (1968)
Souvenir: Tour of USA and Europe (1962)

Flyers and Brochures

(Courtesy, private collection of Shanti Bose)
Tour of USA (1968)
Tour of USA and Europe (1962)

Photographs

(Courtesy, private collection of Shanti Bose)
Early 1940s (Courtesy, private collection of Dr. Ilora Basu)
Photographs of the following productions and tours between 1960 to 1977, as well as other photographs of the period:
Prakriti Ananda (1966)
Samanya Kshati (1961)
Shankarscope (1970)
Tour of USA (1968)
Tour of USA and Europe (1962)

Newspaper Clippings during the Period 1960–1977

Advertisement of *Shankarscope* and *Samanya Kshati* in 1972 in *Amrita Bazar Patrika* on November 10, 1972; *Yugantar* on November 12, 1972; and *Ananda Bazar Patrika* on November 14, 1972.
(Courtesy, private collection of Shanti Bose)

128 *Bibliography*

Dance Critic. "Sur o Chhander Samannay Chinhita 'Prakriti-Anando'." *Ananda Bazar Patrika*, March 25, 1966.
Heller, Zelda. "Outstanding Concert by Uday Shankar." *The Gazette*, October 7, 1968.
Music Critic. "Shankar's Chandalika – A New Approach." *Either from the Statesman or Amrita Bazar Patrika*, 1966.
Phelan, Charlotte. "Dance – A Review: Rattle, Roll and Shankar." *The Houston Post*, November 15, 1968.

Televised Interviews and Documentaries

An Interview of Uday Shankar by Shambhu Mitra on DD Bharati, (Accessed April 28, 2019), url: www.youtube.com/watch?v=JHq-uBio5vE&t=14s
An Interview with Pt. Ravi Shankar on ABP Ananda, (Accessed April 28, 2019), url: www.youtube.com/watch?v=gS4a875tXlg&t=21s
Kathay: An Interview with Shanti Bose on DD Bangla, (Accessed April 28, 2019), url: www.youtube.com/watch?v=4A70mTydsAs
Uday Pather Shanti: A Documentary on the Life and Works of Shanti Bose, by Government of West Bengal and Rabindra Bharati University, (Accessed April 28, 2019), url: www.youtube.com/watch?v=fsYjtDyKFXg

Films and YouTube Videos

Awaara, (Accessed December 28, 2021), www.youtube.com/watch?v=u4mjCJaJe-g
Incredible Choreographer Shanti Bardhan, (Accessed April 17, 2021), url: www.youtube.com/watch?v=Lbh12Ni8ln0
Indian Classical Music: Ravi Shankar, Alla Rakha and Yehudi Menuhin Trio, (Accessed March 2019), url: www.youtube.com/watch?v=hg6nTQFHf78
Kalpana, (Accessed September 15, 2019), url: https://indiancine.ma/BKLU/player
Munimji – *O Shivji Bihane Chale*, (Accessed January 8, 2023), url: www.youtube.com/watch?v=bIGJymRn5tQ
Pt. Ravi Shankar Cherishes Pt. Uday Shankar, (Accessed July 19, 2017), url: www.youtube.com/watch?v=H7GceqHJsUc

Recordings of Music

Prakriti Anando, HMV.

Secondary Sources

Books

Wajid Ali, H. M. *India and the Non-aligned Movement*. New Delhi: Adam Publishers, 2004.
Banerjee, Utpal K. *Tagore's Mystique of Dance*. New Delhi: Niyogi Books, 2011.
Bhattacharya, Shankarlal. *Udayer Pathe*. Kolkata: Sahityam, 2007.
Board of Scholars. *The Natya Shastra*. New Delhi: Sai Satguru Publications (Date of publication not mentioned).

Bibliography

Calhoun, Craig. *Dictionary of the Social Sciences.* New York: Oxford University Press, 2004.
Carr, E. H. *What is History.* London: Penguin Books, 1987.
Chatterjee, Satyen. *Padma Parer Manush Ebong Uday Shankar.* Kolkata: Satyen Chatterjee, 1993.
Dey, Manna. *Memories Come Alive: An Autobiography.* New Delhi: Penguin Books, 2007.
Dubey, Muchkund. *India's Foreign Policy: Coping with the Changing World.* New Delhi: Orient Black Swan Private Limited, 2016.
Erdman, Joan L. and Zohra Segal. *Stages: The Art and Adventures of Zohra Segal.* New Delhi: Pauls Press, 1997.
Ganguly, Sumit, ed. *India's Foreign Policy: Retrospect and Prospect.* New Delhi: Oxford University Press, 2010.
Ghose, Bisakha. *Shankarnama: Smritichitre Amalashankar.* Calcutta: Ananda Publishers Private Limited, 2019.
Guha, Ramachandra. *Makers of Modern India.* Cambridge: The Belknap Press of Harvard University Press, 2011.
Khokar, Mohan. *His Dance His Life – A Portrait of Uday Shankar.* New Delhi: Himalayan Books, 1983.
Kothari, Sunil and Mohan Khokar, eds. *Uday Shankar – A Photo Biography.* New Delhi: Ravi Shankar on behalf of RIMPA and Uday Shankar Festival '83 Committee, 1983.
Mukhopadhya, Ashoke Kumar. *Uday Shankar – Twentieth Century's Nataraja.* New Delhi: Rupa Charitavali Series, 2004.
Mukhopadhya, Sudhiranjan. *Uday Shankar.* Kolkata: Pratya Prakashani, 1991.
Papola, Trilok S. and Gerry Rodgers, eds. *Labour Institutions and Economic Development in India.* Vol. 97. Geneva: International Institute for Labour Studies, 1992.
Said, Edward W. *Orientalism.* London: Routledge and Kegan Paul, 1978.
Tagore, Rabindranath. *Gitabitan.* Calcutta: Viswa-Bharati, 1997.
Tagore, Rabindranath. *Nationalism.* London: Macmillan and Co, Limited, 1918.
Thapar, Romila, Abdul Ghafoor Noorani and Sadanand Menon. *On Nationalism.* New Delhi: Aleph Book Company, 2016.
Vatsyayan, Kapila. *Traditions of Indian Folk Dance.* New Delhi: Clarion Books Associated with Hind Pocket Books, 1987.

Articles in Newspapers and Magazines

Bose, Shanti. "Adhunik Bharatiya Nritye Uday Shankar Er Prabhab." *Special Edition: Desh Binodan Shankhya, Ananda Bazar Patrika*, 1987.
Chowdhury, Satyajit. "Kalpana: Pratham Bharatiya Adhunik Chalochchitra." *Desh, Ananda Bazar Patrika*, June 10, 2000.
Das, Anupama and Lila Roy (Translator of excerpts on Page 40). "Uday Shankar in America: A Photo Album." *Span*, January, 1978.
Ghatak, Aditi Roy. "In the Eye of the Storm." *The Sunday Statesman*, December 14, 1997.
Khullar, Sonal. "Almora Dreams: Art and Life at the Uday Shankar India Cultural Centre, 1939–44." *Marg – The Magazine of Arts*, June – September, 2018.
Sen, Sulakshana. "Shanti Bose: The Journey Continues." *Loud Applause* (2017): 5–7.
Sen, Sulakshana. "Shanti Bose's Synthesis of the Two Worlds of Tagore and Shankar." *Nartanam* XII, no. 2 (2012): 63–69.

Shankar, Mamata (Transcribed by Madhumanti Poito Chowdhury). "Uday Shankarer Ananya Dhara." *Anandabazar Patrika*, December 29, 2021.
Shankar, Ravi. "Shatabder Uday Shankar; Aamar Dada." *Desh*, *Ananda Bazar Patrika*, June 10, 2000.
Shome, Swapan. "Jiban Je Rokom, Shey Bhabei Meley Dhorechhen." *Ananda Bazar Patrika*, August 3, 2019 (Page: Pustak Parichay).

Articles in e-journals

Abrahams, Ruth K. "Uday Shankar: The Early Years, 1900–1938." *Dance Chronicle* 30, no. 3 (2007): 363–426, (Accessed July 10, 2017), url: www.jstor.org/stable/25598119
Bardia, Meena. "Dr. B.R. Ambedkar His Ideas about Religion and Conversion to Buddhism." *The Indian Journal of Political Science* 70, no. 3 (2009): 737–749, (Accessed April 11, 2017), url: www.jstor.org/stable/42742756
Baumer, Franklin L. "Intellectual History and Its Problems." *The Journal of Modern History* 21, no. 3 (1949): 191–203, (Accessed March 11, 2019), url: www.jstor.org/stable/1876066
Beyerbach, Barbara. "Chapter One: Social Justice Education through the Arts." *Counterpoints* 403 (2011): 1–14, (Accessed June 1, 2018), url: www.jstor.org/stable/42981592
Bhat, Janki Nath. "Untouchability in India." *Civilisations* 4, no. 4 (1954): 565–570, (Accessed January 4, 2023), url: www.jstor.org/stable/41377660
Bhattacharya, Ratan. "Satyajit Ray's Documentary Film Rabindranath: A Saga of Creative Excellence." *European Academic Research* 1, no. 6 (2013), (Accessed March 11, 2019), url: http://euacademic.org/uploadarticle/62.pdf
Blight, James G., Joseph S. Nye and David A. Welch. "The Cuban Missile Crisis Revisited." *Foreign Affairs* 66, no. 1 (1987): 170–188, (Accessed November 28, 2021), url: https://doi.org/10.2307/20043297
Brooks, Lynn Matluck. "Dance History: Coming of Age." *Journal of Aesthetic Education* 20, no. 3 (1986): 39–48, (Accessed June 1, 2018), url: www.jstor.org/stable/3332432
Buckland, Theresa. "Definitions of Folk Dance: Some Explorations." *Folk Music Journal*, 4, no. 4 (1983): 315–332, (Accessed June 1, 2018), url: www.jstor.org/stable/4522127
Chakravorty, Pallabi. "Dancing into Modernity: Multiple Narratives of India's Kathak Dance." *Dance Research Journal* 38, no. 1/2 (2006): 115–136, (Accessed February 20, 2019), url: www.jstor.org/stable/20444667
Chakravorty, Pallabi. "From Interculturalism to Historicism: Reflections on Classical Indian Dance." *Dance Research Journal* 32, no. 2 (2000): 108–119, (Accessed June 1, 2018), url: www.jstor.org/stable/1477983
Chatterjea, Ananya. "Dance Research in India: A Brief Report." *Dance Research Journal* 28, no. 1 (1996): 118–123, (Accessed March 10, 2015), url: www.jstor.org/stable/1478122
Coorlawala, Uttara Asha. "The Classical Traditions of Odissi and Manipuri." *Dance Chronicle* 16, no. 2 (1993): 269–276, (Accessed June 1, 2018). url: www.jstor.org/stable/1567933
Craske, Oliver. "Indian Sun: The Life and Music of Ravi Shankar." *Google Books*, (Accessed December 30, 2021), https://books.google.co.in/books?id=KSuzDwAA

QBAJ&pg=PP64&lpg=PP64&dq=prabhat+ganguly+and+simkie&source=bl&ots=qtm83bXqy6&sig=ACfU3U3DdNoBdrGBrPBWseCF_SfNotCskg&hl=en&sa=X&ved=2ahUKEwjDsMfUmIz1AhUPxzgGHf3dCCsQ6AF6BAgnEAM#v=onepage&q=prabhat%20ganguly%20and%20simkie&f=false

Datta, Meenakshi. "The Popular Art of Jamini Roy: Reminiscences." *India International Centre Quarterly* 17, no. 3/4 (1990): 281–290, (Accessed March 10, 2015), url: www.jstor.org/stable/23002469

Eley, Geoffrey. "What Is Cultural History?" *New German Critique*, no. 65 (1995): 19–36, (Accessed May 5, 2019), url: www.jstor.org/stable/488530

Erdman, Joan L. "A Comment on Dance Scholarship." *Dance Chronicle* 31, no. 2 (2008): 306–309, (Accessed July 10, 2017), url: www.jstor.org/stable/25598167

Erdman, Joan L. "Circling the Square: A Choreographed Approach to the Work of Dr. Kapila Vatsysyan and Western Dance Studies." *Dance Research Journal* 32, no. 1 (2000): 87–94, (Accessed March 10, 2015), url: www.jstor.org/stable/1478281

Erdman, Joan L. "His Dance, His Life: A Portrait of Uday Shankar by Mohan Khokar." *Asian Theatre Journal* 3, no. 2 (1986): 275–276, (Accessed July 10, 2017).

Erdman, Joan L. "Inside Tradition: Scholar-Performers and Asian Arts." *Asian Theatre Journal* 8, no. 2 (1991): 111–117, (Accessed June 1, 2018), url: www.jstor.org/stable/1124538

Erdman, Joan L. "Performance as Translation: Uday Shankar in the West." *The Drama Review: TDR* 31, no. 1 (1987): 64–88, (Accessed July 9, 2017), url: www.jstor.org/stable/1145766

Erdman, Joan L. "Society and the Dance: The Social Anthropology of Process and Performance by Paul Spencer." *Pacific Affairs* 61, no. 2 (1988): 322–323, (Accessed June 1, 2018). url: www.jstor.org/stable/2759313

Erdman, Joan L. "Who Should Speak for the Performing Arts? The Case of the Delhi Dancers." *Pacific Affairs* 56, no. 2 (1983): 247–269, (Accessed June 1, 2018), url: www.jstor.org/stable/2758653

Erickson, Mary. "Teaching Art History as an Inquiry Process." *Art Education* 36, no. 5 (1983): 28–31, (Accessed June 1, 2018), url: www.jstor.org/stable/3192729

Frazier, A. M. "The Criterion of Historical Knowledge." *Journal of Thought* 11, no. 1 (1976): 60–67, (Accessed March 15, 2019), url: www.jstor.org/stable/42588543

Gupta, Amit Kumar. "Soft Power of the United States, China, and India: A Comparative Analysis." *Indian Journal of Asian Affairs* 26, no. 1/2 (2013): 37–57, (Accessed June 15, 2018), url: www.jstor.org/stable/43550355

Hall, Fernau. "Honoring Uday Shankar." *Dance Chronicle*, 7, no. 3 (1984–1985): 326–344, (Accessed March 10, 2015). url: www.jstor.org/stable/1567655

Harter, Patricia, Nancy K. Nanney, Andrew T. Tsubaki and Carol Martin. "Report of the American Theatre Association Panel: Asian Theatre through Conferences and Festivals." *Asian Theatre Journal* 2, no. 2 (1985): 212–220, (Accessed March 10, 2015), url: www.jstor.org/stable/1124072

Hoopes, James. "Art as History: Perry Miller's New England Mind." *American Quarterly* 34, no. 1 (1982): 3–25, (Accessed June 1, 2018), url: www.jstor.org/stable/2712785

Huxley, Michael. "Dancing in Utopia: Dartington Hall and its Dancers by Larraine Nicholas." *The Journal of the Society for Dance Research* 28, no. 1 (2010): 125–127, (Accessed March 10, 2015), url: www.jstor.org/stable/40664460

Jacoby, Russell. "A New Intellectual History?" *The American Historical Review* 97, no. 2 (1992): 405–424, (Accessed March 11, 2019), url: www.jstor.org/stable/2165725

132 Bibliography

Kaeppler, Adrienne L. "Dance Ethnology and the Anthropology of Dance." *Dance Research Journal* 32, no. 1 (2000): 116–125, (Accessed June 1, 2018), url: www.jstor.org/stable/1478285

Krieger, Leonard. "The Autonomy of Intellectual History." *Journal of the History of Ideas* 34, no. 4 (1973): 499–516, (Accessed March 11, 2019), url: www.jstor.org/stable/2708884

LaCapra, Dominick. "Intellectual History and Its Ways." *The American Historical Review* 97, no. 2 (1992): 425–439, (Accessed March 11, 2019), url: www.jstor.org/stable/2165726

Levine, Joseph M. "Intellectual History as History." *Journal of the History of Ideas* 66, no. 2 (2005): 189–200, (Accessed March 11, 2019), url: www.jstor.org/stable/3654246

Maxwell, Neville. "Sino-Indian Border Dispute Reconsidered." *Economic and Political Weekly* 34, no. 15 (1999): 905–918, (Accessed September 16, 2021), url: www.jstor.org/stable/4407848.

Mitrović, Branko. "Intellectual History, Inconceivability, and Methodological Holism." *History and Theory* 46, no. 1 (2007): 29–47, (Accessed March 11, 2019), url: www.jstor.org/stable/4502220

Nath Bhat, Janki. "Untouchability in India." *Civilisations* 4, no. 4 (1954): 565–570, (Accessed January 4, 2023), url: www.jstor.org/stable/41377660

Nye, Joseph S. "Soft Power." *Foreign Policy*, no. 80 (1990): 153–171, (Accessed March 14, 2019), url: www.jstor.org/stable/1148580

Nye, Joseph S. "Public Diplomacy and Soft Power." *The Annals of the American Academy of Political and Social Science*, 616 (2008): 94–109, (Accessed May 21, 2023), url: http://www.jstor.org/stable/25097996

O'Shea, Janet. "At Home in the World?: The Bharatanatyam Dancer as Transnational Interpreter." *TDR (1988)* 47, no. 1 (2003): 176–186, (Accessed March 10, 2015), url: www.jstor.org/stable/1147037

Ohtani, Kimiko. "Bharata Nāṭyam, Rebirth of Dance in India." *Studia Musicologica Academiae Scientiarum Hungaricae* 33, no. 1/4 (1991): 301–308, (Accessed February 20, 2019), url: www.jstor.org/stable/902452

Palmer, Norman D. "India's Position in Asia." *Journal of International Affairs* 17, no. 2 (1963): 126–141, (Accessed November 28, 2021), url: www.jstor.org/stable/24381368

Pande, Mrinal. "Last of the Titans." *India International Centre Quarterly* 37, no. 2 (2010): 180–183, (Accessed March 10, 2015), url: www.jstor.org/stable/23006446

Pandey, Gyanendra. "The Time of the Dalit Conversion." *Economic and Political Weekly* 41, no. 18 (2006): 1779–1788, (Accessed April 11, 2017), url: www.jstor.org/stable/4418177

Prasad, Indulata. "Caste-Ing Space: Mapping the Dynamics of Untouchability in Rural Bihar, India." *CASTE: A Global Journal on Social Exclusion* 2, no. 1 (2021): 132–152, (Accessed January 4, 2023), url: www.jstor.org/stable/48643389

Purkayastha, Prarthana. "Dancing Otherness: Nationalism, Transnationalism, and the Work of Uday Shankar." *Dance Research Journal* 44, no. 1 (2012): 69–92, (Accessed June 1, 2018), url: www.jstor.org/stable/23524558

Raghunath, H. "Rajkot Episode of 1938–39: Indian Nationalism in the Princely Context." *Proceedings of the Indian History Congress* 40 (1979): 670–680, (Accessed December 30, 2021), url: www.jstor.org/stable/44142008

Renouf, Renée. "Folk Dances of India." *Dance Chronicle* 2, no. 4 (1978): 327–334, (Accessed June 1, 2018), url: www.jstor.org/stable/1567446

Roditi, Edouard. "Oscar Wilde's Poetry as Art History." *Poetry* 67, no. 6 (1946): 322–338, (Accessed June 1, 2018), url: www.jstor.org/stable/20584621

Rubinoff, Arthur G. "India's Search for Power: Indira Gandhi's Foreign Policy, 1966–1982 by Surjit Mansingh." *The Journal of Asian Studies* 44, no. 3 (1985): 643–644, (Accessed March 3, 2019), url: www.jstor.org/stable/2056319

Schramm, Harold. "Musical Theatre in India." *Asian Music* 1, no. 1 (1968): 31–40, (Accessed June 1, 2018), url: www.jstor.org/stable/834008

Segal, Zohra. "Theatre and Activism in the 1940s." *India International Centre Quarterly* 24, no. 2/3 (1997): 31–39, (Accessed June 1, 2018), url: www.jstor.org/stable/23005429

Stauffer, Joseph R. "Sino-Indian Border Dispute – 1962." *Naval War College Review* 19, no. 9 (1967): 81–117, (Accessed March 15, 2019), url: www.jstor.org/stable/44640979

Stern, Laurent. "Hermeneutics and Intellectual History." *Journal of the History of Ideas* 46, no. 2 (1985): 287–296, (Accessed March 11, 2019), url: www.jstor.org/stable/2709640

Terhal, P. "Guns or Grain: Macro-Economic Costs of Indian Defence, 1960–70." *Economic and Political Weekly* 16, no. 49 (1981): 1995–2004, (Accessed March 15, 2019), url: www.jstor.org/stable/4370452

Vatsyayan, Kapila. "The Future of Dance Scholarship in India." *Dance Chronicle* 18, no. 3 (1995): 485–490, (Accessed March 10, 2015), url: www.jstor.org/stable/1567844

White, Hayden V. "The Tasks of Intellectual History." *The Monist* 53, no. 4 (1969): 606–630, (Accessed March 11, 2019), url: www.jstor.org/stable/27902149

Williams, Louise Blakeney. "Overcoming the 'Contagion of Mimicry': The Cosmopolitan Nationalism and Modernist History of Rabindranath Tagore and W. B. Yeats." *The American Historical Review* 112, no. 1 (2007): 69–100, (Accessed November 24, 2021), url: www.jstor.org/stable/4136007

Wohl, Richard R. "Intellectual History: An Historian's View." *The Historian* 16, no. 1 (1953): 62–77, (Accessed March 11, 2019), url: www.jstor.org/stable/24436203

Wuerfel, Alfred G., Baumer, Bettina and Sen, Geeti. "An Affair with India." *India International Centre Quarterly* 24, no. 1 (1997): 48–66, (Accessed March 10, 2015), url: www.jstor.org/stable/23004631

Zwirn, Susan and Andrea Libresco. "Art in Social Studies Assessments: An Untapped Resource for Social Justice Education." *Art Education* 63, no. 5 (2010): 30–35, (Accessed June 1, 2018), url: www.jstor.org/stable/20799834

Online Resources

A Digital Trip: Strobe Light and the Birth of New Media Art (Trends in Contemporary Art Lecture Series, Department of Art, Art History and Design, University of Notre Dame), (Accessed June 21, 2018), url: https://artdept.nd.edu/news-and-events/events/2016/11/07/dr-tina-rivers-ryan-talk-a-digital-trip-strobe-light-and-the-birth-of-new-media-art-trends-in-contemporary-art-lecture-series/

Ahmed, Imtiaz. "Recognising the 1971 Bangladesh Genocide: An Appeal for Rendering Justice." *Ministry of Foreign Affairs, Government of the People's Republic*

134 Bibliography

of Bangladesh, February 2022, (Accessed January 8, 2023), url: www.ucl.ac.uk/risk-disaster-reduction/sites/risk_disaster_reduction/files/bd_genocide_booklet.pdf

Aiyar, Mani Shankar. "The Non-Alignment Man." *The Indian Express*, January 5, 2020, (Accessed November 28, 2021), url: https://indianexpress.com/article/books-and-literature/historian-jairam-ramesh-v-k-krishna-menon-a-chequered-brilliance-the-many-lives-of-v-k-krishna-menon-jawaharlal-nehru-6199932/

Alonzo King Lines Ballet. (Accessed December 4, 2022), url: https://linesballet.org/wp-content/uploads/2021/03/Ballet-Master-Job-Description.pdf

Arghya Sen. *Oxford Reference*, (Accessed December 30, 2021), url: www.oxfordreference.com/view/10.1093/oi/authority.20110803095423224

Ballet. *The Free Dictionary*, (Accessed July 11, 2017), url: www.thefreedictionary.com/ballet

Ballet, Britannica. (Accessed June 25, 2018), url: www.britannica.com/art/ballet

Bansal, Abhishek. "Indira Gandhi formed 'Vanar Sena' as Child to Fight British." *Inshorts*, November 19, 2016, (Accessed December 30, 2021), url: https://inshorts.com/en/news/indira-gandhi-formed-vanar-sena-as-child-to-fight-british-1479565283086

Beard, Charles A. "Written History as an Act of Faith." *American Historical Association*, (Accessed May 20, 2023), url: https://www.historians.org/about-aha-and-membership/aha-history-and-archives/presidential-addresses/charles-a-beard

Bhattacharya, Ratan, *Satyajit Ray's Documentary Film Rabindranath: A Saga of Creative Excellence*, (Accessed March 11, 2019), url: http://euacademic.org/UploadArticle/62.pdf

Bhutoria, Sundeep. "Humanism and Hope: The Legacy of Film Director Satyajit Ray." *United Nations UN Chronicle*, May 2021, (Accessed January 3, 2023), url: www.un.org/en/un-chronicle/humanism-and-hope-legacy-filmmaker-satyajit-ray

Boissoneault, Lorraine. "The Genocide the U.S. Can't Remember, But Bangladesh Can't Forget." *Smithsonian Magazine*, December 16, 2016, (Accessed June 22, 2018), url: www.smithsonianmag.com/history/genocide-us-cant-remember-bangladesh-cant-forget-180961490/

Celebrating Creativity: Life & Work of Uday Shankar (1900–1977). *A Photo Exhibition on the Life and the Times of the Legendary Dancer 8th December–31st December, 2001 Matighar, IGNCA*, (Accessed July 10, 2017), url: ignca.nic.in/ex_0054.htm

Century 21 World's Fair, Seattle Municipal Archives. (Accessed on June 27, 2018), url: www.seattle.gov/cityarchives/exhibits-and-education/digital-document-libraries/century-21-worlds-fair

Chatterjee, Debjani. "Jallianwala Bagh Massacre: Heroes of Jallianwalla Bagh Remembered." *NDTV*, April 13, 2021, (Accessed November 24, 2021), url: www.ndtv.com/india-news/jallianwala-bagh-massacre-india-remembers-the-heroes-of-jallianwalla-bagh-2412502

Chaturvedi, Kamal Nayan. "Pandit Ravi Shankar as Film Music Director." *Vidur's Blog*, (Accessed March 15, 2019), url: https://mevidur.wordpress.com/2012/12/13/pandit-ravi-shankar-as-film-music-director/

Chowdhurie, Tapat. "Mould it like Manipuri." *www.thehindu.com*, October 18, 2016, (Accessed September 12, 2019), url: www.thehindu.com/features/friday-review/Mould-it-like-Manipuri/article14412584.ece

Collins Dictionary, (Accessed December 1, 2021), url: www.collinsdictionary.com/dictionary/english/maya

Bibliography 135

Cultural History, Department of History, Yale University, (Accessed May 5, 2019), url: https://history.yale.edu/academics/undergraduate-program/regions-and-pathways/cultural-history

Dartington Trust. (Accessed November 25, 2021), url: www.dartington.org/

Dasgupta, Priyanka. "Satyajit Ray Was Obsessed with Kalpana and Loved Amala Shankar's Dance Pieces." *Times of India*, July 24, 2020, (Accessed December 4, 2021), url: https://timesofindia.indiatimes.com/city/kolkata/satyajit-ray-was-obsessed-with-kalpana-and-loved-amala-shankars-dance-pieces/articleshow/77157103.cms

Deva, B. C. "Towards and Indian Orchestra: Interview with Vishnudas Shirali." *Sangeet Natak Akademi, New Delhi*, 1993, (Accessed December 19, 2021), url: www.indianculture.gov.in/towards-indian-orchestra-interview-vishnudas-shirali

Downing, John D. H. (Ed.). *Encyclopedia of Social Movement Media, Sage Reference – Social Movement and Modern Dance (Bengal)*, 2011, p. 462, (Accessed July 10, 2017), url: http://sk.sagepub.com/reference/socialmovement/n205.xml?term=Social%20Movement%20and%20Modern%20Dance%20(Bengal)

Dutt, Sharad. "Father of Indian Symphony Orchestra – Timir Baran." *Millennium Post*, November 30, 2019, (Accessed December 19, 2021), url: www.millenniumpost.in/sundaypost/beacon/father-of-indian-symphony-orchestra – timir-baran-388449

Eighth Pupul Jayakar Memorial Lecture. *Cultural Diplomacy Leveraging India's Soft Power by Shri Shyam Saran*, April 18, 2016, (Accessed November 28, 2021), url: http://intangibleheritage.intach.org/eighth-pupul-jayakar-memorial-lecture-cultural-diplomacy-leveraging-indias-soft-power-by-shri-shyam-saran/

Erdman, Joan L. *Dance Advance – Who Remembers Uday Shankar?* (Accessed July 10, 2017), url: https://mm-gold.azureedge.net/new_site/mukto-mona/Articles/jaffor/uday_shanka2.html

From Endymion by John Keats, Poetry Foundation. (Accessed July 12, 2019), url: www.poetryfoundation.org/poems/44469/endymion-56d2239287ca5

Ghosh, Raya. "When is Rabindranath Tagore Jayanti 2021?" *India Today*, May 7, 2021, (Accessed January 3, 2023), url: www.indiatoday.in/lifestyle/what's-hot/story/when-is-rabindranath-tagore-jayanti-2021-1799787-2021-05-07

Glossary, ITC Sangeet Research Academy. (Accessed June 24, 2018), url: www.itcsra.org/glossary.aspx

Harold "Doc" Edgerton, MIT, (Accessed June 21, 2018), url: http://web.mit.edu/6.933/www/Fall2000/edgerton/www/intro.html

Hoda, Najmul. "Mohammad Iqbal, Who Wrote 'Saare Jahan Se Achha', Made Modernity A Dirty Word for Muslims." *The Print*, November 9, 2021, (Accessed December 30, 2021), url: https://theprint.in/opinion/mohammad-iqbal-who-wrote-saare-jahan-se-achha-made-modernity-a-dirty-word-for-muslims/763165/

How We Met: Yehudi Menuhin and Ravi Shankar, Independent, (Accessed March 15, 2019), url: www.independent.co.uk/arts-entertainment/how-we-met-yehudi-menuhin-and-ravi-shankar-1575503.html

India at the Big Four International Beauty Pageants, (Accessed June 21, 2018), url: https://en.wikipedia.org/wiki/India_at_Big_Four_international_beauty_pageants

"India Missed the Bus for They Threw us under its Wheels: Shashi Tharoor on British Rule of India." *Scroll.in*, September 10, 2017, (Accessed November 28, 2021), url: https://scroll.in/video/850022/india-missed-the-bus-for-they-threw-us-under-its-wheels-shashi-tharoor-on-british-rule-of-india

Indian Council for Cultural Relations. (Accessed May 5, 2019), url: www.iccr.gov.in/content/constitution

Bibliography

Indian People's Theatre Association. (Accessed on December 15, 2021), url: https://ipta.in/

Indian Revival Group. (Accessed July 15, 2019), url: http://indianrevivalgroup.com/?page_id=33

Intellectual History, Penn Arts and Sciences, Department of History. (Accessed March 11, 2019), url: www.history.upenn.edu/undergraduate/undergraduate-courses/concentrations/intellectual-history

Islam, Sirajul. *Uday Shankar*, (Accessed July 10, 2017), url: banglapedia.search.com.bd/HT/U_0003.htm

Jataka. (Accessed June 28, 2018), url: www.britannica.com/topic/Jataka

KarnATik. (Accessed November 29, 2021), url: https://web.archive.org/web/20071104111756/www.geocities.com/promiserani2/c1298.html

KarnATik. (Accessed November 29, 2021), url: https://web.archive.org/web/20071227054028/www.geocities.com/promiserani2/co1083.html

Kothari, Sunil. *Uday Shankar – An Appreciation*, (Accessed July 10, 2017), url: www.narthaki.com/info/profiles/profile2.html

Kumar, Anu. "Thomas Macaulay Won the Debate on How to Shape Indian Education. So Who Were the Losers?" *Scroll.in*, February 4, 2017, (Accessed October 30, 2021), url: https://scroll.in/magazine/821605/thomas-macaulay-and-the-debate-over-english-education-in-india

Kumar, Anuj. "Eminent Dance Scholar and Critic Sunil Kothari Passes Away at 87." *The Hindu*, December 27, 2020, (Accessed December 30, 2021), url: www.thehindu.com/news/national/dance-historian-sunil-kothari-dies-of-cardiac-arrest/article33429773.ece

Lange, Greg. "President Kennedy's Cold War Cold Supersedes Seattle World's Fair Closing Ceremonies on October 21, 1962." *History Link. Org*, March 15, 1999, (Accessed June 27, 2018), url: www.historylink.org/File/967

Miss World: My Protest at 1970 Beauty Pageant, (Accessed June 21, 2018), url: www.bbc.com/news/av/magazine-26437815/miss-world-my-protest-at-1970-beauty-pageant

Modern Dance, (Accessed July 10, 2017), url: www.artindia.net/modern.html

Mufti, Ifrah. "Allama Iqbal: Pakistan's National Poet & the Man Who Gave India 'Saare jahan se achha'." *The Print*, November 9, 2018, (Accessed December 30, 2021), url: https://theprint.in/features/allama-iqbal-pakistans-national-poet-the-man-who-gave-india-saare-jahan-se-achha/147155/

Mukherjee, Bhaswati. "India's Culture Diplomacy and Soft Power." *Ministry of External Affairs, Government of India*, October 18, 2019, (Accessed November 28, 2021), url: www.mea.gov.in/distinguished-lectures-detail.htm?855

Mukherjee, K. C. "Tagore-Pioneer in Education." *British Journal of Educational Studies* 18, no. 1 (1970): 69–81, (Accessed November 22, 2021), url: https://doi.org/10.2307/3120112.

Music, BBC. (Accessed March 15, 2019), url: www.bbc.co.uk/music/artists/697f8b9f-0454-40f2-bba2-58f35668cdbe

Nair, C. Kunchu. "The Kathakali and the Dance Drama of India." *UNESCO, UNESDOC Digital Library*, (Accessed January 2, 2023), url: https://unesdoc.unesco.org/ark:/48223/pf0000060001?posInSet=3&queryId=N-EXPLORE-809a6e21-dea9-4f7c-b916-aea16cfcce2f

Narendranath Mitra. (Accessed December 30, 2021), url: www.goodreads.com/author/show/4859098.Narendranath_Mitra

Nariman, Gushtaspshah Kaikhushro, Moriz Winternitz, Sylvain Lévi. *Eduard Huber Literary History of Sanskrit Buddhism*, (Accessed March 16, 2019), url: https://books.google.co.in

Official Press Book. *Seattle World's Fair 1962*, (Accessed January 7, 2023), url: https://spl.contentdm.oclc.org/digital/api/collection/p15015coll3/id/2199/download

Official Souvenir Program. *Seattle World's Fair 1962*, (Accessed January 7, 2023), url: www.state.gov/wp-content/uploads/2019/04/Seattle-Expo-1962-Guidebook.pdf

Panchatantra. (Accessed December 30, 2021), url: www.britannica.com/topic/Panchatantra-Indian-literature

Panchsheel, Ministry of External Affairs, Government of India. (Accessed April 10, 2017), url: www.mea.gov.in/Uploads/PublicationDocs/191_panchsheel.pdf

Pandit, Srimoyee "Rajasthani-Hindi Lyricist, Musician and Poet Gajanan Verma Died in Rajasthan." *Jagran Josh*, May 19, 2012, (Accessed December 30, 2021), url: www.jagranjosh.com/current-affairs/rajasthanihindi-lyricist-musician-and-poet-gajanan-verma-died-in-rajasthan-1337423417-1

Planning Commission. (Accessed June 21, 2018), url: http://planningcommission.gov.in/aboutus/history/index.php?about=aboutbdy.htm.

Rabindra Bharati University Prospectus 2012, (Accessed on September 12, 2019), url: www.academia.edu/8192030/RABINDRA_BHARATI_UNIVERSITY

Rajan, Anjana. "Body of Work." *The Hindu*, December 15, 2016, (Accessed December 20, 2021), url: www.thehindu.com/features/friday-review/theatre/body-of-work/article16300483.ece

Ramnath, Nandini. "In Dancer Uday Shankar's Rare Film from 1948, A Manifesto for a New India." *Scroll.In*, November 26, 2014, (Accessed December 10, 2021), https://scroll.in/article/691671/in-dancer-uday-shankars-rare-film-from-1948-a-manifesto-for-a-new-india

Ravi Shankar. (Accessed March 15, 2019), url: www.ravishankar.org/-music.html

Roychowdhury, Adrija. *Five States that Refused to join India after Independence*, (Accessed April 25, 2019), url: https://indianexpress.com/article/research/five-states-that-refused-to-join-india-after-independence/

Sachin Shankar, IMDb. (Accessed April 28, 2019), url: https://Www.Imdb.Com/Name/Nm1281193/

Santidev Ghosh, Visvabharati. (Accessed November 25, 2021), url: www.visvabharati.ac.in/SantidevGhosh.html

Saran, Mekhala. "Operation Searchlight: All That Bangladesh Lost on 25 March 1971." *The Quint*, March 25, 2018, (Accessed June 22, 2018), url: www.thequint.com/videos/operation-searchlight-began-on-25-march-1971

Scheduled Castes Population – Census 2011. (Accessed March 16, 2019), url: www.census2011.co.in/scheduled-castes.php

Seattle World's Fair – 1962 – Century 21 Exposition. (Accessed June 27, 2018), url: www.62worldsfair.com/

Sen, Amartya. "Illusions of Empire: Amartya Sen on what British Rule Really did for India." *theguardian.com*, June 29, 2021 (Accessed December 30, 2021), url: www.theguardian.com/world/2021/jun/29/british-empire-india-amartya-sen

Sengupta, Nitish. "Builders of Modern India: Dr. Bidhan Chandra Roy." *New Delhi: Publications Division, Ministry of Information and Broadcasting, Government of India*, 2002, (Accessed January 7, 2023), url: https://archive.org/details/bidhanchandraroy00seng/page/n5/mode/2up

138   Bibliography

Shanti, Bose. (Accessed March 15, 2019), url: www.shantibose.com/home.html

Shanti, Santi, Śāntī, Śānti, Samti, Shamti: 39 Definitions, Wisdom Library. (Accessed December 4, 2022), url: www.wisdomlib.org/definition/shanti

"Shiv Hari Complete Filmography." *Bollywoodmdb.com*, (Accessed March 15, 2019), url: www.bollywoodmdb.com/celebrities/filmography/shiv-hari/4061

Smt. Indira Gandhi, Ministry of External Affairs, Government of India. (Accessed March 15, 2019), url: www.pmindia.gov.in/en/former_pm/smt-indira-gandhi/

Stein, Alan J. *Century 21 – The 1962 Seattle World's Fair, Part 2, History Link. Org*, April 19, 2000, (Accessed January 8, 2023), url: http://historylink.org/File/2291

Sudevan, Praveen. "Who is Baul? Documentary Delves into the Philosophy of Bengal's Musical Mystics." *The Hindu*, April 19, 2021, (Accessed November 22, 2021), url: www.thehindu.com/entertainment/movies/ricky-kej-who-is-baul-documentary/article34359867.ece

Swamy, K. R. N. *Pavlova Steered Uday Shankar towards Indian Dancing*, (Accessed July 10, 2017), url: www.tribuneindia.com/2002/20020922/spectrum/main2.htm

"Tagore Centenary in Bombay." *Economic Political Weekly*, January 7, 1961, (Accessed April 7, 2017), url: www.epw.in/system/files/pdf/1961_13/1/tagore_centenary_in_bombay.pdf

"Tagore Renounced his Knighthood in Protest for Jallianwalla Bagh Mass Killing." *The Times of India*, April 13, 2011, (Accessed November 24, 2021), url: https://timesofindia.indiatimes.com/india/tagore-renounced-his-knighthood-in-protest-for-jalianwalla-bagh-mass-killing/articleshow/7967616.cms

The Concise Oxford Dictionary of Art Terms, (Accessed June 21, 2018), url: https://books.google.fi/books?id=vyiiW3uL49sC&printsec=frontcover#v=onepage&q=%22light%20art%22&f=false

The Seattle Public Library, Special Collections Online, (Accessed June 27, 2018), url: http://cdm15015.contentdm.oclc.org/cdm/compoundobject/collection/p15015coll3/id/2588/rec/7

The World of Indian Performing Arts by Utpal K. Banerjee, Exotic India Collections Culture Creations, (Accessed January 8, 2023), url: www.exoticindiaart.com/book/details/world-of-indian-performing-arts-uae305/

Uday Shankar. (Accessed July 10, 2017), url: www.culturalindia.net/indian-dance/dancers/uday-shankar.html

Uday Shankar. (Accessed July 10, 2017), url: www.iloveindia.com/indian-heroes/uday-shankar.html

Uday Shankar. (Accessed July 10, 2017), url: www.voiceofdance.net/smf/index.php?topic=1931.0

Uday Shankar. (Accessed July 10, 2017), url: www.whereincity.com/india/great-indians/artists/uday-shankar.php

"Uday Shankar: A Tribute." *The Hindu*, (Accessed July 10, 2017), url: www.hindu.com/thehindu/fr/2001/12/21/stories/2001122101030800.html

Uday Shankar and Locating Modernity, (Accessed February 20, 2019), url: https://ecommons.cornell.edu/bitstream/handle/1813/5163/11.%20AESTHETIC%20FUSIONS%20Chapter%201.doc%3F.pdf?sequence=11&isAllowed=y

Ullah, A. H. Jaffor. *Uday Shankar — The Choreographer Par Excellence: A Pictorial View*, (Accessed July 10, 2017), url: www.mukto-mona.com/new_site/mukto-mona/Articles/jaffor/uday_shankar.htm

Ullah. A. H. Jaffor. *Uday Shankar's Short Biography [1900–1977]*, (Accessed July 10, 2017), url: www.mukto-mona.com/new_site/mukto-mona/Articles/jaffor/uday_shankar.htm

Verma, Bharat. "The Indo – Pak War of 1965." *Indian Defence Review*, January 4, 2021, (Accessed January 8, 2023), url: www.indiandefencereview.com/spotlights/indo-pak-war-of-1965/

"Viewpoint: Britain Must Pay Reparations to India." *BBC News*, July 22, 2015, (Accessed November 28, 2021), url: www.bbc.com/news/world-asia-india-33618621

Visvabharati. (Accessed September 15, 2019), url: www.visvabharati.ac.in

Visvabharati. (Accessed September 15, 2019), url: www.visvabharati.ac.in/Visva_Bharati.html

Visvabharati. (Accessed September 15, 2019), url: www.visvabharati.ac.in/EDUCATIONAL_IDEAS.html

Visvabharati. (Accessed September 15, 2019), url: www.visvabharati.ac.in/History.html

What is Satyagraha. (Accessed December 30, 2021), url: www.mkgandhi.org/faq/q17.htm

Why Was Nagpur Chosen? (Accessed July 10, 2017), url: www.columbia.edu/itc/mealac/pritchett/00ambedkar/txt_ambedkar_conversion.html

Winners, Miss World. (Accessed June 21, 2018), url: www.missworld.com/#/past_winners

Index

Note: Page numbers in *italics* indicate a figure on the corresponding page.

Academy of Dance, Drama and Music xi, 15, 74, 82, 84, 117, 123
Act of Parliament, 1951 35
Aesops's fables 77
Akbar, Ustad Ali 46, 50
All India Centre for Dance and Music 6
Almora xxii, xxiv, 4, 6, 9, 16, 19, 36, 115, 119, 120, 121
Ambedkar, Dr. B. R. 76, 118; embracement of Buddhism 76
Amrita Bazar Patrika xvi
Ananda Bazar Patrika xi, xvi
Asamyukta Hastas 14
Ashar 31
Ashramik Sangha 75
Attenborough, Richard 30, 50
Awaara (film) 121

Bagchi, Papia 85
Baij, Ramkinkar 36
Bakshi, Animesh 70
Balasaraswati 116
ballet and dance productions: *Astrapuja* 67; *Brahmaputra* 67–68; *Chandalika* 22, 32, 35, 75–77, 79, 81–82, 84; *Dances of India* 65–67, 70–71; *Dream of Rhythm* 102; *Drum Dance* 102; *The Great Renunciation* 66–69, 76; *Harvest Dance* 66; *Indra* 67–68, 86; *Kartikeya* 5, 15, 90, 102, *122*; *Khadya* 67; *Krishna Ni Begame Baro* 66–67; Labour and Machinery 66, 81; *Labour and Machinery* 116; *Naga dance* 102; *Panthadi* 66, 68; *Rhythm of Life* 116; *Shiva Dance* 2, 102;
Udara Charitanam 22–23, 30, 33, 52–53, 76, 84, 122
Bandana, Bani 84
Bandopadhya, Kanika 36
Bandopadhyay, Ashoketaru 75
Banerjee, Brojo Bihari 5
Bangladesh 7–8, 27, 99, 110
Bangladesh genocide 110
Baran, Timir 5, 73, 117
Barbier, Simone (Simkie) 4–7, 9, 121
Bardhan, Gul 120
Bardhan, Shanti 120–121
Basu, Dr. Ilora 7–9
Beard, Charles A. xxi
Bharata Jai Jai 34, 102
Bharatiya Gana Natya Sangh 120, 123
Bharatnatyam viii, ix, xxvii, 7, 23, 116–117, 123
Bhattacharya, Ramgopal 75, 89
Bhaya, Jana Gupta 89
Bidai 10
Boaz, Franz xv
Body Expression 14–15, 22–23, 35, 38, 43, 45, 47, 114
Boner, Alice 4–6, 42, 118
Bose, Amarendra *xvii*, xviii, 70
Bose, Purnima *xvii*, 70
Bose, Shanti xx–xi, *xii*, xv–xvi, 2, 10, 12, 15–16, *18*, 26, 39, 43–44, 46, 48–50, 52, 61, 63, 70, 73, 75, 81, 84–85, 91–93, 94, 96–97, 99, *100*, 101, 103, *109*, 111, 115–116, 118–119, *119–120*, 122, *125*; as Ballet Master xvi, xxii, xxv, 75
Bose, Sunanda 12, 20, 85, 89, 118, 122–123

Index

Brahmacharyasrama 35
Brahmins vii, 1, 5, 76, 116
Brahmo Samaj 35
Bramhavidyalaya 35

Calcutta Youth Choir 75
Calhoun, Craig xv
Cannes Film Festival, 2012 8
Carr, E. H. xxi
Century 21 World's Fair 61
Chakravorty, Dr. Pallabi, vi
chamars 1, 76–77, 81
Chandalika xxiv, 22, 32, 35, 75–79, 81–82, 84
Chandra, Ramesh 90
Chandranath 84
Chaplin, Charlie 30
Chatterjee, Asit 70
Chattopadhya, Kamaladevi 118
Chekov, Anton 6
Chekov, Mikhail 6
Chekov Theatre Studio 6
Chelmsford, Lord 34
China: military preparedness of 63; Sino-Indian war of 1962 58, 63–64, 88
Chinna Bichhinna xxv, 27–28, 107, 110
Chitrangada 75, 123, 124
Choudhury, Amiyah Lal 7–8
Chowdhury, Salil 121
cinematic creativity 15
Clausen, George 2
Cold War politics 58–59, 63
colonialism vi, viii, 59; Indian dance during, vi–vii
costumes and *paagdis* ix–x, xxii, 6, 10, 24, 27, 36, 39, 43, 46–49, 69–70, 85, 92–94, 112
creative dance style of Uday Shankar viii–ix, xv, 12, 32, 74, 114; *ballet* form 14; *bhav nritya* 13–14; body expressions 14; choreography in films 121; classical and folk dance forms 35; dance movements 20–21, 114; devotional dances 22; evolution of movements 26; exercises for body joints 16, 19, 37; facial expressions 15; formations and patterns on stage 22; impact on society and performing arts 116; improvisation 19–20, 114; markings for position of dancers 25; *mudras* 14–15, 114; portrayal of socio-political and economic turmoil 115–116; postures 16, *18*; preparing body for dance 16; single-handed gestures 14; tenets for beauty, simplicity and power 16, 23; usage of stage space 114; use of stage lights 25
Creativity in Independent India: Uday Shankar, 1960–1977 xv
Cuban Missile Crisis xxiii, 58, 63
Cultural ambassador vi, 30, 35, 67
cultural diplomacy 59, 61
Cultural History, xv
Cyclone Bhola 109

Daji, Yasmin 105
Dalit deprivations 76–77
dance forms of India–classical vii–viii, x–xi, xxiv–xxv, 7, 14, 15, 23, 38, 74;devotional dances vii; enactment of myths and epics vii; folk vii–x, xxv, 2, 15, 24, 28, 35, 36, 43–44, 46–47; functional and occupational dances of peasant vii; related to fertility rites, rituals, magic propitiation and trance vii; nomads and food gatherers vii; related to seasonal cycles vii
Dartington Hall 6, 36
Das, Anupama 89, 102
Das, Rabin 70, 92
Das, Sudhi Ranjan 36
Debi, Pratima 30
Desai, Yogendra Sunder 73–74, 123; in freedom struggle 73
Devi, Hemangini 1
Devi, Kalavati 123
Devi, Maharani of Jaipur Gayatri 36
Dey, Soumen (Suman) *xvii*, 70, 92, 96
Dubey, Muchkund 58
Dutt, Guru 8
Dutta, Barun *xvii*, 73, 75, 84–85, 90
Dutta, Ganesh 70
Dutta, Jharna 82, 84, *94*
Dyer, Colonel Reginal 34

East Pakistan 98–99, 107, 109–110
Edgerton, Harold 106
education systems in India 27, 34–36

142 Index

Elmhirst, Dorothy 6
Elmhirst, Leonard 6
Erdman, Dr. Joan x, xii–xiv, xxxi, 4, 123–124

folk dance forms vii–x, xxv, 2, 15, 24, 28, 35, 36, 43–44, 46–47
foreign policy of India 58–59, 64, 88
freedom struggle 32, 73, 86n2–3
free exchange of views 6

Gandhi, Indira xxiv, 36, 53, 54, 88, 110, 121
Gandhi, Mahatma 30, 73, 118
Gandhi, Rajiv 53, 54
Gandhi, Sanjay 53, 54
Ganesan, Shivaji 66
Ganguly, Bandana *xvii*
Ganguly, Prabhat 121
Ganguly, Sumit 58
Ganguly, Tarun 70
Gemini Studios 8
George V, King 2
Ghosh, Haren 6
Ghosh, Kishore 85, 90
Ghosh, Shantideb/ Shantidev 36–37
Ghosh, Shefali 89
Ghosh, Shubhra 84
Ghosh, Soumen 85
Ghosh, Sukomal Kanti 16
Golf Club Road, Kolkata 19
Goswami, Himangshu 75
The Great Renunciation 10
Guha, Polly xi, *xii*, 84, 102
Guha, Ramchandra 33, 118
Guha, Sadhan xi, 84
Gupta, Arati 75
Gupta, Krishna 85
Gupta, Pranati Sen 84
Gupta, Sunanda Sen 84
guru-shishya parampara 117
Guruvayoor temple 5

Hara Parvati 5
Harvest Festival 5
Hindi film music 50
The Hindu Marriage 2
HMV (Sa Re Ga Ma) Record Company 75, 90
humanism 32, 34
Hurok, Sol xxiv, 4, 65, 88, 94

improvisation classes 7, 19, 66, 114, 121
Indian Ballet Troupe (IBT) xxiv, 73–75, 84, 92, 123; dancers 84; Fishermen's Dance 74; folk dances 74; *Kirat Arjun* 74; *Madia* 74, 90
Indian Council for Cultural Relations (ICCR) 59
Indian People's Theatre Association (IPTA) 28
Indian Revival Group (IRG) 73, 74, 75
Indian society, then-contemporary 104–105
Indo-Pak war of 1947 and 1965 xxiv, 88
Indra 3, 5, 67–68, 86, 91
Intangible Cultural Heritage of Humanity 31
Intellectual history xiv–xv
International Beauty Pageant 105
Iqbal, Mohammad 63

Jalan, Shyamanand *120*
Jataka tales 77
J.J. School of Art, Bombay 2

Kalakendra 19
Kalia Daman 6
Kalpana (film) x, xiii, xxii, 6–10, 19, 26–27, 33, 55, 66, 74, 82, 85, 92, 100, 102, 104, 116–117, 121; humanity in 33; personification of *Bharat Mata* 34; reflection of Shankar's dream for India 35; sequence on *Labour and Machinery* 33
Kanaklata 37, 116
Kandy dance 36
Kankaria, Ranjit Mull xxv, 98, 100
Kapoor, Raj 121
Kartikeya xxv, 5–6, 15, *17*, 90, 93
Kastaur, Jayant *120*
Kathak viii, xxvii, 73
Kathakali viii, xi, xxvii, 5, 7, 13–14, 36, 73–74, 81, 84, 116–117, 120
Kennedy, John F. xxiii, 61, 63
Khadya 32, 66–67, 78
Khambatta, Persis 105
Khan, Baba Allauddin/ Ustad Allauddin 5, 7–8, 50, 117
Khan, General Agha Muhammad Yahya 109
Khokar, Mohan x, 4, 28

Kirat Arjun 7, 74
Kotal 36
Kothari, Dr. Sunil *125*
Kumar, Mahindra 99
Kundu, Hirendranath 100

Labour and Machinery 7, 32, 81, 116
La Compagnie d'Uday Shankar Hindoue Danses et la Musique 5
Lalitha 116
Light Art or Luminism 106
lighting techniques 41, 46, 51–52, 106, 114–115
literacy rate 58
Little Ballet Troupe (Ranga Shri Little Ballet Group) 120–121
Locarno Film Festival 30
love affairs 104

Macaulay's *Minute on Indian Education* 35
Madia x, xxvii, 74, 79, *80*, 90
Mahendra of Nepal, King 74
Maihar 7
Maitra, Kamalesh 23, 73, 75, 84–85, 90–91, 97, 99, 102, *108*
Manipuri dance viii, x–xi, 7, 36–37, 73–74, 117
Martin, John ix
Matadin 1, 5, 33, 76, 81
Maxwell, Neville 63
Mazumdar, Gouri Prasanna 99
Mazumdar, Ranjan 70
Mehanati Manush 28
Mekas, Jonas 106
Menon, Balkrishna xi, *xii*, 75
Menon, V. K. Krishna 58
Menuhin, Yehudi 50
Methodology iv
Mistri, Meher Castelino 105
Mitra, Debi Prasad *xvii*
Mitra, Narendranath *124*
Mitra, Shambhu xx, xxii, 1–2, 10, 16, 21, 70
Mitra, Shikha 89
Mitra, Suchitra 36, 91, 122
Modern Dance 13
mudras vii–viii, xxii, xxvii, 13–15, 22–23, 35, 38, 47, 48, 92, 114
Mukherjee, Ambika Charan (*Mastermoshai*) 2, 99
Mukherjee, Shambhu 85

Mukherjee, Shikha 89
Mukherjee, Tapati 89
Mumtaz, Uzra 37
My Love for Dance 2–3, 10, 31

Nag, Shakti 75
Nag, Tarun *xvii*
Naga Chief 10
Namboodri, Shankaran xi, 5, 7, 15, 93
Namboodri, T. S. G. xi, *xii*
Nandi, Amala 6, 116
Nandi, Asoke 61–62, 65, 70
Nandi, Meena 61
Nandita 65
Nasrathpur 1, 5
Nataraj pose 2
Nath, Anju 89
Nation, national, nationalism, nationalistic, nation-hood, nation-states, nation building vi, ix, xiii, xxvi, 19, 27, 107, 109, 110, 116, 118
Natyashastra vii, ix, xxvii, 13, 15, 38, 114; categories of dance (*Nrutta, Nritya* and *Natya*) vii, 38
nautch girls vi, xxiii
navarasas vii, xxvii
Nehru, Jawaharlal xxiii, 6, 30, 53, 54, 88, 118
new cosmopolitanism 34
Nirikshan 10
Nritya xxvii
Non-Alignment principle 59
Nrityangan 16, *17*, 122, *123*, *124*, *125*
Nye, Jr,, Joseph S. 59

Operation Searchlight 28, 98, 110
oriental dances viii
Orientalism viii

Padma Parer Manush Ebong Uday Shankar (Satyen Chatterjee) x
Padmini 116
Pakistan 107
Panchatantra 77
Panchsheel principles 59
Patel, Sardar Vallabhbhai 73
Patha Bhavan (House of Studies) 35–36
Pavlova, Anna ix, xxii, 3, 13, 31, 117
performing arts traditions in India 36, 51, 118
Phule, Jotirao 118

144 Index

Pillai, Kandappa 7
Pillai, T. K. Maruthappa *xii*
Planning Commission of India 103
Politics 9, 58, 59
poverty 58, 88
Powell, Reita Faria 105
Prabashi Bangiya Sanskriti Sammelan 30
Prakashan, Gyan 107
Prakriti Ananda x, xiii–xvi, xxiv, 7, 19, 22–23, 32–33, 35, 75–77, 82, 89–92, 102, 124; act of kindness 79; characters 78, 85; choreography 78; Curd Seller and Bangle Seller 81–82; "*mantra*" scenes 78, 81, 84–85; *Mati toder daak diyeche* 78, 79; *maya arpana* 81; movements of Madia 79, *80*; Prakriti's mother dances 81; production of 76; Shankar as Lord Buddha 82, *83*; songs and instrumental music 84; stage rehearsals 85; story outline 77; tour and performances 86; troupe members *91*
provincialism, regionalism 33–34, 37
puppetry dance 120

Rabindra Bharati 11, 19–20
Rabindranath Tagore (film) 30Rabindra Bharati Act of 1961 xi
Rabindra Bharati University xi, xx
Rabindra Nritya 14
Rabindra Rachanabali 33
Rabindra sangeet (Rabi Babur *gaan*) 31
Radha Krishna 2
Radhakrishnan, Dr 54
Ragas xxvii
Raghavan, Pappu 70, 73–74, 92
Ragini 116
Rajput Bride 10
Rakha, Ustad Alla 46, 50, 117
Ramayana 120
Ram Leela 7
Ray, Satyajit 30, 100; Apu Trilogy 50; *Jana Aranaya* 104; *Pratidwandi* 104; *Seemabadhha* 104
Rehman, Indrani 105
Rehman, Sheikh Mujibur 110
research vi, xiii, xiv–xv
Rhythm of Life 7, 32
Rolland, Romain 6
"rooted" or "realistic" cosmopolitanism 34

Rothenstein, Sir William ix, xxii, 2, 6, 31
Roy, Dr. Bidhan Chandra xi
Roy, Kalpana 61
Roy, Ram Mohan 118
Roy, Subinoy 84

Saare Jahaan Se Achha 63
Sadhukhan, Vishnu Das 90
Said, Edward W. viii
Salvage Ethnography xv–xvi, xxi
Samanya Kshati x–xi, xiii, xvi–xvii, xxiii–xxv, 12, 21–23, 25, 30–31, 33, 37–38, 65, 70–71, 76, 78, 84–85, 99, 111, *112*, 114, 122, 124, *125*; callousness of queen towards villagers 33; cast *54*, *63*; characters 42; choreographic movements and style 43–44, 47–48, 50; costumes 71; fire dance 45–46, *47*; King's Court scene 41–42, *42*; lighting 41, 51–52; music and musicians for 46, 50, 70; performances 53–55; poem of 39–41; portrayal of queen, maids and companions 44–45; preparation for production 38–39; representation of rural life 44; setting and props 51; souvenir of 30–31, 38–39, 49; storyline 45–49; tempo and pitch of music 43; as tribute to *Gurudev* 30
Samyukta Hastas 14
Sananda xi
Sangeet Natak Akademi 5, 16
Sanyal, Pali 89
Saran, Shyam 59
Sarkar, Manjushree Chaki 75
Seattle World's Fair, 1962 xxiii, 61, 63, 88
Second World War 7, 106
Sehgal, Uzra 6
Sehgal, Zohra 4, 6, 8, 37, 116, 121
Sen, Amartya 36
Sen, Arghya *124*
Sen, Chitra 75
Sen, Dhurjati xi, *xii*, 73, 84, 111
Sen, Sulakshana *122*
Sen, Tapas 25, 51
Sengupta, Pranati xi, *94*, 102
Sengupta, Santosh 91, 122

shadow play productions: on Life of Buddha 65–66, 99–100; *Ram Leela* 99–100
Shah, Chiranjilal 71, 85, 97
Shankar, Amala xi, xxiv, 6–7, 9, 16, 21, 26, 45, 49, 60, 61, 86, 92, 97, 118–119, 121
Shankar, Ananda 61, 65, 70, 96
Shankar, Bhudeb 61, 93, 96
Shankar, Devendra 5, 37
Shankar, Kedar 5
Shankar, Laxmi (Lakshmi) 46, 50, 61, 63, 65, 70, 117, 121
Shankar, Mamata 26, 61, 65, 107, 119, *119*
Shankar, Rabindra (Ravi) xx, 5, 37, 50, 96, 117; music composition 52–53
Shankar, Rajendra 5, 7, 37, 121
Shankar, Sachin *120*, 121
Shankar, Shyam 1
Shankar, Uday xxi–xxii, 60, 61, 65, *100*, *109*; A.R.C.A. Diploma 2; art form as a mirror of modern India xii–xiii; choreography 1; concerns with education 36;; contribution to Indian dance and impact 14, 117–118, 123–125; on creativity 13; as cultural ambassador of India 30; fire accident 10; five-year programme in arts 36; formal education 1; ill health 86, 88, 96–97, 111; Indian-ness of art ix, influencing people 1–2; marriage 6; movements 4; in Olympic game ceremonies 92; parents 1; social consciousness and sense of social justice 32; storytelling viii, xxiii, 13, 44, 47, 114; use of instrumental music 35; *see also* creative dance style of Uday Shankar; tours and performances
Shankarnama (Swapan Shome) xi
Shankarnama: Smritichitrey Amala Shankar x–xi
Shankarscope x, xiii, xv–xvi, xx, xxv, 10, 21, 25, 28, 31–32, 35, 48, 111–112, 115–116, 124; Announcer and Belly Rolling 103–104; Beauty Competition 102, 104–106; *Chinna Bichhinna* 98, 107, 110; clips from film *Kalpana* 102; *Dance Mad* 104; Epilogue 106, 115; *Eternal Song* 102; film and stage, use of 102–103; items included 102; *Kartikeya* 102, 107; *Lady and the Thief* 104; lighting techniques 106; *mantra* sequence 102; music recording for *108*; *Prakriti Ananda* 102; production planning 99–101; *Scope Scope Shankar scope* 102; shooting location *100*; sketch of stage and screen *101*; souvenir of 98
Shantiniketan 30, 36–38, 52, 73, 75, 117
Shardulakarna Avadana 77
Sharma, Narendra 119, *120*
Sharma, Pandit Shiv Kumar 50, 117
Shastri, Lal Bahadur 88
Shinde, Tarabai 118
Shirali, Vishnudas 5–6, 117
Shivashankaran, N. K. xi, *xii*, 27, 73, 84
shloka vii, xxvii, 35
Shyama 75
Singh, Ambobi 7
Singh, Guru Bipin 123
Singh, Guru Nadia xi, *xii*
Singh, Maharaj Kumar Bhopal 1
Singh, Maharaj Rana Bhawani 1–2
Sino-Indian war of 1962 xxiii–xxiv, 58, 63–64, 88
Snanam 5
society ladies 104
soft power 59, 64
Speculative history xxi
stagecraft 24–25, 32, 38, 46, 51, 111, 115, 118
Stages: The Art and Adventures of Zohra Sehgal (Erdman and Sehgal) 4
Stotra xxvii
Straight, Lady Daphne 6
Sword Dance 2

Tagore, Debendranath 35
Tagore, Rabindranath xi, xxiii, 6, 21–22, 30–37; abhorrence for divisiveness 33–34; *Balmiki Pratibha* 75; *Bhanusingher Padabali* 75; *Chandalika* xxiv, 22, 32, 35, 75–77, 79, 81–82, 84; *Chitrangada* 75, *123*; concerns with education 35; cosmopolitanism of 34; dance

dramas 13, 36–37, 75; greatness 31; humanism 32; humanity 32; influence of Indian and Western folk music 31; *Nationalism* 32, 34; nationalism of 34; patriotism 33–34; *Rabindra Rachanabali* 33; return of Knighthood 33; *Samanya Kshati* 33; school for children 35; *Shyama* 75, *119*; social consciousness 32; *Udara Charitanam* 22–23, 30, 33, 52–53, 76, 84, 122
Tagore, Shyamasree 122
Tagore, Surendranath 32
technology 25, 51, 99–100, 106
Terhal, P. xxiv
Thakurta, Ruma Guha 75
Tharoor, Shashi 58
Tilottoma 10
Tirtha, Sri Vyasaraja 66
tours and performances xviii–xix, 86, 88; Africa 10; Canada 12, 60–61, 63, 65; China 10; costumes and *paagdis* 69; Europe 12, 31, 45, 60–61, 63, 64, 65, 70–71; Germany 61; London 61; music and musicians for 46, 50, 70; the Netherlands 61; Oslo 61; Poland 61; Sweden 61; use of waterproof and fireproof boxes 69–70; *see also Prakriti Ananda;* Samanya Kshati; Shankarscope; USA performances
troupe members 37, 69–70, 89; dancers 70; disbandment of 73; punctuality and professionalism in behaviour 117

Udara Charitanam 22–23, 30, 33, 52–53
Udayer Pathey (Shankarlal Bhattacharya) x
Uday Shankar (Sudhiranjan Mukhopadhya) x
Uday Shankar–A Photo Biography (Dr. Sunil Kothari and Mohan Khokar) x

Uday Shankar–Twentieth Century's Nataraja (Ashoke Kumar Mukhopadhyay) x
Uday Shankar Ballet Company xi, 4
Uday Shankar Culture Centre, Almora xxii, 4–7, 16, 36, 71, 85, 119
Uday Shankar Culture Centre, Kolkata xxiv, 74, 92, 118
The Uday Shankar Hindu Dancers and Musicians 59
Uday Shankar Shatabdi Samaroh 16–17, *120, 125*
Uday Shankar–Twentieth Century's Nataraja (Ashoke Kumar Mukhopadhyay) x
unemployment 103–104
united India ix
universal appeal 22, 35, 81
untouchables 76
USA performances 5, 12, 31, 45, 49, 60–61, 63, 65, 88–89, 94, 94–95; costumes and *paagdis* 92–93; *Deva-Dasis* 92; *Indra* 91, 93; *Kartikeya* 90, 93; *Laiharoba* 90, 92; music rehearsals 90; *Prakriti Ananda* 90–92; promotional material used 96; *Punjabi* folk dance 91; *Raag Mohan-Kosh* 90; rehearsals 89–90; *Sari* 91–92; *Tabla Taranga* 91; troupe members 89, *89*, 95

Vasudevan, Raman Nair 70
Vatsayan, Kapila vii
Viji 65
Village Festival 10
Vinode *xvii*
Vishwa Bharati 35

Wembley Exhibition Theatre 2
West Pakistan 107, 109–110
Williams, Raymond xv

Yatra visvam bhavatieka nidam 35
Young Father 27
Yuddha Yatra 5
Yugantar xvi

Printed in the United States
by Baker & Taylor Publisher Services